PALGRAVE MACMILLAN'S
CRITICAL STUDIES IN GENDER, SEXUALITY, AND CULTURE

Highlighting the work taking place at the crossroads of sociology, sexuality studies, gender studies, cultural studies, and performance studies, this series offers a platform for scholars pushing the boundaries of gender and sexuality studies substantively, theoretically, and stylistically. The authors draw on insights from diverse scholarship and research in popular culture, ethnography, history, cinema, religion, performance, new media studies, and technoscience studies to render visible the complex manner in which gender and sexuality intersect and can, at times, create tensions and fissures between one another. Encouraging breadth in terms of both scope and theme, the series editors seek works that explore the multifaceted domain of gender and sexuality in a manner that challenges the taken-for-granted. On one hand, the series foregrounds the pleasure, pain, politics, and aesthetics at the nexus of sexual practice and gendered expression. On the other, it explores new sites for the expression of gender and sexuality—the new geographies of intimacy being constituted at both the local and global scales.

Series Editors:

PATRICIA T. CLOUGH is Professor of Sociology and Women's Studies at Queens College and The Graduate Center, CUNY. Clough is on the editorial boards of *Women's Studies Quarterly*, *Body and Society*, *Subjectivity*, *Cultural Studies/Critical Method*, *Qualitative Inquiry*, and *Women and Performance*. Clough is the coeditor of *Beyond Biopolitics: Essays in the Governance of Life and Death* (with Craig Willse, 2011); author of *The Affective Turn: Theorizing the Social* (with Jean Halley, 2007); *Autoaffection: Unconscious Thought in the Age of Teletechnology* (2000); *The End(s)of Ethnography: From Realism to Social Criticism* (1998); *Feminist Thought: Desire, Power and Academic Discourse* (1994); and *The End(s) of Ethnography: From Realism to Social Criticism* (1992).

R. DANIELLE EGAN is Professor and Chair of the Gender and Sexuality Studies Program at St. Lawrence University. Egan is the author of *Dancing for Dollars and Paying for Love: The Relationships between Exotic Dancers and Their Regulars* (2006) and coauthor of *Theorizing the Sexual Child in Modernity* (with Gail Hawkes, 2010), both with Palgrave Macmillan. She is also the coeditor of *Flesh for Fantasy: Producing and Consuming Exotic Dance* (with Katherine Frank and Merri Lisa Johnson, 2006). She is on the editorial board of *Sexuality and Culture*.

Titles:

Magnus Hirschfeld and the Quest for Sexual Freedom: A History of the First International Sexual Freedom Movement
Elena Mancini

Sex, Ethics, and Young People

Moira Carmody

SEX, ETHICS, AND YOUNG PEOPLE

First published in 2015 by
PALGRAVE MACMILLAN®
in the United States—a division of St. Martin's Press LLC,
175 Fifth Avenue, New York, NY 10010.

Where this book is distributed in the UK, Europe and the rest of the world,
this is by Palgrave Macmillan, a division of Macmillan Publishers Limited,
registered in England, company number 785998, of Houndmills,
Basingstoke, Hampshire RG21 6XS.

Palgrave Macmillan is the global academic imprint of the above companies
and has companies and representatives throughout the world.

Palgrave® and Macmillan® are registered trademarks in the United States,
the United Kingdom, Europe and other countries.

ISBN 978-1-349-49169-8   ISBN 978-1-137-40597-5 (eBook)
DOI 10.1057/9781137405975

Library of Congress Cataloging-in-Publication Data

Carmody, Moira, 1953–
    Sex, ethics, and young people / Moira Carmody.
        pages cm.—(Critical studies in gender, sexuality, and culture)
    Includes bibliographical references and index.

    1. Sex crimes—Prevention. 2. Youth—Sexual behavior. 3. Sexual
ethics for youth. I. Title.

HV6556.C37 2015
176'.40835—dc23   2014043566

A catalogue record of the book is available from the British Library.

Design by Newgen Knowledge Works (P) Ltd., Chennai, India.

First edition: May 2015

10 9 8 7 6 5 4 3 2 1

For young women and men beginning their sexual lives and those who work with them

Contents

Acknowledgments

A research and education project of this size that has been ongoing since 2005 would not have been possible without the support of many individuals and organizations. First, I wish to thank the young women and men who opened up their sexual lives and relationships to reflection during the interview stage of my research. The young people who participated in the Sex & Ethics Education Program made the research ideas come alive. Without their involvement, there would have been no project. I am extremely grateful to them for sharing their wisdom with their educators and me.

A number of organizations have provided funding of different aspects of this work, and I am very grateful for all their support. The Australian Research Council provided the initial funding (2005–2008) as part of a Linkage grant. The Management Committee of Rape and Domestic Violence Services, Australia (formerly NSW Rape Crisis Centre), provided funds and in kind support as part of this initial grant and provide an ongoing commitment. Karen Willis, executive officer of the services, has been a generous and enthusiastic supporter of the approach to Sex & Ethics since its inception, and continues to advocate and promote the ideas and the importance of evidence-based primary prevention of violence at state and national levels. We have had the pleasure of training educators together over the last ten years and continue to learn much from each other. The New Zealand Ministry of Justice provided additional funding in 2009–2011 for the Sex & Ethics Program to be implemented and evaluated in Wellington; the former Australian Department of Families, Housing, Community Services and Indigenous Affairs provided two rounds of funding for a rollout of the Sex & Ethics Program in NSW and in Queensland in 2009–2010. The University of Technology also provided funding in 2012–2013.

I have had many invitations to present my ideas on Sex & Ethics at universities across Australia, New Zealand, and the United Kingdom and at national and international conferences. I have also spoken at dozens of community organization conferences and professional meetings and run master workshops. All of these settings have been crucial to testing the findings of the research, receiving feedback, and honoring my commitment to taking engaged research back to communities of scholars and practitioners. Over the life of the project, I have had the opportunity to work with many skilled educators who enthusiastically embraced the ideas and skills from the Sex & Ethics Program and shared them in their home communities across several states in Australia and New Zealand and in the United Kingdom. Particular thanks to Kath Albury and Clif Evers, who have facilitated educator training with me along with Karen Willis, and to Kay Humphreys who has championed the program in rural areas.

I am blessed to be part of a university culture that values applied and engaged research with a strong commitment to social justice. I have received much support over the years, in a variety of ways too numerous to mention here, from colleagues at the University of Western Sydney. Gar Jones, manager of research, deserves special mention for his enthusiastic encouragement of my research over many years. In particular, I want to thank my close colleagues Kerry Robinson, Peter Bansel, Nida Denson, Lesley Wright, and other members of the Sexualities and Genders Research Group and the School of Social Sciences & Psychology. Georgia Ovenden worked with me as research associate on many of the projects discussed in this book, and I am indebted to her for her skills and insight in many areas and her ability to make numbers sing for me.

I received enthusiastic support for this work in its early stages from Elizabeth Vella, former publisher from Palgrave Macmillan in Australia. More recently, I have received much encouragement and assistance from Mireille Yanow, Lani Oshima, and Mara Berkoff from Palgrave Macmillan, New York. Danielle Egan, series editor, with Patricia Clough, of the Critical Studies in Gender, Sexuality, and Culture Series, has been extremely generous in her support of the ideas I am working with, and provided an important opportunity for the Sex & Ethics work to reach a wider audience. On a personal level, Michael Hurley, adjunct professor from the Australian Research Centre in Sex, Health and Society at La Trobe University, Melbourne, Australia, has greatly assisted me with editing and so much more in terms of critical dialogue as we worked together on the final manuscript. Finally, to Louise Shortus who makes every day a blessing; provides spirited and ongoing conversation about the work as it unfolds; and is so calm, patient, and skilled when the "computer says no" and I run screaming from the room. Thank you all for the many and varied ways you have supported me and the Sex & Ethics research and education projects.

Part I

Young People, Sex, and Sexual Assault Prevention

Chapter 1

Thinking Critically about Sexuality Education

One afternoon in the mid-1960s at my high school in Sydney, Australia, all the girls were taken to the assembly hall. We were shown a film that contained many diagrams of the male and female reproductive systems. There was no movement in the slides used, no sense of context—just as there was no discussion, nor any call for questions. As we filed out, we were given a booklet with a picture of a bride on the front cover. Inside was information about menstruation and how to manage it. We returned to the classroom to the bemused curiosity of the boys. They wanted to know what had happened. Most of us refused to tell them. We had no idea. We were mystified, but we knew enough to not tell the boys. At my school, there were no sexuality education classes for boys. My friend Michael tells me he went to a father-and-son night in about 1965. He didn't get it either. There were no discussions in classes about what we heard in the hall, and there was certainly no mention of sexual assault, date rape, or domestic violence.

Sometime later, my friend Jenny and I were in a domestic science class, decked out in our white starched caps and white aprons. We looked like a cross between a domestic servant and a nurse. The teacher was droning on about the need to prepare good, wholesome meals for our husbands. Husbands seemed a long way off. We were much more interested in reading the latest book I had got hold of— Mary McCarthy's 1963 novel, *The Group*. With the novel tucked inside my exercise book, I read a passage that, for the first time in my life, explained what sex between a man and a woman involved. It described Dottie, one of the female characters, losing her virginity to Dick, a married man. I passed it to Jenny. We couldn't wait to get out of class. We talked about it endlessly; we puzzled at the mechanics, pondered the biology, and, for a while, we were convinced it wasn't true. Being avid readers, we sought out many other books and finally concluded it was true. We were left feeling somewhat underwhelmed. What was it that caused so much unspoken anxiety around us?

These stories seem far removed from the options available to young women and men today. With the click of a mouse, they can find sexual information and see videos of sexual acts on the Internet. All is graphically revealed, at least to those who can bypass the various filters that might be in operation. There also seems to be greater openness to discussion. Government-funded state schools in Australia, and in many other countries, mostly have some form of personal development curriculum with opportunities for both women and men to interact, ask questions, and expect direct answers from teachers.

Despite this, the young women and men who participated in the research that underpins this book found much of what passes for sexuality education lacking. As a schoolgirl, I was struggling to get even biological information I could relate to—let alone anything that addressed the feelings and confusions I experienced. Similarly, despite the apparently more open discussion of sexuality today in the community, and within school curricula, the young people in my study reported feeling confused and pressured. They saw themselves as lacking in knowledge and skills to safely begin their sexual lives. Some of this can be attributed to the anxiety of moving into new territory. Whatever its name, sexuality education for young people is still often contentious, still too often done only in the name of biology or risk, and still caught up in moral anxiety. Sex often remains embedded in a romance narrative that has little room for the practical circumstances of everyday life.

Yet the facts are clear. The age of first sexual experience continues to get lower, even as the range of sexual activities involved widens. Parents, sex educators, teachers, youth workers, researchers, and politicians continue to worry. The latter often frequently see it as an indication of the "moral" decline of contemporary society. At the same time, high levels of pregnancy, sexually transmitted infections (STIs), coerced or pressured sex, and sexual assault among young people suggest that current approaches to preparing young people for sexually active lives is limited in reaching them on their terms.

Those terms are, of course, what are at stake in the wider discussion. In the wider context, they create the interface between sexuality, sexuality education, and violence prevention. How can young people be heard in any dialogue about the realities of their lives, sexuality education, pleasure, and danger? How might such a dialogue affect violence prevention? And how might it include pleasure and desire?

Sexuality and Violence Prevention Education in Dialogue

A unique feature of this book is the bringing together of research and other scholarship on both sexuality and violence prevention education. You may be wondering why a book with a title about sex is concerned with sexual assault prevention, or why sexual assault prevention includes consideration of issues regarding sex. There are several reasons. First, I argue that, for too long, sexuality education has denied the full range of young people's (and other's) experiences of sexual intimacy. It is more than biology. It covers a wide range of experiences, from the desire for and the negotiating of pleasures—physical and emotional, committed and casual—to the downright ordinary ("is that all it is?"). Sadly, for many, it also includes varying degrees of pressure, coercion, and sexual assault. This book identifies new ways of thinking about sex, sexual assault, and the prevention of violence. Violence prevention strategies are developed inside a sexual ethics framework that values pleasure at the same time as it acknowledges danger.

My argument is not that anything goes. Rather, I'm interested in what young people do when negotiating intimacy, sex, and love, and how they might be supported to do this well. There are some good sexuality education materials that take similar approaches. These too are often limited in their impact by restrictions on what can occur in schools, by inadequate training, and the constant need to defend them against attack. These conversations, or the lack of them, reflect the social and political contexts that frame what it is possible to speak of in any given historical moment. This is the wider contested field where discussion of sexual ethics takes place. It is not, as some would have it, simply a matter of sexuality education versus abstinence.

The evidence says that abstinence-based programs do not produce positive, sexual health outcomes. Nor do they prevent sexual violence. Quite frankly, I'm fed up with sex getting a bad rap, and the education for young people being primarily focused on the risk of STIs, or sexual assault. While risk matters, and is part of any sexual ethics framework, it is neither the only story, nor representative of the bigger picture. For too long, STIs, fear of pregnancy, and sexual assault have been used to narrate sex negatively, to the exclusion of the positive aspects of sex and what this means to many young people and others.

This book positions violence prevention in relation to these wider questions of sexual ethics and sexuality education, especially for young people. This required me to rethink what was being done in the name of violence prevention. In the process, I drew on many sources. I reflected also on what had occurred over the 30 years I have been involved in the field, as a social worker, program developer, and researcher. I listened to what practitioners told me, and to young people and what they said, and to what I learned from my own research and that of others. I drew my own conclusions.

Put bluntly, violence prevention education has focused on the "bad" things that can happen, and it too provides only a partial perspective on intimacy in all its forms. In a sense, how could it not? This partial perspective was crucially important historically. It allowed all of us in the feminist movement to name sexual assault and other forms of intimate violence, and make them visible in the media, in the law, and to policymakers. It allowed us to challenge social denial (of domestic violence, rape in marriage, and date rape) and the ways in which women were made responsible for "inciting men's lust" that resulted in rape (Carmody 1992).

We argued that rape and sexual assault were not about sex, but about power and control. From that perspective, rape represented the ultimate operation of a male patriarchal system that benefited all men—whether they committed rape or not. I now see that as a deeply pessimistic view that held out little hope for change, apart from a complete restructuring of society. While some aspects of this restructuring are evident in increased gender equality for women in the public sphere, it is the private sphere of intimate relations that proves so resistant to change.

Over time, we have also realized that the power and control evident in sexual violence has many different forms. An earlier assumption that rape was most frequently committed by strangers was refuted by Diana Russell (1990), in her study on wife rape, and by Mary Koss (1988), who investigated date rape on US college campuses. This enabled change to the law and to policy environments and arguably had considerable effects on wider society. Those effects, however, did not seem to stop sexual assault, or even lessen its occurrence. Sexual assault within marriage, for example, was not made a crime until the early 1980s in many democratic countries. Even so, there are very few charges laid or prosecuted under this legal provision. Indeed, most sexual assaults of any kind are still not reported. Estimates vary, but they are low. In Australia, only 10–20 percent of actual offences result in reports to the police, and the attrition rate is high for those cases that go before the courts (Australian Bureau of Statistics 2004; Jordan 2001; Lievore 2003; Neame and Heenan 2003). In the United States, a 2009 analysis of the US Department of Justice rape crime statistics found that, contrary to media reports, the rate of rapes and the conviction rates for rape in the United States haven't improved since the 1970s. According to the study, even today, in only roughly 2 percent of rapes reported to police in the United States will a rapist go to jail (Lonsway and Archambault 2012). Some of the reluctance to report may be due to fear of legal proceedings—especially what it means to give evidence in court. However, most researchers and practitioners agree that many women still feel they are responsible, and this inhibits them from reporting the crime.

As the definition of rape widened, researchers began asking women about other forms of subtle coercion—from an unwanted kiss to unwanted sexual intercourse—as a result of verbal pressure. Koss (1988) and Gavey (1991a, 1991b) both found that 50 percent of women reported having some experience on this continuum of sexual victimization. Gavey's (2005a) study further documented the experiences of women who felt pressured or were coerced directly by partners or their cultural conditioning to accept unwanted sex.

These shifting approaches to sexual assault resulted in prevention education incorporating an understanding of risk as occurring "closer to home." However, as I discuss in chapter 5, many prevention efforts utilized a risk model that individualized the problem for women. Women are made responsible for learning to manage their own risk of sexual assault. Men are not seen as part of the solution because they are the problem. In this model, the educational spotlight is on stopping unethical behavior. In the process, gender relations are made central. It all seems to make sense on the surface, given the statistics on who mostly perpetrated the violence.

Yet, over time, research indicated it just wasn't this simple. There is now a substantial body of evidence from the United States and Canada that this approach does not prevent sexual violence (see Carmody and Carrington 2000, for a detailed overview of this research).

In addition, it produces an account where women are doomed to potential victimhood and men to be inherently exploitative. There is no recognition of the diverse ways in which women and men negotiate sexual intimacy based on mutuality and ethics. Not surprisingly then, I believe that we need alternative ways of conceptualizing our primary prevention education in the field of sexual violence.

As part of this rethinking, we need to consider how prevention materials for young people have incorporated risk and fear. Young people are often associated with ideas of risk (Furlong and Cartmel 2007). However, the sexual cultures in which they operate are less well understood. Research in the United Kingdom by Attwood and Smith (2011) among a range of specialists from sexual health, childhood, youth, and media and communication studies identified a number of gaps in their understanding of young people.

These included a considerable lack of actual knowledge about young people's sexual cultures, a need for more qualitative research, and a concern to move beyond young people and danger to a consideration of the ways in which young people can and do have good experiences of sex. This lack of knowledge is strongly evident in the official resources provided to young people. If we listen to the talk about sex, we come away with an overwhelming sense that sex is always dangerous and that young people need to be fearful of it. This, however, is not how they see sex. For them, sex has much more complex relations with going out, dating, forming relationships, and feeling their way. It sometimes seems as though film, television, and much else in popular culture better understands this. This mismatch or "gap," as Louisa Allen (2005) calls it, between official sexuality talk, popular culture, and what young people say about their experiences has negative effects. Sexuality education is, therefore, seen as irrelevant and out of touch with their concerns.

I remain optimistic in spite of the damning worldwide evidence of sexual and other forms of intimate violence reported by the United Nations (2005), in the United States (Black et al. 2011), and in Australia and other countries (Mitchell et al. 2014). I do not think my optimism is misplaced. As evidence for this, I think we need to reflect on the many women and men who do not resort to violence in their intimate relationships.

We can do better in relation to preventing sexual violence before it occurs. My optimism is underpinned by the possibility of a more comprehensive approach to violence prevention education that places positive sexuality education at its heart. We need to think differently about both sexuality and violence prevention education, and produce links between them that enable more positive prevention results.

In this book, I position prevention education within a sexual ethics framework that values sexual pleasure. It involves social and collective perspectives on how people negotiate sex. It is not used simply to refer to morals and morality. The general purposes of prevention education in this framework are twofold: to support people in constructively achieving their goals in sexual contexts and to lessen the frequency of negative outcomes.

This approach allows us to explore the risks of sexuality, including emotional as well as physical risks, but it does so in relation to the pleasures involved. That is, it acknowledges what the participants bring to sex and the contexts where it occurs. It steps back from prescriptive approaches that primarily tell young people what they should do. Rather, this project involves asking them: "What is it you are concerned about? What knowledge and skills do you need?" It then offers practical ideas and techniques that help them work out their own ethical stance in a multiplicity of contexts. Let me spell out my theoretical rationale a bit more fully.

Conceptual Frameworks

I have worked for more than three decades around a range of strategies to prevent sexual violence. These include law reform; clinical support for survivors of sexual assault; policy reform to improve institutional responses to survivors; and community education to challenge community denial of the trauma and cost of sexual violence to the whole community. This has been matched by academic research and teaching. In 1999, I realized that, despite our best efforts, sexual assault had not diminished and, in some areas, it seemed to have worsened. Despite this pessimistic evaluation, I also knew many women and men who were appalled at the gross inhumanity and lack of concern for others evident in sexual assault. Much of the time, as a community, we have seen education as the answer, whatever the issue: drink driving, smoking, obesity, parenting, environmental protection, and sexual and physical violence, to name a few. However, education is not a value-free enterprise and sexuality education, in particular, is highly contested terrain: "Discourses of sex education are important because they include and exclude, empower and disqualify, facilitate and stigmatise" (Scott 2005, 168).

As I began to critically examine educational approaches to sexual assault prevention, it became evident that a primary focus on awareness of the existence and impact of sexual violence had little hope of significantly altering the cultural and individual gendered practices in communities. Collectively, thousands of hours of work had gone into this enterprise by thousands of women and some men, but there was little evidence of lasting social change. I think many of us naively believed that, if people just understood how devastating crimes of sexual violence are, they would stop. A growing community awareness and government lack of tolerance of this behavior has resulted in increased penalties for offenders. However, these changes have failed to address the underlying problem before the crime is committed.

My continued musing and research in the area led me to question how it is that some men and women who are exposed to the same cultural messages as others are able to resist using violence to achieve sexual intimacy. It seemed that, for years, we had been talking about the excesses of some forms of masculinity, but had heard little about the productive ways in which some men had negotiated gender performance within intimate relations. In a study conducted with my colleague Kerry Carrington, we concluded there was a "need to develop multi-level prevention strategies which promote an alternative cultural landscape of sexual practices and norms" (Carmody and Carrington 2000, p. 355).

This book reflects on further research and education I have undertaken since that time. It focuses on exploring alternative ways to prevent sexual violence and working with young women and men of diverse sexualities, cultural groups, and geographic locations to build ethical sexual practices. I propose an alternative way of working with young people based on the concept of sexual ethics. This concept is drawn from Michel Foucault's work (1990, and as cited in Rabinow 1997) on developing ethical subjectivity, as well as other work on gender and sexual diversity. It includes a consideration of the multiple ways in which both women and men perform gender and sex, and resist or conform to dominant cultural discourses.

Foucault's work seems compatible with other recent changes. The World Health Organization (WHO), as cited by Mitchell (2007), has moved away from a factual information model in terms of young people and sexuality education. It argues, instead, that young people need to learn how to make sound decisions about relationships and sexual pressures, use negotiation skills, recognize risky situations, and identify how and where to get help. Other sexuality researchers such as Allen (2005), Cameron-Lewis and Allen (2013), and Powell (2007a, 2007b) have identified the need for a shift in approach. However, there has been a limited uptake of positive sexuality education models that promote and develop these skills and include more than a passing mention of sexual assault or other forms of gendered violence.

This book aims to address this gap. The Sex & Ethics framework I have developed does not "tell" young people what they should or shouldn't do in relation to sexual intimacy, but provides them with a set of tools to help them make informed ethical decisions. One hallmark of the Sex & Ethics framework used in this study is how it links the ways in which a young person can take care of themselves and be mindful of the needs of a potential partner, irrespective of whether it is a casual encounter or an ongoing relationship. Like Louisa Allen (2005), I see young women and men as active sexual subjects who have the potential to shape their own lives. However, I take this further and argue that young people are not only sexual subjects, but also are and have the potential to become ethical sexual subjects. Fundamental to this approach is a conceptualization of young people that moves beyond either universalizing or demonizing them. This approach provides a space in which to consider both the pleasures of sex and some of the dangers and, as such, it provides a more wide-ranging approach based on ethical subjectivity.

Theoretically, the book is written from a feminist poststructuralist perspective. For me, this means following the challenge from Audre Lorde (1984)—that is, as feminists and researchers we need to dis-cover and utilize differences between women and men as a source for creative change. I have been strongly influenced in my work by Foucault's reworking of power and the feminist applications of his work (see, e.g., Ramazanaglou 1993; Sawicki 1991). Power is cen-tral to all social relations and it is Foucault's reworking of traditional conceptualizations of power that have proved most useful to many feminist scholars. He argued that power is exercised rather than pos-sessed and, therefore, foregrounds the relational and productive pos-sibilities of power. Jana Sawicki (1991, 23) describes the impact of his approach. She suggests that Foucault's conceptualization of power to include its impact on the microlevels of society provides the possibil-ity of resistance against the many forms of power that are exercised at the everyday level of social relations.

I would argue that debates around sexuality education and the sexual lives of young people involve the exercise of disciplinary power on the lives and bodies of young people. Not surprisingly, this is often experienced negatively. The challenge for prevention education is how to support young people in their use of their own power to shape their sexual lives as ethical sexual subjects. What this book explores is how sexual ethics can assist young people to reconfigure everyday forms of power in sexual intimacy.

TheR esearchS tudies

While the following chapters are theoretically informed, they are also substantially supported by a series of empirical research stud-ies conducted between 2006 and 2012. Phase one of the research was funded by an Australian Research Council Grant for the period 2005–2008. The data are drawn from two areas of work with over 100 young people. The first involved in-depth interviews with 56 cul-turally and sexually diverse young women and men aged 16–25 years from rural and metropolitan areas in New South Wales (NSW),

Australia, in 2006. One of the key findings from this stage of the research (Carmody and Willis 2006) was that young people wanted sexuality and violence prevention education that moved beyond the "mechanics of sex" and "just say no" approaches. Rather, they wanted an opportunity to explore the dilemmas involved—both between and within being sexual or not being sexual. These included how to deal with friendship pressure to be sexually active, where they could learn skills in negotiating consent and safe sex, and how to address conflicting desires and expectations in intimate relationships. This research forms the basis of Part I of the book and includes many excerpts from interviews with young women and men.

Data derived from interviews with young people informed the development of a three-hour per week, six-week educational program based on sexual ethics. Using sexual ethics as the organizing principle, I wanted to assess its primary prevention potential. That is, I wanted to assess how useful it would be to support young people in preventing unwanted, coerced, or pressured sex within casual or ongoing relationships. This goal was not only about reducing unethical behavior. More importantly, it was about increasing their confidence in ethical negotiation of sex.

From this work, the Sex & Ethics Program was born. The program was piloted with six groups, involving 47 young women and men of diverse sexualities, aged 16–25 years, in two rural and three city locations in NSW in 2007. A rigorous process and outcome-evaluation approach was embedded in the pilot. Young people completed pre- and post-test surveys, provided feedback on weekly sessions and activities, and comments on what they had gained from the groups and what they thought could be improved. All participants agreed to be contacted six months after completing a group. This follow-up was conducted to try to assess the longer term impact on the participants' sexual lives beyond the life of the program. The findings from Phase One of the research were published by Palgrave Macmillan, Australia, in two books: *Sex & Ethics: Young People and Ethical Sex* (Carmody 2009a) and a workbook of the program, *Sex & Ethics: The Sexual Ethics Education Program for Young People* (Carmody 2009b).

Since the original research was completed, I have received additional funding from multiple sources to continue the research to implement and evaluate the Sex & Ethics Program. This has included funding, in April 2009, from the Australian Commonwealth (federal) Department of Families, Housing, Community Services, and Indigenous Affairs (FaHCSIA) for training of educators to deliver the program in five locations across the state of NSW including one rural area, and to evaluate its impact among young people. In late 2009, further funding was provided by FaHSCIA to extend the program to trainee junior footballers in the state of Queensland and to evaluate its impact specifically on the lives of young men. The New Zealand Ministry of Justice also provided funding for 2009–2010 for the training of educators who subsequently ran multiple groups for young people in Wellington. This period I refer to as Phase Two.

Data were collected during Phase Two from 2009 to 2011. Since the program's inception, over 220 personnel from a variety of disciplines including social workers, psychologists, youth workers, sexual health educators, sexual assault and domestic violence workers, and footballers have received formal five days of training prior to running the six-week Sex & Ethics Program with young women and men. Data collected included feedback from the educators' training that is discussed in detail in chapter 9.

Data have also been collected from all Sex & Ethics Groups run with young people. This includes pre- and post-group surveys and six-month follow-up data from participants who took part in the program from 2009 to 2011, as well as feedback received during the six-week group program. Data were collected from multiple sites across Australia and New Zealand. In chapter 8, I discuss the findings and the lasting impact of the Sex & Ethics Program on their lives.

The following chapters will weave these empirical research findings with theoretical discussions of the challenges that emerge in working at the crossroads of sociology, sexuality, gender studies, and violence prevention to find new ways of ethical intimacy.

Audience for This Book and the Structure

There are several main audiences for this book. I have written for both—practitioners who work directly with young people and for academics that research and teach in the fields of sexuality, gender, and violence against women. It is also for students who are preparing to work with young people or who are studying these topics. I also have in mind that the work will be of interest to a range of disciplinary contexts particularly sociology, social work, psychology, sexual health, criminology, education, cultural studies and gender, and women's and masculinities studies. I have placed a lot of importance on providing space for you to hear directly from the young people who have taken part in interviews and education groups and the educators who worked with them. While I provide theoretical and critical analysis throughout the text, for those less interested in these approaches, there are a number of chapters that focus more on the direct experience of the women and men who took part.

The book is presented in two parts. The first part (chapters 1–5) describes the initial interview research and a consideration of international literature on sexuality and violence prevention. Chapter 2 considers how young women and men understand and experience sexuality and sexual intimacy. This is followed by chapter 3, where young people talk about their experiences of negotiating sexual intimacy and sexual consent in casual sex and sex in relationships. I explore the competing pressures experienced by young people as they begin their sexual lives. Moral or ethical frameworks provided by schools or family may be rejected in lieu of a young person finding their way in social and sexual relationships. Chapter 4 considers young people's experiences of sexuality education within schools and offers a critique of education and other strategies based around risk. This is explored from the perspective of how well young people feel school prepares them for sexual intimacy, and what they say would help them in developing ethical sexual lives. Chapter 5 provides an international overview of sexual assault prevention education. In this chapter, I describe the competing discourses operating within the field, and how they have impacted in both Western and emerging nations. I consider some of the unintended consequences of these discourses and their limitations in terms of the primary prevention of sexual violence. I also highlight promising areas of work to more actively engage men and boys.

The second part of the book (chapters 6–10) describes and explores the development of education based on sexual ethics. While it has been very important to document the experiences of young people and sexuality, there is a need to find alternative approaches to sexuality and violence prevention education that move beyond risk discourses and deficit models of educational intervention. The focus of chapter 6 is the Sex & Ethics framework that is offered as an alternative to previous educational models. This chapter explores the origins of my new approach and how it has been implemented in Australia and New Zealand in several research and educational studies (Carmody and Carrington 2000; Carmody 2003, 2005, 2006; 2009a; 2013a; b). The key elements of the model are explored, including care of the self, care of the other, negotiation, and reflection. Feedback from young people who took part in the Sex & Ethics groups, in rural and city locations, conclude this chapter.

Chapter 7 outlines the values that underpin the Sex & Ethics Education Program, its structure and philosophy, and provides an overview of the six-session interactive format. It explores how the issues raised by young people in interviews have been incorporated into the program content and activities to provide real-life situations that speak to the concerns of young women and men. Their response to these activities is also discussed briefly.

Chapter 8 documents the impact of the Sex & Ethics Education Program on the lives of young people who have participated in groups across Australia and New Zealand since 2008. From the inception of the program, research data have been collected from participants at three time intervals, including at the six-month follow-up. Results across diverse population groups consistently reveal statistically significant changes in how people understand caring for themselves and caring for another. Many reported continued use of ideas and skills from the program in casual and ongoing sexual relationships, with friends, and intervening as ethical bystanders.

Chapter 9 reflects on my experience of training educators since 2008 to deliver the Sex & Ethics Education Program. The conceptual approaches underpinning training are discussed as well as theories of change utilized in training. Central to the approach taken is an invitation to educators to move beyond the role of expert and to critically reflect on their own values and attitudes to gender, sexuality, young people, and their pedagogical practices.

Chapter 10 is the final chapter. It draws together the overall findings of the research and considers some of the wider impact of the research and education since its initial developments. I also consider the importance of the Sex & Ethics Program and research as one part of a multi-systemic approach to primary prevention. I conclude by discussing future research needs.

Chapter 2

Listening to Young People's Experiences of Sexuality

Throughout the life of this ongoing research project, it has been important to provide space to hear the experiences of young people. Although they are often the consumers of sexuality and violence-prevention education, they are rarely involved in shaping the programs delivered to them or in critically evaluating them. I was keen to explore how young women and men, aged 16–25 years, negotiate sexual intimacy, and to assess their views on sexuality and violence-prevention education, its usefulness to them, and what they thought should be included. This is the focus of the present chapter. I was also aware of the diversity in young people's lives: where they live; what they do; and the effects of gender, sexuality, ethnicity, and race. In the initial phase of the research, this commitment was put into practice through interviewing a sample of young women and men from three metropolitan locations and three regional towns in the state of New South Wales (NSW), Australia.

Recruiting for Individual Interviews

The recruitment materials—inviting young people to take part in a one-to-one interview about intimate aspects of their lives—needed to speak to them on their own terms. We had to capture their interest in the project. We used a variety of methods to engage participants for interview. These included a postcard and poster using a comic format for distribution at key sites, personal promotion at interagency meetings, print and radio articles and television spots about the project, and building relationships with a wide range of organizations working with young people.

We had decided to not actively recruit in schools, as our sample went beyond school-age young people. Recruitment of participants who were younger than 18 years of age was constrained by the University of Western Sydney's Ethics Committee.[1] It required parental consent, as well as that of the young people. We knew this would rule out most of that cohort, as many young people are reluctant to raise the issue of sex with their parents. Despite these limitations, we were able to interview a number of young people, aged 16–18. They formed a much smaller cohort than we had hoped for when the project was designed. Overall, we found that the most productive recruitment strategy in actually getting young people to consent to interview was working with someone the young people already knew and trusted. They could vouch for our credentials and actively encourage young people's involvement. Without their support, hard work, and commitment to violence prevention and working with young people, we would not have been able to access young people in the time frames we had allocated.

Recruiting a Diverse Range of Young People

Sampling was not designed to be "representative." That only applies to large-scale quantitative samples, and is not feasible in qualitative sampling. However, we did want the recruitment to engage with issues of diversity. This meant we wanted a spread of ages, genders, socioeconomic backgrounds, sexualities, and cultures. In addition, we wanted sexually experienced and inexperienced young people from metropolitan and regional locations. This was important to ensure we could access a range of different experiences. We did not assume, for example, that young people in different parts of the city had the same concerns as each other or with those in regional rural areas.

We determined the choice of recruitment sites by factors such as demographic information on the numbers of young people in the region in the specified age cohort, level of reported sexual assault, culturally diverse regions, and identified youth groups. We tended to focus on existing collaborative arrangements with education, police, and health and community services. Given the high incidence of violence within Aboriginal communities, we aimed to recruit in at least one rural region with a high indigenous population of young people (Bolger 1991, Cox 2008, Robertson 2000).

We interviewed 56 people. The interview sample included a higher proportion of young people from regional/rural areas (63 percent) compared to those from metropolitan areas (38 percent). This was not problematic. In Australia, the NSW state Bureau of Crime Statistics and Research (BOCSAR) reports on sexual assault offenses identified the top 50 towns with the highest rate of reported sexual assaults. Two-thirds were in regional and rural locations (BOCSAR 2004, 2005). This was consistent with Hogg and Carrington's (2006) research on rural crime that showed a higher rate in rural areas per population than in metropolitan areas—contrary to long-held beliefs about the comparative safety of the country compared to the city. This profile of higher assault rates in rural and regional towns has remained consistent across many years. There is also less published research on young people and sexual intimacy from rural areas in Australia—something I was keen to redress.

Of the young people we spoke to, 71 percent were female and 29 percent were male. (There were no self-identifying transgender people.) This lower representation of young men reflects an ongoing difficulty researchers have of attracting male participants into sexuality research. University students made up 60 percent of the sample, but almost a quarter (23 percent) were not in any form of education. A smaller number (14 percent) were at high school and 4 percent were in post-school vocational education (TAFE). This meant the sample was broader than in many North American studies that tend to be dominated by university and college participants.

Australia is a culturally diverse country with an indigenous population and a history of immigration. A quarter of the population was born overseas (ABS Census 2001). Census figures from the Australian Bureau of Statistics (ABS) for 2001 indicated that 3 percent of young people were identified as Aboriginal or Torres Strait Islanders (ATSI). This study included 12 percent of people from an ATSI background. That was very pleasing in its own right, and because it was more than consistent with national demographics. They were all from regional areas. Compared to the ABS figure of 15 percent, 21 percent of the participants also indicated a cultural background other than Anglo-Australian. They included many second- and third-generation young people of migrant parents from South America, Sri Lanka, Malta, Greece, Italy, Poland, Laos, Korea, India, New Zealand, and the United States. The data indicate how hard it was to recruit young men from culturally diverse backgrounds and suggest specific recruitment techniques may be necessary to reach this group.

It has been suggested that Generation Y is reluctant to claim a fixed sexual identity, refusing labels (Wilkinson, 2014). Although four participants indicated a reluctance to claim a sexual identity label, the majority of participants claimed an identity when asked the open-ended question: "How would you describe your sexual identity?" The sample was predominantly heterosexual, with 66 percent identifying in this way. However, these identity categories should not be taken as fixed, as a few of the heterosexual women had some same-sex experience, the gay men had some experience with women, and the lesbians had some sexual experience with men. This indicates sexual exploration across heteronormative boundaries and may be pertinent to discussions of the pressure on lesbians and gay men to conform to dominant forms of sexuality, especially between 16 and 25 years of age.

Interviews

Interviews were held between March and June 2006. Karen Willis, my co-researcher, and I conducted all interviews face-to-face, except for two telephonic interviews. All interviews were audio-taped or digitally recorded, and then professionally transcribed. Interviews averaged about an hour, although some went on for up to two hours. Participants were provided with information about local resources or were encouraged to access the NSW Rape Crisis Centre's 24-hour toll-free telephonic counseling or online counseling service if issues arose as a result of the interviews.

An interview schedule was developed to guide the semi-structured interviews. The process of the interviews, however, was conducted more as a conversation—with key areas explored without the rigidity of a structured interview schedule. Demographic information was collected at the beginning of the interview and, after that, paper and pen were put aside.

Areas for exploration in the interviews included:

- Experiences of formal and informal sexuality education.
- Sexual history of consensual and unwanted sexual experiences.
- Sexual intimacy and participants' feelings about how things happen in sexual encounters, using scenarios to trigger conversation.
- Reflection on their own sexual experiences and how they work out what they will or won't do in any sexual encounter and how their partner would know this, including the impact of safe-sex education on their sexual practices and how they negotiate this.
- Experience of sexual assault or other violence-prevention education strategies, and what they thought were the strengths and weaknesseso ft hep rograms.

Data were analyzed using the Nvivo® V. 6 software package to code and organize the 56 interview transcripts thematically. The primary focus of the data analysis was to highlight similarities and differences across the sample to gain an understanding of the lived experience of participants. The theoretical orientation of the analysis was informed by a poststructuralist gender analysis that examined multiple ways in which women and men of diverse sexualities and backgrounds experienced sexual intimacy.

Young People's Experiences of Sex

I was particularly interested to explore with the interview participants how they felt about sex, how they worked out whether to be sexual or not, what kind of pressures they had to juggle in negotiating whether to be sexual or not, and what the experiences were like for them. I begin by exploring the data about gender and age of first sexual experience, the impact of education on the age of commencing sexual activity, and the number of sexual partners young people reported as well as the gender of these partners. All participants have been given pseudonyms.

Studies that explore young people's first sexual experiences focus primarily on heterosexual intercourse (Hall 1995; Hickman and Muehlenhard 1999; Humphreys 2004). My approach was somewhat different for several reasons. First, this approach fails to examine the wide range of sexual activities that young people can engage in or are possible. In this study, sex was defined by young people in response to an open-ended question: "What happened when you had your first sexual experiences with another person?" It also relegates sexual activity outside of heterosexual intercourse to "foreplay," thus denying the meaning given to it by young people, and reinforces a focus on heterosexuality. As Nicola Gavey (2005, 124) argues, "a coital imperative operates, which provides a cultural nest in which penetration of the vagina places it as central to sex; the defining feature of sex; the main act." Second, a focus that is exclusively on heterosexual activity denies the experiences of same-sex-attracted young people and others who explore sexuality outside of a fixed sexual identity. Given my concern about preventing sexual violence, such a focus makes invisible possible sites of sexual assault or unwanted sex. A broader definition of sexual activity allows exploration of how sex is defined and experienced by young people. It is also consistent with varying definitions of what constitutes sexual assault or rape in different jurisdictions.

The issue that concerns many parents, and others working with young people, is the declining age of first sexual experience and what they fear young people are doing. The data indicate young men commence sexual activity at a younger age than most of the young women, with ages 15–16 being the most common age for commencing activity for both young men and women. This study did not actively seek details of sexual acts engaged in, but the transcripts reveal a range of acts including oral and anal sex and sexual intercourse. Cumulative rates of first sexual experiences by gender indicated that 90 percent of the young women and men included in the research were sexually active by age 18. Involvement in education was explored to see if it had any impact on age at first sex. The data indicated some interesting findings. There was no difference in the age at first sex for young women, if they were in education or not, with the average age being 16.6 years. However, for young men, the average age of first sex for those who were not in education was 14.7 years, compared to 17.0 years if they were on a track to university. This suggests that young men with university in mind may be less focused on early sexual activity than boys who leave school earlier. The educational implications of this are important to ensure that sex education deals explicitly with sexuality and sexual assault-prevention issues before some boys leave school.

Sex occurred in both casual encounters and ongoing relationships. An analysis of the data on total numbers of casual and ongoing-relationship partners for regional and metropolitan participants indicated some minor differences. Rural participants reported a slightly higher number of casual partners compared to the city sample (7.0 compared to 6.3). The numbers of ongoing-relationship partners were slightly higher for metropolitan young people (3.2 compared to 2.7 for the regional sample). A comparison of the different rates of casual and ongoing relationships for the total sample by gender revealed little difference between women and men. Men had, on average, 7.3 casual partners compared to 6.0 for women. Women had an average of 2.8 ongoing relationships compared to 3.1 for men.

The data do not indicate that the younger you are when you have sex, the more partners you have—despite community fears about the decreasing age of first sexual activity. I also examined any differences between young people of different sexual identities, and whether this influenced the number of partners. The data indicate five to ten partners as the most common number. There were some exceptions including two gay men, two heterosexuals, and one bisexual female. In this study, apart from a few outliers, heterosexual-identified young people had the most partners. This has significant implications for targeted sex education including safe-sex information provision and violence prevention.

Of the total sample, six or 11 percent indicated they had no sexual experience. This included four young women, ages 22, 19, and 17, and two young men, ages 17 and 22. However, three of the women had sexual contact with a partner, but they had not had heterosexual intercourse and felt they were not sexually experienced. They felt sex was important in the context of a special relationship that they were yet to find, and they resisted partner and friendship group pressure to become sexually active. One young man was yet to have the opportunity for sexual intimacy, and the other was a committed Christian, and it was against his beliefs to have sex before marriage.

Feelings about the Experiences of First Sex

Participants indicated a range of feelings and impacts of their first exploration of sexual activity. These included disappointment, feelings about virginity, feelings of regret, and positive feelings about first sex. I'll now consider each of these in turn.

Disappointment

Moira: So how was it?
Lorraine: It was three minutes
Moira: That long? (laughs)…So not a romantic storybook kind of thing?
Lorraine: No, definitely not.
(Lorraine, from a regional area, aged 16)

Given the focus on the need to be sexually active among many friendship groups, expectations about what it might be like were high. Lack of experience in knowing what to do and how to make it pleasurable for both involved is a common feature of first sex. However, it seems that participants expected more and were not prepared for the awkwardness involved, as Donna, from a regional area, aged 18, described:

It's not what I expected…like you know how people make out "oh it's the best thing ever" sort of thing, and I think it was a bit awkward the first time.

This was similar for Mike from the city, aged 16:

I don't know life changing and the best thing ever…the first time was just like yeah, this isn't that good.

Looking back on it now, Helen from a regional area, aged 17, could see the humor and awkwardness:

> No, more like one of those teenage movies where you bump heads and [you are] sitting on your hair and it was really bizarre and like just all that…nothing bad it was just silly and I giggled in the middle of it because he didn't have a clue and I didn't have a clue, I didn't have a clue at all, and I was like still shy afterwards and couldn't even look at him and everything and I'd known him forever and it was head down and not talking.

Being older didn't seem to reduce expectations of the experience, as Kerry from a regional area, aged 20, recalls:

> I was at my parents' house and I went and woke up my sister and I said, "I've just had sex," and she goes, "well, did you like it?" I said, "nah, I was expecting like something magnificent to happen" and she goes, "oh well, you'll get used to it." Um, but it wasn't fantastic, but it wasn't…like it wasn't God that was so bad, I was just like oh okay.

Feelings about Virginity

For those participants who defined their first sexual experience as heterosexual intercourse, there was a mixture of feelings about virginity. Some, as Carpenter (2002) describes, saw it as a stigma and a negative status they wished to remove. Marion, a Laotian-Australian woman from the city, aged 16, said:

> I was really hyped up about it. I just knew I was ready and it was just part of, um, I don't know…just the way I thought was a bit strange because I was just like, okay, I didn't really care who it is with I was just like okay I'm ready for sex.

For Sasha, a Korean-Australian woman from a regional area, aged 18, getting rid of the label "virgin" was important:

> Honestly, it got to the point where I thought, I just want to get rid of this whole label of being known as a virgin and just get it over and done with and see what the big deal is.

The need to feel like her friends and be able to participate in discussions about it was a deciding factor for Kirsten, aged 16, from the city:

> So that's the only reason I ever decided to have sex was because I hadn't done it and all my friends had done it. They all talked about it together and I felt left out.

However, for others, virginity was seen as a gift (Carpenter 2002) or something special that they valued and wanted to hold onto, and had not yet found the right person to share this with. For Doug, aged 22, a committed Christian from a regional area, this is something he wants to keep until he is married:

> I guess when you get to that point where you're thinking seriously about marriage with a partner, a girlfriend,... that's not going to be always the case, but you're more than likely going to share the same values, the same beliefs as your partner, so you both respect that you both want to wait until you can give that gift, 'til after you're married and you consummate the marriage basically with that gift from sex.

The recognition that virginity is special requires some serious consideration, as Zoe from a regional area, aged 19, explains:

> I suppose it's a special type of thing, especially when it's, I don't know, it's hard to explain um...it's just something you should consider [being] serious about, like in all seriousness about because once it happens you can't get it back and that's something that I reckon, in my opinion, should be exercised thoroughly. Like if you want to, yeah fine, just go but make sure it's with somebody very special or who you think is very special.

Feelings of Regret

A number of young people expressed feelings of regret about the experience of first sex once it was over. Their expectations either weren't met or they felt confused about their feelings and unable to talk about them. Judy, aged 16, from the city described her feelings:

> Oh it was awful. It was dreadful...I'd honestly, um, had maybe a bottle of vodka. I felt really dirty...I didn't have time to have a shower and I just felt so awful. I was just guilt-ridden walking around with her [mother] going oh God mum you've got no idea, and I was uncomfortable and I was confused and...generally upset.

Other participants who felt that they had not really thought about it enough at the time expressed similar feelings of regret. They wished they had been sober and waited longer for it to happen with someone they felt more connected to. Stuart—who was 14 at the time he first had sex, from a regional area—indicated:

> If I could change it I probably would...to keep it a bit longer and find someone more to connect with. I was pretty pissed [drunk] so don't

even remember most of it, so yeah something I regret being drunk for the first time.

For Ellen, aged 17, from the city, who has since come out as a lesbian, her feelings of regret resulted from feeling she had to prove she wasn't gay:

> I don't think I was ready and because well I did come out being gay a year later when I moved here, I realized then I didn't want to do it, I was just trying to prove something to myself...I didn't really like it and afterwards it was very regrettable, I guess like I did regret it a lot.

The lack of a space to be able to talk through feelings and doubts about first sex was exacerbated for Rod, also from a regional area, as his first experience at 17 was with another man in a casual encounter:

> Well it was with a guy, my first time, and so there was that added to it as well, so I'd just lost my virginity and that I'd just done it with a guy as well...I didn't really know how to deal with it and I had no-one to talk to about it because it was just that one time with him.

Positive Feelings about First Sex

The context in which participants expressed positive feelings about first sex was different, depending on gender. The men's positive feelings were linked to a sense of achievement related to their masculinity, for example: "I was just being a male, all excited and happy," "I thought I was on top of the world," and "scored man." Their feelings indicate a sense of personal and gendered achievement that seemed to have little to do with whom they had the sexual experience.

This was noticeably different for women, whose positive feelings of first sex they attribute to the sex occurring with someone they were in a relationship with—either as partners or as friends. This was the case for lesbians, heterosexual, and bisexual women. Meryl, from a regional area, who is now married and describes herself as bisexual, had her first sexual experience at 16 with a woman who was a good friend:

> It was really natural, we were good friends and had travelled together...it wasn't a premeditated thing it just seemed like a natural projection of our friendship at the time. Um, yeah it was it was great. In terms of a first serious sexual experience it was really positive...probably one of the most positive sexual experiences I've ever had.

The need to feel comfortable with the person was highlighted by a number of women, as was the ability to talk about sex in the context of the broader relationship, as Carol, aged 19, from the city, explained:

> This was someone I'd known for a very long time and I think, more than anything, I just felt very comfortable with him and probably, because we'd been friends for such a long time, there was like a good deal of openness. For 19, we were still very awkward, but despite that, [we had] a good deal of openness about, you know, did we want to have sex and when and how and yeah, so we talked about it and then we decided to do it.

These narratives from young people reveal the complexity of feelings around first sexual experiences. For many, their expectations about what it was supposed to be like and the reality of what occurred were somewhat different. The most positive experiences occurred within the context of a relationship or with someone who was known well. What is noticeably absent from many of these stories is any indication of sexual desire. Rather, we see an almost inevitable "let's get it over with" approach, which suggests that some of them felt compelled to engage in sexual acts as a rite of passage, or as a way to demonstrate their sexual credentials to their friendship groups and to themselves. Despite this, their reflections suggest that for some, at least, they would have liked more time to consider taking this step. This suggests a lack of emotional and cultural space for young people to explore sexual desire. Sex is reduced to a biological act that needs to be achieved and the feelings, emotions, and bodily responses to it seem to be secondary. This is not just an individual matter of choice, but reflects the way cultural patterns concerning gender and sexuality are embodied by individuals.

CasualS ex

Young people describe casual sex using a variety of terms including "hooking up" or "picking up." Whatever term is used, they describe sexual relationships in ways not based on romance, as often spontaneous and impulsive, and that frequently involve alcohol or drugs (Grello, Welsh, and Harper 2006). Hooking up or picking up for casual sex was experienced by 64 percent of both male and female participants. Of the city sample, 33 percent had experience of casual sex and this increased to 66 percent for participants from regional towns. This indicates that, in our sample, there were higher levels of casual sexual relationships for regional young women and men. However, caution needs to be exercised in considering these figures. There were some differences between regional young people and the metropolitan sample in relation to casual sex.

The rural young people engaged in casual sex, but this was rarely with someone who was unknown to them or their circle of friends. This may have been a function of living in smaller communities where people the same age may be known to them at least as acquaintances. In the city, casual sex involved more pick-ups at clubs, where they were less likely to have any knowledge of the person beyond that night.

Although some participants had experiences of casual sex during their school years, this presented some risks for young women, as discussed. They needed to balance the peer pressure to be sexually active, to fit in with friendship norms and not be seen as "a loser" but, at the same time, they needed to avoid being condemned as sexually promiscuous. Therefore, most sex in the school-age years happened in the context of a relationship, however brief. This did not hinder experiences of casual sex at parties, however, where underage drinking was common.

By age 18, when access to licensed premises is legal in Australia, the opportunities for hooking up for casual sex increased markedly. Alcohol consumption was a key factor in both women's and men's stories of hooking up. They felt it gave them courage to be sexually assertive. For both women and men, it appeared alcohol allowed them to express the desire for a sexual encounter and to be quite assertive about achieving it. Young people who left country areas and went away to university and lived in residential colleges found a new freedom in which high levels of alcohol consumption and casual sex were expected. In one setting, this was actively encouraged by practices in a residential college where everyone had to weekly recount their sexual experiences and pay a monetary fine if they had failed to pick-up. Despite positive initial feelings of freedom, a number of participants were left with negative feelings afterwards, as Judy, aged 23, from the city indicates:

> Personally it makes me feel shit, but my friends think that it's empowering and, you know, that's cool and that's what they wanted and I feel like crap.

Similarly for Kerry, aged 21, from a regional area:

> I didn't like the fact that, ah, the next day I was like "and what was his last name?" and "what else do you do?" And I had all these questions and I was like, "oh dear, that was bad".

And also for Ellie, a 17-year-old Aboriginal young woman from a regional area:

> [I've] never been frightened, 'cause I've always been able to defend myself, but sometimes you just feel…sometimes you just feel used. Sometimes you feel like a piece of meat and it's a lot of the time especially with alcohol 'cause the next day you feel so degraded and it's just something you deal with 'cause if you sit and whinge [whine] about it, like if you stew on it and think about it, it just gets worse.

While the heterosexual men in the study did not express negative feelings about casual sex, one gay man found it difficult:

> We had a good night, it was good sex but, um, I kind of felt…there was something strange about [it] afterwards…I just, um, I kind of felt dirty and I didn't know why. I eventually put my finger on it; it was because it was completely meaningless. That whole encounter had nothing behind it for me, even if it had for him, it had nothing for me. I felt horrible for doing that to myself and to him and then I had this sort of moment of, "oh my God, I don't even know if he used a condom." I had no idea, you know, and I just went, "oh my fucking God, how could you have been so stupid…all because you, um, you got drunk and felt lonely and wanted to party." I felt irresponsible and so I hope never to do something like that again.
>
> (Alex, from a regional area, aged 24)

This sense of not being really aware of what happens when you are drunk and have sex is of particular concern for this study. Condom use appeared to be well accepted in casual encounters—both to protect against disease and, in the case of heterosexual partners, to prevent pregnancy. However, casual sex combined with alcohol did increase the risk of unprotected sex and the potential for sexual assault or unwanted sexual acts.

Experienceso fA buse

The project was advertised as a project on sexual ethics and violence prevention and, as such, may have been of more interest to participants who had experience of sexual assault or other forms of violence in their lives or were committed to preventing it. Active recruiting through designated sexual assault or domestic violence services was avoided, as I wanted a broader population sample and did not consider it appropriate to interview recent survivors of sexual violence.

Of the total sample, 66 percent did not disclose any experience of abuse. In this study, 32 percent of women and 15 percent of men reported experiences of sexual assault. Of these, 25 percent of the city sample of women reported sexual assault or domestic violence compared to 20 percent for regional women. This may have been an effect of recruitment methods in the city and their slightly older ages than the regional women. The women who reported experiences of violence were from a range of cultural groups including Anglo-Australians.

Three young women reported experiences that would meet the definition of a domestic violence relationship. All were younger than 18 years at the time of the abuse. As these relationships were the first for them, they had little understanding of what was happening and no awareness of the possibility of domestic violence among young people. Brenda—age 22, from the city—reflects on the confusion she felt about this relationship:

> I just thought he was a really sweet guy, but I also feel, when I look back on it now, that, um, I was sympathetic to him because every time that he'd blow up at me or he'd get really annoyed about something because he'd be very hurtful he could say rude, horrible things and I'd be shocked that you know someone who's supposed to be in love with me could say something like that, so I'd be really upset and then he'd come back and apologize later and well never said I'm sorry, but just said you know oh I'm just frustrated because my parents have done this or my dad's done this and always passed it off sort of thing but at the time I just, I always felt sorry for him. So every time I took him back and, um, and also because we had fabulous sex all the time so that was kind of the focus.

The impact of her boyfriend's controlling behavior affected her sense of self, but she felt bound to him:

> The bad thing was is that, um, he kind of, like I've always been my own person, and he's the first person that's ever come along that's been able to make me feel vulnerable and no one ever has been able to do that to me before...so in a way I ended up becoming quite afraid. I don't know of him, but of a power that he seemed to hold over me.

The experiences of sexual assault covered a range of ages and situations; most had occurred some years ago, but several had occurred in the last 12 months. The nature of the abuse varied from child sexual abuse, unwanted sexual experiences that made the person feel uncomfortable, through to multiple categories of sexual assault as defined in the NSW Crimes Act 1981. All of the participants had received some professional support in dealing with these issues from police, sexual assault services, or counselors, although for some there was a delay. All participants were actively encouraged to reconnect with these services or to access the NSW Rape Crisis Centre if the interview caused them any distress.

The impact of the abuse varied for young people who experienced it. For some, it involved ongoing distress. For others, it hindered them developing sexual intimacy with their partners. Other young people spoke about how the experience helped them set clearer boundaries and explicitly negotiate what they were willing to do sexually with their current partners.

Jane—age 22, from the city—was sexually assaulted at 13 and was unable to disclose this until two years ago. She explained that she was diagnosed with post-traumatic stress disorder and has been working to rebuild her life. She explains how she is now reclaiming her sexuality:

> I'm starting to get back to the point now where sex is not this big scary thing that it was like a year ago, because people are interested and I thought of something to do with it, but now I'm getting back to where I was…a lot more comfortable, a lot more kind of willing to explore things and discuss it with my partner and things like that.

For Thomas—age 20, from a regional town—his experience of sexual assault as a child has sensitized him to the need to be very careful in his sexual relationships with women:

> Um well, when I was a kid I was raped, so I just figured that really sucked…it was really a painful experience and it took a long time to get over it and such so that's, you don't want to, if you suffer something why would you want to go putting that on someone else, so I've always been very cautious about my behavior in such a manner. You never want something like that to happen, it's a horrible experience, but I think that was a key factor in it. I've always been very cautious to make sure that the woman wanted it and if she didn't I would stop instantly because, yeah, I know what it's like when they don't stop and it ain't friendly at all.

All of the participants who had experienced abuse in their lives felt very strongly about the need for other young people to understand sexual assault, and they feel that many don't realize what is involved, as Carla, age 23, from the city indicated:

> I was just disorientated and I couldn't believe that someone felt that it was okay to violate me, you know, and I mean, although I didn't get raped, I was assaulted, you know and I just couldn't believe the position, you know like that I was just in…like it, when it was happening I felt like I was outside of myself because it happened when I was drunk. It's so like, I just don't want other people to have to go through something like that, to be put into that position and just made to feel like you have no say over your body or what you want you know.

Friendship Groups—"You Don't Want to be Seen as a Loser"

Particularly in high school, friendship groups become fundamental to shaping how a young man or woman thinks about, and creates the beginning of, a sexual life. They are powerful sites in reinforcing or challenging gender expectations about relationships and sexual intimacy. It is therefore disappointing, after 30 years of feminist campaigning, to find in this study that young women and men continue to report that gender equality was absent in relation to attitudes to sexual activity of women and men. Men and women in the study consistently talked about how, on the one hand, women were seen as "sluts" or "slags" (promiscuous women) if they engaged in casual sex, or appeared to know too much about it. On the other hand, the more those men had sex with women, the more they were seen as "studs" (sexually virile men).

The need for men to prove their heterosexual identity was evident in men's discussion with their male friends that centered on with whom they had had sex, what acts they had performed, and how many times they "had scored." Their sexual identity was maintained by the need to report back to male friends, as Frank, an 18-year-old Italian-Australian from the city, explains:

> I think it is like a big thing to have sex when you're in high school…there's that big push for that and I remember with my mates if you went out with a girl and you didn't seal the deal as such, you would cop it at footy training and stuff like that, and even people I didn't play footy with they would give it to you too.

Young women's stories of their high school experiences were marked by conflicting and competing discourses of acceptable behavior. These varied, depending on friendship group norms. Developing a sense of who you are or who you want to be as a sexual being is complex, and our participants recounted how you could be simultaneously idolized and condemned. Carol—age 21, from the city—recalls her feelings:

> I think it was, I think it was all pretty awful, like…there wasn't a lot of, um, kind of friendly chat, it was more like oh my God, last night she gave so and so a blow job, or a hand job and it was all very accusatory and…snide and gossipy and, I don't know, maybe that's just a feature of being a teenage girl but like it's kind of, um, it targeted women or girls I should say who were having sex or intimate relationships, but at the same time kind of idolized them. It was a very strange thing going on so everyone wanted to be in that sort of situation or the majority of girls did, but at the same time they kind of made those girls out to be sluts, so it was very strange…

Missing from the narratives is any sense of young women's own sexual desires and pleasures as part of their decision to have sex with someone, as Carol also remembers:

> When you were at home alone, when they were at home alone with their partners and they were in bed they just had sex like not necessarily because they really wanted to but just because that's what you did.

The woman's pleasure was focused on giving the male partner pleasure, and her sexual pleasure was invisible or irrelevant and reconfigured into the pleasure obtained by increasing your social status with your friends. Karen, an 18-year-old Aboriginal from a regional town, explains:

> The girls that I hung around with, I don't know, it was more…like sex was to pleasure the male, to make him happy, to, um…it was like if you had sex with your boyfriend or if you had a crush on someone and you had sex with them they'd like you and they'd want to stay with you and you'd become more popular or more cool or have more friends or things like that…that's the way you looked at it when you were younger.

These narratives reveal the highly gendered expectation of traditional heterosexual intimacy, where the female's role is to provide pleasure to the male and earn social status for this gendered behavior. This, of course, was a dangerous strategy, as the young woman ran the risk of also being condemned as a "slut."

At the same time, young women needed to be aware of the social etiquette of their friendship group and be aware of the fine line between status and denigration if they had sex too soon or too often with their boyfriend, or if they delayed too long. Fitting in with the group was seen as crucial to your own success as a person. The idea that a young woman could (and did) have a choice about when to have sex or not to have sex was generally not valued. Rather than respecting this as her decision, group pressure was used as a means to enforce group and gender norms by condemning her as not sexually desirable. Judy—age 23, from the city—explains:

> Girls are brutal. Oh, I hated high school. Um, I think we're awful...I think you would've been torn to shreds if you actually said, "Oh I don't want to have sex with anyone." I think it would be more that people would be thinking that no one probably wants to have sex with you.

The gendered nature of intimate relationships highlights the added pressure experienced by young women, in particular. For men, their reputation would be enhanced but, for women, they had to manage their reputation—not only with individual sexual partners, but with their social group and the wider community. For example, Doug, aged 22, from a regional area, explains:

> Um, in high school I guess, yeah, you would be sort of encouraged to do it, um, among your male peers. Among your female peers they would discourage [sex] because they knew, like, there was this whole, "if you're the male then you're a stud, if you're the female then you're pretty much the, um, the town bike or something like that," which is pretty bad, pretty disgusting, but yeah.

Social reputation can be enhanced for men by recounting their "conquests" but, as Thomas—age 20, from a regional area—suggests, women mark their "conquests" by being seen publicly with their partners:

> Um, guys are very much going out, getting laid; chicks very much have boyfriends, yeah, that's it. The guys are just out for...a lot of the guys they'll all sit there and brag about chicks so they're like yeah I scored with this one and but the girlfriends do it in the same...they do the same thing but instead of bragging about it they walk with the man hanging off their arm—that's their trophy.

Same-Sex-Attracted Young People

The schoolyard is tough for many young people with its demands on social conformity. It is especially tough if you are a same-sex-attracted young man or woman in a rural community. Alex, a 24-year-old gay man, reflects on his experience at school:

> Definitely in high school I was bullied a lot and the word [that] was used, the insult primarily was "faggot" and it was, it was about being gay and 'cause I was a singer and actor.

Apart from bullying because of perceived difference, same-sex-attracted young people felt the pressure to conform to the dominant hetero-sexual culture of sexuality in their schools. This meant that the emerging feelings they had were repressed, and they attempted to fit into the culture in their schools and in the wider community. Alex indicated how he handled this:

> I do remember a moment of realization...I was just thinking about a guy and immediately repressing that and being quite successful at repressing that for quite a while and then there would be the odd time when it would, um, come out as a kind of I need to prove to myself I'd, you know, pash [kiss] a girl at a party or get myself into an awkward situation and then have to back out of it pretty quickly 'cause something didn't feel right and I couldn't put my finger on what it was 'cause I wasn't willing to face it.

A similar need to fit in by having some sexual experiences with women was discussed by Rod, a 20-year-old gay man, who also grew up in a regional area:

> I don't know, I just didn't enjoy it. I did it just for the normality I think. There was no interest there, but I just wanted to see what it was about...um, and once I got into a situation I didn't really want to be there but I just let it continue so I didn't hurt any feelings.

This pressure to conform was not only felt by young men who now describe themselves as gay, but also by young women who struggled to work out their feelings of same-sex attraction. As Melissa, a 25-year-old lesbian from a regional area, explains:

> I wasn't ready to even contemplate getting with a woman. Um, it was a lot easier to contemplate being with a guy than it was to contemplate

being with a girl. It was like, if boys don't do it for me, I'm not going to know if boys don't do it for me until I've been with a guy for starters and if they don't, if this doesn't work out, well, then that's fine, I'll find something else. It didn't work out, so I found something else.

For some same-sex-attracted young people, getting out of their rural communities and away from school allowed them the opportunity to escape peer pressure and to work out what was right for them. Ellen, a 19-year-old lesbian, explains:

It is very hard and I realize that now coming away and meeting new people you can be your own person, especially at university 'cause they're a lot more understanding and oh there is still judgment and there always will be but like it's not as bad I guess. And especially the peer pressure's not as bad.

Despite this, there were still times when Ellen's developing self-confidence was challenged by the disapproval of friends and led her to attempt to conform:

Yeah, um, one night a couple of my friends have pulled me aside and said look you're drunk you don't want to do this, um when I first came out and a couple of my friends didn't accept it, I went out, got drunk and I was going to pick up a boy well they pulled me aside and said you're gay, you've already told us, don't do this, you'll regret it and for that I really appreciate it.

Her experience underlies the complexity of friendship. On one hand, some friends undermined her self-confidence by disapproving of her lesbian sexuality. However, other friends confirmed her identity and encouraged her to not deny it by involving herself in an encounter that she may have regretted.

Understanding Young People's Experiences of Sex

The young people's experiences indicate that gender continues to be a major influence on how both young women and men conceptualize and experience sexual intimacy in casual and ongoing relationships. The negative connotations attached to young women's developing sexuality are most marked in the high school years, where they negotiate a fine line between idolization and condemnation among their peers. This is consistent with findings by many feminist researchers over a number of years (see, e.g., Allen 2003; Gavey 2005; Lees 1997; Thompson 1995; Tolman 1994, 2002).

The power of friendship groups to mark out acceptable and unacceptable sexual behavior was significant and resulted in quite different gender expectations for women and men. This also had an impact on same-sex-attracted young people, resulting in invisibility, isolation, and, at times, bullying and harassment. The desire to gain the approval of peers as well as for sexual activity to be focused on pleasing male partners was strongly evident among heterosexual young women. This is consistent with other studies of heterosexual young women (Tolman 1994; Walker 1997).

The reality of sex was different from young people's expectations about what sex would be like. As indicated in this chapter, some were disappointed, others were regretful, and some felt positive. Attitudes to virginity varied. For some, it was seen as a gift to hold onto until the right person or a committed relationship came along. Others felt stigmatized and wished to rid themselves of the negative status they felt it bestowed on them. A number of other young people wished to avoid being different from their friends. Alcohol was often mentioned as giving confidence to be sexual. This raises the question of how this impacted on their ability to make ethical choices about sexual intimacy. Evidence of their own desire was noticeably absent in many of the narratives, similar to Fine's (1998) finding, which she called the missing discourse of desire. The participants who were most able to resist these pressures had higher levels of guidance from parents in developing self-esteem, confidence, respect, and faith-based values.

A simple analysis may suggest that, if young people feel all these pressures, they should just resist sex and wait. However, such an approach fails to recognize that individual young women and men do not grow up in a social vacuum. Rather, from the moment we are born, we are perceived to be a particular gender. Until very recently, there were strong cultural assumptions made about how we should perform gender and, indeed, how we should behave sexually. Sexuality is imbued with diverse and competing discourses or bodies of knowledge that impact on us as individuals, and are transmitted culturally by family, peers, and government policies and media representations. A young person beginning their sexual life has already been exposed to these cultural expectations long before sexual intimacy is up for discussion. When they move toward sexual experience, they bring these messages and expectations to their encounters, often without even realizing it.

Note

1. University of Western Sydney Human Ethics Committee Approval Number HREC 05/123, August 22, 2005. Criminal record checks were also completed for both researchers.

Chapter 3

Negotiating Sex

How do we work out what we want from sex? This is a particular challenge for young women and men as they begin their sexual lives. Central to concerns about ensuring sexual encounters are ethical is an understanding of sexual consent and how we may ensure both parties are freely agreeing to what occurs. This chapter discusses how young people explore issues of sexual consent within casual and ongoing relationships. I want to extend this discussion beyond a legal focus on consent. I consider this limited, in that it fails to address how individuals—as sexed and gendered bodies—constitute themselves as ethical or unethical subjects within the social body and within interpersonal relationships (Carmody 2004, 45). I, therefore, want to extend the discussion of consent to focus on young women and men negotiating consensual sex. I also consider the differences young people report in negotiation, depending on the context of sex. Young women and men reveal different practices in how they indicate what they want or don't want from a sexual encounter. Certain relationship attributes were found to significantly increase the ability to negotiate ethical intimacy. I then consider what young people told me about their experiences of negotiating sex in casual and ongoing relationships during the interview stage of the research. Their stories highlight the strong reliance on nonverbal communication, especially in casual encounters, that is consistent with other research in this area. However, a broader range of communication strategies is used in the context of relationships. I conclude the chapter by considering the challenges these findings raise for educators working in sexuality and violence prevention education.

Understanding the Process of Consent

The gendered context in which we decide to be sexual with another person (or people, for that matter) significantly impacts on how we understand and experience our own sexuality, and how we imagine it will be. In the previous chapter, we have seen how young women and men's experience of first sex, for example, was imbued with romantic expectations or seen as a rite of passage that needed to be experienced for their own self-identity and/or their position within friendship groups. While the issue of consent is one that is of crucial concern in sexual assault matters, I would argue it is often not foremost in many young people's minds as they begin to engage in sexual intimacy. Rather, their concerns are about relationship status with friends, managing their developing bodies and the feelings these provoke, and, for some, how to achieve bodily pleasure. The dominant and commonsense story of rape and sexual assault is still one in which these things are done by strangers—not by someone known to the victim. Therefore, deciding to be sexual with someone is viewed as potentially pleasurable. In this framework, pleasure is not primarily related to an embodied sense of sexual desire, especially for women, but rather, it is linked to the expectations and desires about what the sexual experience might mean besides bodily pleasure. As Deborah Tolman (2002) found with the young women she interviewed, "sex just happens." Many of them did not have the language to express the bodily sensations they felt in relation to sexual desire.

What I found in the young people who took part in research interviews and the sexual ethics education groups was that they had little conception that there were variable state laws about sexual consent. They did not seem very aware that these were aimed at protecting them from exploitative sex, and were an avenue for criminal redress if they were sexually assaulted. They knew that rape and sexual assault existed, but it was "something that strangers did," and was not something they needed to think through as they began to be sexually active. Their sense of consent was not framed in legal terms, but rather was more about managing their sexual reputation, how much bodily access they would allow another to have, and what form this intimacy would take. This was particularly so for young heterosexual women.

Young heterosexual men, on the other hand, saw convincing women to have sex as achieving a mark of their masculinity—not only for the individual man but in relation to their position with their male peers (Holland, Ramazanoglu, and Thomson 1996). So this raises the question of how men understand sexual refusal. Kitzinger and Firth (1999) have shown through conversational analysis that men and women have demonstrated competency at communicating refusals in many social situations and, therefore, for men to say they do not understand sexual refusals is to lay claim to a surprising ignorance of conversational patterns. These findings were extended in research with men by O'Byrne, Rapley, and Hansen (2006) who found men did understand "refusals" in a variety of forms, but often ignored them.

It has been a popular strategy in sexual assault prevention work to teach young women refusal skills such as "just say no." This approach constructs sexual negotiation as primarily negative, especially for young heterosexual women. The refusal strategy has also been used in drug education to promote abstinence in both sexual activity and drug use. As a strategy to communicate non-consent, this approach fails to understand the complexity of the process of consent as well as the different communication styles used by women and men in sexual encounters. There are several concerns here. Negotiating sex from a starting point of refusal reflects a traditional model of heterosexual sex, in which the woman is expected to accept a passive role or, at best, a secondary rather than equal role in the negotiation process— she must be convinced or coerced to indicate consent. This model of consent assumes that it is always the woman who is consenting or giving something to a man. This denies any agency to the woman and places the man in a role of aggressive pursuer. There is no space in this model of consent for women to say "yes" to sex or "maybe," depending on what is on offer. As these refusal messages are framed within a heterosexual discourse, same-sex desire and negotiation is made invisible. This construction of consent continues to replicate a highly gendered, rigid form of dance rather than a process of mutual exploration and agreement, where both parties' desires—regardless of gender—are considered and agreed upon.

The need for the prevention of sexual violence in all its forms is underscored by both Australian and US data about young people. The first large-scale Australian Study of Health and Relationships (ASHR Smith et al 2003) of 19,307 people, aged between 16 and 59, found that 4.8 percent of men and 21.1 percent of women had been forced or frightened into having sex. They also found that homosexual and bisexual respondents were more likely than others to have been sexually coerced. The level of coerced sex among young people was specifically identified in 2002 by the third national Australian sexual health survey of 2,388 students in years 10–12. The findings indicated that over a quarter (25.9 percent) of all sexually active students had had unwanted sex at some time in their lives. Being drunk and pressured by their partner were the most common reasons they gave. These results were first reported in 2003 (Smith et al. 2003) and similar results have been reported in the latest study (Mitchell et al. 2014).

Sexual coercion has negative impacts on psychological, physical, and sexual health. It is often associated with higher levels of anxiety, depression, suicide, and anger (de Visser et al. 2003, 198). Studies of US college women over a number of years have found that 50 percent experience some form of unwanted sexual activity, with approximately 3 percent reporting the most serious forms of sexual violence (Abbey, Ross, and McDuffie 1996; Fisher, Cullen, and Turner 2000 as cited in Banyard, Plante, and Moynihan 2004; Koss, Gidycz, and Wisniewski 1987). More recently, an August 2014 initiative—*Not Alone: Protecting Students from Sexual Assault*—by the US White House reports one in five women is sexually assaulted while in college (www.whitehouse.gov). Continued low reporting of sexual assault to police and the attrition that occurs after a charge is laid (see Kelly 2007 for UK figures) suggests there are large numbers of women, in particular, in the community who experience various forms of sexual violence and do not seek help. These findings suggest a pressing need to address the underlying reasons for these behaviors and to find ways to prevent violence before it occurs.

Given all of the above factors, it seems important—if we are trying to encourage young women and men to have ethical sex and to reduce unwanted, coerced, or forced sex—that we understand more fully the process of consent. The confusion that many young people feel about consent is not unique to them. I would argue that many people in the community are confused about this—a point poignantly explored by Nicola Gavey's (2005) interviews with women of diverse ages.

Confusion about the meaning of sexual consent is not unique to the general population. Even researchers in the field are confused. Melanie Beres (2007) provides one of the most comprehensive overviews to date of how scholarly work addresses issues of sexual consent. She argues there is a general lack of explicit definition of what the authors mean by consent, accompanied by a lack of questioning of popular and assumed understandings of consent. Rather, the concept is taken up "spontaneously" following the arguments of Bourdieu, Chamboredon, and Passeron (1991). This refers to an adoption of commonsense meanings of concepts without critically reflecting on the cultural, historical, and social forces that produce these meanings (Beres 2007, 95). She highlights the variety of ways in which researchers deploy consent and problematize these definitions, arguing they fail to understand how dominant heterosexual discourses impact on the understanding and communication of consent. In her most recent work, Beres (2014) has continued to interrogate how young people understand consent. She found that the young people in her study did not understand the concept of consent and many of the descriptions of consent in the interviews were not consistent with legal definitions of consent in Canada or New Zealand.

Nicola Gavey (2005) demonstrates how the cultural scaffolding of our communities creates situations where women experience forced, unwanted, and coerced sex that they do not define as sexual assault, yet it is difficult to see as "just sex." She argues that we need to listen to these stories from women as they raise fundamental questions about how we understand sexual choice and consent (Ibid., 136). Similarly, Anastasia Powell's (2007a) study of over 100 young women and men in Victoria, Australia, found high levels of pressured sex. These researchers, therefore, locate the need for consent to be understood in the highly gendered context in which we live. Without this context, our understandings of consent will at best be partial and will fail to grasp the dynamic and complex nature of sexual intimacy. This has significant implications for how we work with young people, in particular, if we are committed to developing ethical sexualities and practices.

Given the key place consent plays in determining sexual assault matters, I want to return to my earlier point about understanding the process of consent. There has been a paucity of literature on the process of consent, as Cowling (2004) reminds us. Exceptions to this have been Hall (1995), Hickman and Muehlenhard (1999), and Humphreys (2004, 2007). Apart from one study by Beres, Herold, and Maitland (2004) on same-sex-attracted partners, previous studies have only considered heterosexual couples and focused primarily on heterosexual intercourse, thus excluding a diversity of sexual activity. Beres and her colleagues found that nonverbal communication was the preferred method of communicating consent for men who have sex with men and women who have sex with women. Hickman and Muehlenhard (1999) investigated how young women and men inferred and conveyed sexual consent. They found four categories of signals: direct, indirect, verbal, and nonverbal. Therefore, all of these studies found nonverbal behaviors are used more frequently than verbal behaviors. Bearing these insights in mind, I was interested to explore the processes used by young people in my study to negotiate sex in both casual and ongoing relationships, to see if I could interrogate the broad categories of verbal and nonverbal behavior more deeply.

Negotiating Sex in Casual Encounters

The rules of sexual engagement have shifted over time (Powell 2007a). While sex within marriage between opposite gender partners may still be a dominant form of preferred sexual expression among a number of cultural groups, faith-based families, and young people, the reality is somewhat different. As discussed in chapter 2, young people are having sex at an earlier age and outside the constraints of traditional marriage.

A number of young people also revealed that their choice of sexual partners was not solely tied to opposite-gendered partners, regardless of their self-described, primary sexual identity. In my study, 64 percent of young people indicated they had had experiences of casual sex. Men had, on average, seven casual partners and women had six. This was very similar for both rural and city-based young people. This may suggest some equalizing of traditional gender differences. However, there remain differences in how women and men experienced casual sex—despite a belief that "raunch culture" is embraced and even expected of young women—as the following discussion highlights (Levy 2005).

Young people who engaged in casual sex almost always indicated that little verbal negotiation occurred in these encounters, either at the pick-up stage or during sex. Rather, there were direct and indirect nonverbal indications of interest in the other person—for example, kissing the person, dancing with them, touching them, going outside the club or party with them, or having a cigarette with them. The overall impression people gave was that "it just happened":

> I don't think it's even talked about at that stage; it's more like maybe standing outside the pub—unless something's happened inside the pub, you know, the dance floor and start dancing with a girl and then it starts there—[but] it's more like you've left the pub, you're out in the taxi rank or buying your pie to munch on or something, and they'll come and say, or you'll go to them and say, where are you going now, what's going on? And if you happen to end up in a taxi together and end up in the same place it goes from there. Once again, I don't think there's too much communication involved, well there might be communication, but it's not about what's actually going to happen.
>
> (Don, aged 19, from a regional area)

In a small rural town, it could be as simple as cruising in your car past a group of young women hanging out: "You just drive up and down the main street and pick up a one-night stand" (Stuart, aged 19).

The use of social media including phone apps (applications) has increasingly become a main method to meet and connect for friendship, possible sex, and/or a relationship. One gay man, Michael, who grew up in a small rural town but had been in the city since he was 17, developed his own guidelines to ensure his safety in dealing with online pick-ups. These included engaging in online dialogue and seeing them on a web cam; they needed to provide three photos, be willing to talk on the telephone, and meet for the first time in a public place. The online environment also actively encouraged a clear description of the kinds of sexual activity they were interested in, ruling in or out people of similar interests. While this kind of procedure was quite common among gay men, it was not common in the heterosexual hook-up environment of clubs, hotels, and parties where most people met casual partners.

Young people indicated there was little discussion before, during, or after sex in the casual encounter. This didn't seem to vary substantially for regional or urban young people, despite the former having some passing knowledge of the person, as discussed previously. Going home with someone was assumed to imply consent to sex. However, it is not clear what either party thought they were consenting to. What sexual practices were they imagining? What was actually being offered or expected? There is a consistent lack of embodied sexuality education that young people are exposed to within families and school programs. Therefore, young people's sources of information about sexual behavior may be obtained from friends, television programs, movies, and porn. All of these may provide unrealistic, highly gendered expectations of how women and men behave that can create unspoken beliefs about sexual intimacy, with implications regarding consent.

The need to establish whether it was a casual encounter or the possibility of something else may lead to some verbal discussion:

> Well it'd depend; really on what my intentions were, whether my first intention was a one-night stand or she's actually a nice girl and this could go somewhere. If it was a one-night stand you basically have to let them know that's what it is straightaway...you don't want to get their hopes up and thinking that it's going to go somewhere else...so if you end up taking a young girl home you have to let them know that this is as far as it's going to go if you decide to go there, and then it's up to them really.
>
> (Simon, aged 19, a Polish Australian from the city)

Simon initiated the rules of engagement here, bringing to this encounter a belief that the young woman might possibly be assuming more than casual sex. His honesty does provide a space for her to make a decision, if that is what she wants. However, this initiation does not include any discussion of what kind of sex either of them is interested in and, therefore, what they are actually consenting to. In other situations, consent was primarily assumed by, for example, the production of a condom, the removal of clothes, and how both parties interpreted other nonverbal communication such as body language. What then followed was assumed to be okay with the other person unless boundaries were overstepped. Establishing the boundaries may involve pushing the person off, changing position, and, rarely, explicitly saying no. For these young men, the focus of casual sex is, therefore, primarily about the sexual act, and their partner's needs or preferences become less important:

> Yeah, you can just go wild, you know…if it's just like a one-night thing you just go for it, pretty much.
> (Bobbie, aged 17, a Torres Strait Islander from a regional area)

Other men indicated a similar view: "In one-night stands 'cause it's usually get your rocks off and get out of there" (Darcy, aged 20, a gay man from a regional area). The focus on self-pleasure was also commented on by Bill, a 19-year-old heterosexual man from the city:

> I think with a one-night stand or your casual sort of thing it's just to pleasure yourself and then see you later…that's the way I see the difference, anyway.

These examples suggest that casual sex initiated by these men was primarily about self-gratification rather than mutual exploration. The difficulty here is not self-gratification per se, but whether both parties understand this before they agree to have sex. As nonverbal communication is so common in casual sex, it is not clear how a potential partner would know the male's intention. It seems that verbal communication is primarily seen by these men as something that happens within a relationship:

> If there were to be communication it would be in a formal relationship that's turned into a sexual relationship. I don't think you'd find any form of communication in casual sexual encounters…I guess it's something that might get said, but only in the moment…it's not like something you'd sit down and discuss I don't think. At the time of the sex, if there's something that they don't like they might say something,

or if there's something they want then they might say that but it's not something I'd say you'd have a formal discussion about.

(Don, aged 19, a heterosexual man from a regional area)

Women recounted similar experiences, but there was a sense in which the women felt the lack of knowing the person hindered being able to say how they felt about what was happening. To speak would offend the other person and result in an end to the encounter:

In a casual one you're more likely to let it go on...'cause you don't have that, you don't feel like you can communicate to them in that way that I don't feel comfortable with this or it hurts or something or you might try re-adjusting your body and stuff but you don't actually feel that you have that relationship with them to be able to say that without them going oh right and walking off sort of thing. In a relationship it's a bit different...you can actually tell the person and they don't get as offended.

(Sasha, aged 22, a Korean Australian from a regional area)

The implications of these experiences suggest that while sexual pleasure may be the primary goal of casual sex for both partners, it is a bit of a lottery as to whether it works out well, or if the situation results in unwanted sex, sexual assault, or discomfort emotionally or physically. Some people commented that not knowing what was going to happen was part of the pleasure of the encounter and talking about it could be "a passion killer." The interpretation of nonverbal language to ascertain and express desire is a complex one without knowledge of the people involved. If the encounter occurs while drunk, judgments may be impaired and bodily cues misread. This would suggest that the context in which the sexual encounter occurs needs to be considered in order to gauge more adequately how consent is obtained.

Negotiating Sex in Relationships

Casual sex was a feature of both regional and metropolitan young people's experiences. Despite this, most young people in this study had most of their sexual experiences within the context of a relationship—a similar finding to that seen in Powell's research (2007a). Metropolitan young people had slightly higher numbers of ongoing relationship partners; that is, 3.2 compared to 2.7 for their rural counterparts. Both women and men had similar numbers of relationship partners, with the men having slightly more partners. Definitions by young people of what constituted a relationship varied from several weeks to months and years, and also included marriage. Five young women had children. Of these women, three had two children, all except one were in a committed relationship with a male partner, and, interestingly, all lived in regional areas. The level of commitment to sex within the context of a relationship challenges some speculation in media stories that young women and men are having more casual, random sex and are less interested in relationships. The data in this study do not support this speculation, as was also found by Allen (2005) and Powell (2007a). Of some concern was a failure to use safe-sex practices once a relationship had commenced. If a heterosexual woman was using another form of contraception instead of condoms, there was a sense that sexually transmitted infections (STIs) were of less concern, even if the relationship had just begun. Perception of risk is, therefore, based on romantic assumptions about their partners rather than objective information. Despite the similar numbers of relationships between women and men, the processes women and men used to negotiate sex differed.

Given the high levels of reliance on nonverbal communication to negotiate consent in casual sex, it is interesting to consider whether this changed in relation to young people having sex in the context of relationships. Humphreys (2007) researched 415 Canadian university students to try and find out how important relationship experience and gender were to beliefs about the need for sexual consent. He was interested to ascertain if relationship history had a bearing on whether couples continue to ask for consent. The findings indicated that the more established a relationship becomes, the more people assume consent without verbal confirmation. However, he did find gender differences. Compared with the men, the women in the study interpreted explicit sexual consent as more necessary during sexual encounters, regardless of the relationship. He posits this may be due to women's overall heightened awareness of sexual assault among his sample, where campus rape prevention programs are common, and that women take this more seriously than men. As he points out, this is not surprising given that women are more likely to experience coercive sex from male sexual partners. Given these findings, I was interested to explore what an Australian group of young people drawn from community, as well as university, contexts had to say about negotiation and consent in the context of relationships.

Talking in Relationships

Young people's experiences of negotiating sex in ongoing relationships revealed a higher level of verbal communication compared to that experienced in casual sex. Nonverbal communication was enhanced by explicitly talking about the relationship and its sexual component. However, in this study, it was lesbians, heterosexual women, and gay men who talked about the relationship. This may occur outside of a sexual encounter, or during or after sex. This style of communication reflects a mutual and exploratory process that potentially enhances negotiation and equality:

I'm pretty straightforward and what not, and I just…I just expect to be honest and want them to know what you want and stuff like that, so you know *we talked about it a lot* [my emphasis].
(Simone, aged 17, from a regional area)

The importance of talking about the relationship is highlighted:

For me, discussion is a big thing. Like if you want to know where that person stands, or where you stand, talk about it. If you're not going to *talk about* it [my emphasis] how are you really going to know?
(Mary, aged 22, a South American Australian from the city)

One Aboriginal woman reflected on the need to talk about sex in a long-term relationship once children are part of your life:

I suppose when you're first just having sex and anything's great…but, well, now after the kids and everything else, we have to try to keep a little bit in there and *talking about* it [my emphasis] makes it just heaps easy and being so open about it…he's just as open, so it's great, yeah.
(Joanne, aged 22, from a regional area)

Talking about planning to be sexual was also important. Richard, 17, from a regional area, spoke of the process of entering his first sexual relationship with another man:

The majority of it was unspoken, kind of just actions leading up to that decision I guess…we did talk just beforehand if it was okay and if we were ready and stuff like that and we *talked about* [my emphasis] our sexual histories beforehand.

Lesbians, heterosexual women, and gay men indicated that talking about the overall relationship was important to them in relation to negotiating what would happen sexually. However, this was different for heterosexual men. They continued to rely heavily on nonverbal communication to ascertain their partner's willingness to participate in sex or not. When verbally communicating, they also showed higher levels of a closed questioning style of communication than other groups, by asking if something was okay. This allowed them to ascertain consent and to make a judgment about their partner's wishes. Asking was seen as important to ensure that the partner wasn't being pressured:

> I say "what do you want to do?" sort of thing, or "do you feel comfortable?", 'cause I don't believe in pressure, like I, like if some girl said no I'd completely stop—that's me. I'd never hurt anyone like that and I'm being honest, really honest.
>
> (Bill, aged 19, from the city)

Asking a question implies that you will listen to the answer and be willing to act on it:

> We had discussions like if we were doing stuff like if I was mucking around with her and she was mucking around with me and that, and she'll always stop before it and I'll just ask her [my emphasis] once and she'll go no, are you sure, why not, she told me the reasons why and I go okay then.
>
> (Frank, aged 18, an Italian-Australian from the city)

Speaking about What You Want and Don't Want

Women used nonverbal communication to indicate interest, as well as to set boundaries if they felt uncomfortable. Several women and men commented that speaking about sex was difficult, and there was a sense in which they expected the other person to know what they wanted:

> I know and when I just ask her she's like, you weren't supposed to ask me, I'm like okay. You're just supposed to know.
>
> (Marty, aged 20, a lesbian from a regional
> area with a Maori background)

This example highlights a common feature of sexual encounters for many. There is a sense of the idealized lover who will know exactly what we want and, when we ask, it is viewed negatively. This may be a particularly female response echoing ideas from romantic fiction, but also may indicate how some women find difficulty in verbally expressing their desires.

However, other women's style of communication primarily involved telling their partner their wishes. This meant that women of all sexual identities used a directive form of communication that had two different purposes. The first purpose of telling was to indicate a boundary setting to sexual activity. So women used this form of direct communication to indicate what they did not want to happen. One young woman highlights this boundary setting and how she is able to set a limit but not able to speak about what she wants them to do:

> If they're doing something to me that I don't want them to do then I'll say stop but I won't tell them what I want them to do to me, do you know what I mean?
>
> (Louise, aged 20, a lesbian from the city)

This point was also raised by a bisexual young woman who also sees telling as important to indicate what she thinks is needed:

> I think it makes a relationship a lot easier if you can say it out loud, "no, I don't want to do that," because then you don't have someone sitting there going do you think they might do it, I don't know kind of thing, and discussing it with their friends as opposed to discussing it with you.
>
> (Janette, aged 18, from a regional area)

But she tempers this with a positive aspect of telling someone what you want:

> It's, it's not just if you don't like something tell me; it's if you don't like something tell me and then tell me what you do want

Similarly, another young woman says "They're not going to know there's anything wrong if you don't tell them" (Wendy, aged 17, from a regional area).

Negotiation was explored in interviews from many different angles, including asking young people if they had ever been disinterested, frightened, uncomfortable, or bored and how they handled it. Few reported being fearful, except those who experienced sexual assault, as discussed earlier in chapter 2. Discomfort was generally addressed by moving their bodies or by verbally redirecting their partners. One young woman used indirect messages to indicate a lack of interest in sex:

> When I lived with my partner I would just say something like, "I'm having a really bad day." So you know you prep yourself so by night time you don't expect it 'cause I told you what a shit day I had.
>
> (Judy, aged 23, from the city)

While most people indicated they had never been bored during sex, some did. The young people I spoke with found this question very amusing. Those who had been bored reported a range of strategies to deal with it. Interestingly, most of the women, and a few men, who had the experience of boredom were concerned about protecting the feelings of their sexual partners and, therefore, avoided directly saying it during or after sex.

One lesbian woman had a more extreme way of addressing boredom:

> I pretended I was going to vomit or something if I was drunk...I didn't want them to feel bad.
> (Ellen, a 19-year-old lesbian, from a regional area)

One young Aboriginal man also indicated he wouldn't say anything:

> If I was bored I wouldn't say anything, just keep going along and get them so they're happy. Or if it hurts or something, yeah, damn straight...you might not have to say something you just fix it up so it won't hurt and reposition yourself so it's comfortable and it works.
> (Thomas, aged 20, from a regional area)

Other men were more direct:

> If I get bored I usually speak my mind and say, "nah, sorry this is not happening," but that's usually me, I just speak my mind.
> (Darcy, aged 20, from a regional area)

Participants also explained their feelings about the difficulty of speaking up about their needs and the impact on them of not telling:

> With my ex-boyfriend I felt that there were times when I wasn't able to speak up and so I didn't really feel like I was in the room...It wasn't rape or anything like that, I was consenting to it, but if he'd talked to me and asked, "oh is this really what you want?" then I might have been able to say "no, not today."
> (Donna, aged 20, from a regional area)

This story indicates the operation of assumed consent in which some women find themselves in relation to sex with an ongoing partner. Her disembodied response to non-negotiation: "I didn't feel like I was in the room" but "I was consenting" supports Gavey's (2005) finding that women talked to her about experiences that weren't about rape, but were more than just sex. Donna's experience, her inability to find her voice, and her partner's apparent failure to notice her bodily response suggests this was not satisfying for her. This raises questions of consent and whether or not sex is ethical if one person is so unaware of the other person's feelings or is aware of them and ignores them?

However, another young woman felt able to stand up to being pressured by her sexual partner and was quite direct about telling him she didn't want to have sex with him. Despite her assertiveness, he kept pressuring her:

> He wanted to have sex with me, but I was like no and he was all why, why? I said because I don't want to, I said to him I don't want to and he kept on persisting and I just thought no, what part of that aren't you understanding? When, you know, he thinks its okay because at the time he was drunk and he thinks it's okay, but it's like no it's not okay because you're going to wake up and then you're going to realize maybe you don't care, but I sure as hell do care so I don't want to give that to you.
>
> (Carla, aged 23, a Sri-Lankan Australian from the city)

The second purpose of direct communication was to indicate positive things they wanted. One young Aboriginal woman said:

> I stated what I wanted and if they weren't happy then see you later.
>
> (Kirsten, aged 22, from a regional area)

The concern of heterosexual women to protect the feelings of their male partners was also evident:

> We do talk about it but generally it tends to be more positive reinforcement like I really like that position as opposed to that position wasn't good...I personally do that a lot more because I'm just so wary about him, already having this bad image of his sexual capacity...as I say I don't want to put a downer.
>
> (Susan, aged 22, from the city)

While there were a few men who used this second style of communication, there were no examples of men, apart from one gay man, using telling to establish limit setting.

Relationship Aspects that Enhanced Sexual Intimacy

Overall, young people felt that their ability to negotiate pleasurable sex was enhanced by being in a relationship. One young woman commented on the difference in comfort levels between casual sex and sex in a relationship:

> I think there is a difference in the sex … if you're in a relationship you're more comfortable to experiment, whereas if you're having casual sex usually there's alcohol involved so you're a bit freer but you're probably not as comfortable.
>
> (Maureen, aged 21, from a regional area)

Women in this study expressed a variety of issues or characteristics that they valued and wanted in their relationships. These included physical attraction, intelligence, humor, honesty, respect, caring, and commitment. Underpinning these were a desire for mutual expression of feelings and a demonstration that they could trust the person. These findings are very similar to Powell's (2007a), who found trust respect, communication, honesty, and humor as important qualities that participants wanted in their relationships. In my study, the values women were looking for had different meanings for the women concerned. For some, monogamy was central, while being reliable and being in paid employment were linked to trusting them. For one young Sri-Lankan Australian woman, trust is closely linked to love:

> Love, oh, I'm not sure … it's quite weird for me to say it and then still actually, myself, not know what I think it means. I just feel like it's a complete trust in that person, not just small trust like, "I trust you with everything, I'll tell you all my secrets," and stuff like that. It's more like you'll give anything and everything for that person, you'll know that they won't judge you and they'll be there for you and they'll care and I think all of that is what I see as love.
>
> (Mary, aged 22, from the city)

For one young woman, romantic gestures enhanced her feelings for her partner:

> I like it when they bring up ideas like, "let's go to the park and watch the clouds," you know, stuff that doesn't even cost, or like, "I'm going to steal a flower on the way over to see you and give it to you when I get to you."
>
> (Kerry, aged 21, from a regional area)

The need for sexual pleasure to be mutual, and how this is connected with love, was also seen as important by several young people, including an Aboriginal woman:

I think when you get older you realize it's not about them. Sex is shared between two people who have a genuine love for one another and sex isn't a one-way street.

(Karen, aged 18, from a regional area)

This sense of mutual exploration and equality was also discussed:

I like people who you can be in a relationship with and talk and be honest and just say how you feel. You should feel that you have the right to say what you want and how you feel, and not let them sort of decide what they want and then just go from there...there has to be sort of an equal companionship—you need to both speak, not just one.

(Simone, aged 17, from a regional area)

There was also recognition that relationships take work and are not something to just end when things are difficult:

My relationship is great and it's bloody hard work sometimes. I mean it pisses me off and I think what people don't realize is when someone pisses you off you don't have to dump them straight away, you say, " you're pissing me off, go away." But I think there's that whole idea of love...you want the commitment and you want someone to be there for you and truly take care of you and take care of them at the same time.

(Freda, aged 18, from the city)

Men in the study expressed some similar ideas about what was important to them in a relationship. Similar issues about monogamy, trust, and love were highlighted:

Marriage isn't just something you go into thinking, " I'm going to be married forever." It's something that you go into thinking this is going to be a fair bit of work; there's going to be work as well as pleasure, and there's going to be pain as well, and there's going to be things that are going to turn up and you've got to be able to trust each other enough to work together to face those things that come up.

(Doug, aged 22, from a regional area)

For some young people, love, respect, and companionship are important:

Just knowing that she respects me and loves me and she would do anything for me and that she's always there when I roll over in bed or you know look over and she looks after us knowing what I like and I can talk to her all the time and you've just got someone to keep you company and talk about things with.

(Stuart, aged 19, from a regional area)

One young man demonstrated how, in the context of a relationship, it is possible to challenge beliefs:

I'm in a relationship with a woman and she's really wonderful. She talks freely about her opinions and ideas and she challenges my ideas. I like that; I like that she challenges my ideas because it forces me to think and even rethink and I have to replace some part of my ideology...I've got to rethink through and come up with something that will work because she's challenged one of my previous ideas and proven it to be a false kind of method to work off.

(Thomas, aged 20, from a regional area)

These examples highlight that, at least for some young men, sex in the context of a relationship was as important as it was for women and that, within the privacy of the relationship, men can and do want to speak about emotional issues and are open to challenging their belief systems. This is consistent with other research with young men by Allen (2005) and Powell (2007a).

Implications of Young People's Experiences for Thinking about Ethical Sex

The preceding narratives from young women and men demonstrate diversity in the responses and skills they use to negotiate sex, including consent. Some young people indicate that casual sex is dominated by nonverbal communication, unless personal boundaries are overstepped. The difficulty they experience is that nonverbal communication is open to being read inaccurately, ignored, or misinterpreted, especially when alcohol is involved. Assumed consent to sex by an interpretation of nonverbal cues did not provide them with any way of knowing what might happen. For some, this added to the pleasure of the potential experience; for others, it made them vulnerable to unwanted sexual acts and disappointment. This was especially the case for heterosexual women. When we enter into a casual encounter with another person, we bring with us gendered expectations about what it means to be sexual and how we experience that within our bodies. Further, there is the influence of our family background. How confident are we in knowing we have rights and responsibilities, let alone being able to voice them? We bring our own sexual history with us and so does the person with whom we have sex. This may be an idealized or romanticized form of what we believe is possible or an unrealistic one based on pornography. Without knowing something about the other person—for example, how they relate to their male and female friends—it is often hard to make informed judgments about sexual consent. Instead, there is a reliance on nonverbal communication, in which much is inferred and hoped for. It is a lottery whether the other person treats you with consideration, respect, and concern for your desires or purely focuses on their own needs being met. The strong reliance on nonverbal communication suggests that one way to enhance the quality of consent negotiations and mutual enjoyment is to increase women's and men's skills in giving and receiving nonverbal gestures and signals in sexual contexts.

Concerns about lack of clarity around nonverbal communication were less evident in young people having sex in the context of relationships. Higher levels of trust, taking risks, and openness to mutual exploration were possible for some young women and men in this context. However, this was not universally positive just because they knew the person better. It depended on the people involved in the relationship and their willingness to move beyond nonverbal communication to ascertain consent including when, how, and what kind of sexual behavior took place. Women recounted numerous examples of verbal communication used to tell their partner what they didn't want to do. A few women were able to find their voice to move beyond limit setting to speak about what they did want. Heterosexual men indicated that they still relied a lot on nonverbal cues, but they also asked their partners "is this okay?" This suggests more comfort in asking and implies a greater awareness of tuning into the other person's needs. Lesbians, heterosexual women, and gay men recounted the importance of talking about sex as part of the overall relationship. Is this because they demonstrated higher levels of interest in emotional intimacy—an interest not shared by numbers of heterosexual men? Or was this a reflection of the kind of people who signed up for research on sexuality and violence prevention? It is hard to know the answer to these questions, but it does point to some of the constraints that many heterosexual men may feel in relation to how they perform their masculinities. This has implications for how they understand consent and what is required of them to ensure that both parties are consenting to what might happen. Despite the heterosexual men's reliance on nonverbal communication, plus some verbal asking or checking in with their partners, young men in this study strongly valued sex within the context of a relationship. Like the young women I spoke to, they valued trust, love, respect, and communication as what they wanted or had in their current relationships. Both women and men believed this enhanced their sexual experiences and their ability to negotiate for their own needs and to work out the needs of their partner.

Some young people I spoke with had developed ethical ways of negotiating sexual intimacy. However, for many, they were on a sharp learning curve trying to balance cultural narratives and expectations, affection, and maybe romance and, at the same time, manage their bodily response and, hopefully, some understanding of the other person. Those who had developed ethical practices had often developed these as a result of increased experience over time. Some of this was due to strong self-confidence encouraged by their family background; others found ways to do this in the context of a loving relationship. For others, it came as a reaction and led to a reflection on unwanted or unpleasant experiences—either emotionally or physically. The challenge this data presents to all educators is how to increase the knowledge and skills of young people in negotiating sex in either casual or ongoing relationships. This is the challenge of primary prevention work—to provide education that will reduce undesired, negative, and exploitative experiences and maximize the positive ones before harm is done. This is important not only to prevent unwanted sex or sexual assault, STIs, and unwanted pregnancies, but also to enhance the pleasure of the sexual experience for both partners.

In chapter 4, I discuss how well current sexuality education assists young women and men to address the complexity of ethical sexual relationships.

Chapter 4

More than Plumbing: Sexuality Education

They just described the mechanics of it; they didn't discuss how you went about picking up; they didn't discuss how you come to the agreement to have sex; they never discussed any of the actual arrangements, they just described the mechanics and the effects of the mechanics.

(Thomas, a 20-year-old Aboriginal man, from a regional area)

Sexual intimacy can be extremely pleasurable, fun, ordinary, and even disappointing. It can also be confusing and scary, especially when you are beginning your sexual life. Biological facts may be much more easily obtained than for previous generations. However, many young people in this research felt ill-prepared with the knowledge and skills needed to successfully navigate their way through sexual intimacy. In this chapter, I explore young people's experiences of the sexuality education they received from school, friends, and parents, and how well they felt it prepared them. The young women and men I spoke with had many ideas about how both sexuality and violence prevention education could be improved. These ideas form the basis for the second part of the chapter. The chapter concludes by considering how anti-sex discourses impact on the kind of education young people receive.

The preparation for adult sexuality by formal sexuality education is highly contested, with more-conservative groups arguing that it destroys children's innocence and awakens desires that are best left sleeping (Luker 2006; Scott 2005). Others may acknowledge the need for some educational input, but this is primarily seen as being focused on sex within heterosexual marriage and the production of children. Those who are suspicious of the intervention of the state into family life see parents as the only people who should be responsible for transmitting knowledge and values to children. As Scott (2005, 180–181) points out, these restrictive discourses staunchly promote "familial values," youth abstinence from sexual activity, and avoiding disease. They focus on reproductive heterosexuality and conformity to moral absolutes. In contrast, sex-positive approaches emphasize pleasure, self-fulfillment, and physical and psychological health. Sexual development is seen as a dynamic sociocultural process in which children and adolescents have rights to receive sexuality education, make choices about their sexuality, and have sexual autonomy (Scott 2005, 181). In reflecting on the politics and debates around sexuality education in the United Kingdom, Alldred and David (2007, 7–8) suggest concerns around the category of "child" aimed to maintain the purity of idealized objects, rather than the wellbeing of actual, flesh and blood children. Related arguments are made by Robinson (2013), who argues that denying access to sexual knowledge by children actually makes them more vulnerable, and by Egan and Hawkes (2010), who point to the long history of social anxieties and moral panics associated with sexuality and children. Regulation of children and young people's sexuality is, therefore, of long standing duration (Haydon and Scraton 2002).

In this study, I was keen to understand what exposure participants had to both formal sexuality education and violence prevention education through primary/grade school and high school and from their parents or friends. Of particular interest was how the young people who had received school-based education viewed the education, and how well they thought it prepared them for dealing with the complexity of sexual relationships. In government schools in New South Wales (NSW), Australia, as in many countries, personal development—including sexuality education—is part of the Personal Development, Health and Physical Education Curriculum (PDHPE). Students are required to study 300 hours of the total PDHPE curriculum as part of their successful completion of high school to gain a School Certificate at the end of Year 10 (Board of Studies NSW 2003). Despite this promising policy, what happens in practice is extremely variable. Individual schools can determine how many hours are allocated within the broad curriculum and what emphasis is taken. This is influenced by staff interest and willingness; professional skills of teachers; available resources; and demands of the crowded curriculum (Mitchell 2007).

Matters Included In, and Impact of, School Sexuality Education

An examination of the NSW state school curriculum indicated a wide range of topics and issues that can be explored with students throughout their school years. Few participants were able to recall anything of their school sexuality education that went beyond lessons that covered biological aspects of male and female reproduction. Participants recalled safe-sex messages with amusement, as some teachers—embarrassed by the content—tried to explain the perils of sexually transmitted infections (STIs). Many young people had lasting memories of bananas being used to demonstrate how to apply a condom. While bananas have little to do with the actual physical structure of the penis, the message was transmitted and received. The overall impression received was that sex was dangerous—either due to unwanted pregnancy or disease. The majority of participants had very little memory of input that addressed relationships, how to negotiate them or how to make decisions about whether or not to have sex, and what things to consider in making these decisions. Young people in regional areas fared somewhat better than their city counterparts in gaining some knowledge about relationships. However, only three participants could recall any information about date rape or sexual assault.

Young people who attended Catholic schools primarily received the message that sex outside marriage was unacceptable. They appear to have received little instruction apart from this message; although one participant did indicate a degree of pragmatism on behalf of her teachers:

> I think the teachers were obliged to tell us [that] it is the Catholic Church's view, um, for you to try to abstain, try to realize other implications. They definitely gave us an anti-abortion slant when we were learning about that...but overall they were fairly realistic. They knew that we were going to be having sex and they weren't telling us we'd all go to hell.
>
> (Debbie, aged 19, from the city)

Most young people who attended state secular and religious coeducational schools experienced sexuality education in mixed-gendered groups. The reason for this may have been to encourage discussion between the genders or simply may have been administrative. However, this had an impact on how young people felt about asking questions in front of their friends and classmates:

> I think it was easier; it's easier when you're younger to discuss it if it's just one gender-based group. You don't have to. I think when you're younger you more or less worry about how the other sex is going to see you and at that time I was only still young I didn't want to say I'd

done anything if I hadn't done it…I didn't want to give anybody the wrong impression kind of thing.

> (Karen, aged 18, an Aboriginal woman from a regional area)

Another Aboriginal young woman, Kirsten, added to this need for comfort based on shared cultural values:

> Um, I didn't feel very comfortable talking about sex in class with people I wasn't really comfortable with…so yeah it was better in that way for me that I was with other Aboriginal people.

The current study found that 30 percent of women and 50 percent of men are engaging in some form of sexual activity under the age of 16 years. This suggests there is a pressing need to address how current sexuality education programs in schools are failing to prepare young people for sexual intimacy. Gourlay (1995, 39) argues that sexuality education is being taught by "teachers who invariably feel under-trained, under-resourced and often under siege." There is nothing to indicate much has changed since the time of this observation. An overcrowded curriculum may result in pragmatic decisions to teach the basics of biological knowledge and adopt a harm-minimization approach to safe-sex education. This leaves untouched the key issues that young people are struggling with as they begin their sexual lives.

Another area that is absent from most young people's memories is information on the diversity of relationships—including same-sex relationships or attraction in the lives of young people. Given that 34 percent of this sample indicated same-sex attraction or a lesbian or gay identity, this left them with little information to understand their emerging feelings during their time at school. Hillier, Turner, and Mitchell (2005, n = 1,749) found that fewer than 10 percent of young people in Australia had accessed information about gay and lesbian relationships from school or family. Hillier and Mitchell (2008), using data from the 2005 study, found that same-sex-attracted young people thought their sex education "was as useful as a chocolate kettle" because it was not inclusive of difference or their particular needs. Same-sex-attracted young people in my study also felt excluded from sexuality education discussions, with significant negative effects on their health. Ellen, a 19-year-old lesbian, who grew up in a regional area, indicates:

> It was actually really hard for me. I became really depressed, especially from the age of 15 to 16, and I had to go see a counsellor about it and they didn't know what was wrong with me. They thought it was

depression and then after that I actually met someone and that made me realize, well, maybe its okay.

Parental Influence on Sexuality Education and Sexuality

Parents may comfort themselves that sexuality education is in the hands of teachers and this means that they don't need to have what, for some parents and young people, can be difficult and confronting discussions about sexuality. In this study, I found that the family's role in imparting sexuality education was primarily limited to basic biological information, some advice about looking after themselves (although not always clearly defined or elaborated), and some advice about contraception. If input was attempted, it was almost always by mothers talking to their daughters. Fathers rarely were involved, except when children were younger, and input was restricted to basic biological information. A few fathers had brief talks with daughters or sons about " being careful," but fathers and sons rarely engaged in discussions about sexuality. This is consistent with surveys in Australia, Great Britain, and the United States that indicate that teenagers receive very little, if any, sexuality education from their parents (Scott 2005, 179). Parents, however, are not all the same. Dyson and Smith (2012) found that a wide range of values and attitudes were represented among parents in their study. Regardless of the varying approaches parents used, all participants expressed a desire for their children to be well informed about sex, sexual health, and relationships, yet many felt inadequate to the task of providing high-quality sex education to their children.

For those parents who did discuss sexuality matters with their children, these discussions were linked to imparting values that they felt were important; for example, abstinence. In the case of Debbie, a 19-year-old from the city:

> My parents were really very good talking to us about sex . . . always told us the truth from when I was very small . . . they very much pushed abstinence and they still do. They don't want us to be having sex before marriage but they always talked to us about, you know, how sex worked, and we always got the correct names for our body parts. It was always, you know, when, when a man and a woman love each other very much, but they did go into it and answer our questions frankly.

When Debbie later came out as a lesbian, she was not surprised by their reaction:

> Um well . . . they're Catholic, they are really committed Catholics and brought me up the same and you can't, like . . . there is no grey area in

Catholicism. If you have homosexual feelings you don't act on them and then even that's a recent development to admit that it's okay to have them, so when I told my mother she reacted...the way I thought she would. They love me very much and I'm very close to them so there was no "we disown you."

For Meryl, a 22-year-old married mother from an Indian-Australian background, her parents had an open approach that valued sexual exploration not tied to gender:

My parents had an open relationship for a few years before they decided to, you know, to have a monogamous marriage. I mean they always told us the possibility that human love it doesn't really matter what body they're in...the fact that you have either a penis or vagina doesn't prevent you from doing anything; it might prevent other people from seeing you in a certain way but that's not your problem, that's their problem...I have a lot to thank them for, like they were never really gender specific, they never gendered any conversations with us or any activities that we did or didn't do.

Kelly, aged 25, who grew up in a regional area, remembers the messages she gained about gender equality from her parents:

I've more or less been taught that if a male is to treat a female like they are nothing, like dirt under their feet or whatever they think, there's no point in even knowing that person, that's just wrong. Everyone should be, like everyone should be um...what's the word I'm looking for?...Um...that should be equal, male and female should have everything the same, everything should be the same for both sexes.

In Stuart's (aged 19, from a regional area) family, his father made it very clear that women need to be treated with respect:

Well me (sic) mum got raped at a young age by her uncle so we always knew about the situation and me (sic) dad always told us kids it's wrong to touch a woman or raise your fist to a woman. It doesn't matter what they do they don't deserve to get a fist raised to 'em...I've always been a strong believer of women shouldn't be hurt by men whatsoever so I usually stick me (sic) nose in [intervene] whenever I see an incident that I don't think is respectful.

The need for a foundation of values is something that several participants felt was important, even if they didn't agree with their parent's values. Dianne, a 22-year-old from the city with a Maltese-Australian background, describes her views:

Um, I think it also depends on where you're coming from, like what your upbringing was like and, like I said, I've always come from a place where morals were very clear and I knew exactly what they were and, like you said, although I sort of, I changed them to suit myself and you know the world I've grown up in rather than the world my parents grew up in...the foundation's still the same.

Despite the calls by conservatives for parents to be the primary source of information about sexuality, it appears in this study that many parents felt incapable or unwilling to take on the task, or they felt the matter was being dealt with by schools. This may also reflect on their own lack of education in this area, therefore, resulting in an inter-generational silence between parents and their children. Given that young people are experiencing more and more pressure to be sexually active at younger ages, lack of parental guidance leaves them with little support. It also leaves young people at increased risk, as they attempt to negotiate a mixture of biological changes, peer pressure to conform to their social group's rules about "what is cool," a myriad of conflicting parental messages, and the power of the broader cultural messages that shape gendered expectations about sexuality. As indicated above, school information had a limited impact on the participants' knowledge and preparation for sexual intimacy. Parents too had a limited role. This meant that friends became a powerful source of information on how to negotiate a developing sexual life.

Sexuality and School-age Friends

For young people who feel that a discussion of sexual issues with parents or teachers is out of the question because of conflicting value systems or even embarrassment, their friends become a major source of factual information, advice, and guidelines as to what is acceptable or unacceptable sexual behavior. Moral frameworks provided by schools or family may be rejected in lieu of a young person finding their place in social and sexual relationships. Especially in the high school years, fitting in becomes a crucial and often distressing challenge. Friendship groups, therefore, become fundamental to shaping how a young man or woman thinks about and creates the beginning of a sexual life. As discussed in chapter 2, depending on the social norms of the group, young people may have sex before they feel ready, or perform certain sexual acts to gain status or to avoid being seen as a "loser." Friendship groups are powerful in reinforcing or challenging gender expectations about relationships and sexual intimacy. The lack of specific attention by school programs to the knowledge and skills that young people want, then places young people in a position of negotiating among their own needs, parental expectations, and the needs of their friendship groups. There seems to be little relevant information coming their way from official sources, and this increases their reliance on the advice of people the same age or on information gleaned from television programs, websites, or DVDs (information that is often misleading and may replicate highly traditional gender roles for women and men).

Ideas about Improving Education on Violence and Sexuality

Young people's thoughts about sexuality and sexual assault prevention education included a wide range of ideas from the individual to the wider community. They saw it as important to include both men and women. The themes identified here are: communication; consent; ethical intimacy; challenging violence and supporting victims; and the delivery of education. While the themes are discussed separately below, they need to be considered as overlapping and informing each other.

Communication

A number of participants felt that young people needed more opportunity to learn how to communicate effectively with potential partners, whether in a casual encounter or an ongoing relationship. They were quite specific in what they felt some people missed. For example, Thomas, aged 20, an Aboriginal man from a regional town, said:

> No matter how they do it, couples do need to communicate. There's got to be some level of communication, whether it's direct talking about the relationship or just listening to what the other person says and likes and does, and paying attention to that and figuring out what they like from that and then...consideration is the key—pay attention to the other person.

Active listening was seen as an important part of effective communication and several male participants indicated that they felt men, in particular, didn't really understand how to do this. Both women and men felt there was a need to teach people how to pay attention to verbal and nonverbal communication in intimate encounters, and to recognize the mismatch between the two. There was an awareness of how it is often difficult to talk in intimate situations and that people shouldn't just rely on nonverbal cues. Kirsten, aged 21, a Greek Australian from the city, describes this feeling:

> I just think that, you know, kind of talking about it, but it's hard to talk about it and there are times you don't want to talk about it...like I might want to be with you but not the whole way, and it's sort of like my experience of pushing the hand away...I think non-verbal was really sort of a key aspect of it because you're going to get kids that don't want to talk about it.

Consent

The issue of consent is fundamental to non-coercive sexual encounters. Participants were very aware of this and, while some were aware of prevention messages, such as "no means no," they felt this was not adequate to address the complexity of the issues involved. For example, Louise, a lesbian aged 20 from the city, suggests more attention needs to be given to how to address questions such as: "What are you consenting to, in what way are you consenting and why are you consenting?"

Young people felt they had been ill-prepared to address the complexity; for example, Carol, aged 20, also from the city, said:

> I feel like that whole part is entirely missed and, for me, like, certainly when I had sex with someone who I like, really felt awful...I didn't really know how to deal with that because no-one had ever really talked really to me about consent and what that meant and how you grant it or don't grant it and, because all of my previous relationships had been so kind of nice and negotiated, it was very hard for me to deal with 'cause you don't have any coping mechanism that's given to you.

While a clear "no" needs to be respected, participants indicated an awareness of how negotiating consent is more fluid than this:

> I guess basically there's "no means no" but the only real way that people want it is "yes means yes." That's it, there's no in-betweens or shades of grey.
>
> (Ellen, a 19-year-old lesbian from a regional area)

For Christine, a 23-year-old from the city, learning how to handle ambivalence in a relationship and how this impacts on consent is something she thinks is missing in current sexual assault information:

> This is why I came, because I really do believe that the current sexual assault information is really great. What it isn't great about, the

messages that don't get across is that stuff...that really grey compli-
cated stuff that happened between (my partner) and I. How do you tell
someone that when you give permission, but you don't want to give
permission, you know, that's such a grey area?

Having the skills to deal with the fluidity of consent in any sexual
encounter is something that most sexual assault prevention education programs don't address. The impact of this is that young people
are confused about how to negotiate encounters. It may appear that
a woman has indicated consent by agreeing to accompany her partner home, but what she is consenting to once she's there can't be
assumed, and there is a need to ascertain willing agreement to what
follows:

> Ooh, I wouldn't say "no means no" but I think most of the time
> I think it's just not understanding maybe the signals that girls give,
> being more aware that maybe something she says or something she
> does doesn't necessarily mean that's what she wants. She may just be
> reacting to what you...like what the guy would say or something like
> that...like just what I would say is that I'd make...sure that it's some-
> thing she wanted.
> (Mary, a South American Australian, aged 22, from the city)

In the heat of passion and possible intoxication, participants felt it was
important to take time to be sure that both parties wanted not only
sexual intimacy, but understood what form it was going to take. This
requires awareness of your own desires and the impact of those desires
on the other person. The emotional impact of sexual encounters,
both consensual and non-consensual, was an area that participants
commented on frequently. For example, Doug, a 22-year-old from
a regional center, felt there was a need to consider the impact on the
whole relationship and how gender can shape attitudes to consent:

> There is the whole respect and the dignity that's attributed to it and
> there's that emotional attachment and emotional relationships between
> men and women. I think it should also be emphasized in sex educa-
> tion because there's a lot of people who are hurting out there and a
> lot of women especially who are hurting out there because men only
> see them as an object...when they do go and decide that they want
> to have sex because not only are they going to see the physical side of
> things, they're going to see the emotional side of things and they're
> going to think, well, maybe I don't really want to hurt this person in
> an emotional way and I really do care about this person and maybe I
> shouldn't go this step forward.

Feelings about sexual intimacy can change quickly, and there is a need to equip people with the skills to recognize this and respect the changes that can happen:

> So she puts it out there, she decides to say no...you should respect her decision and stuff and just wait till she says whether to keep going or not and just, yeah, it should be vice versa, though, as well...if the guy doesn't want to do it, the same thing but we should always listen to what the other person wants and respect the other person.
>
> (Stuart, aged 19, from a regional area)

He adds that respect is not just about two people relating, but that there is a need for men, in particular, to stand up to other men who aren't treating women well. While we may not agree with his use of violence, his intention to intervene in another male's violence toward a woman is clear:

> I was walking to another mate's place with a group of mates and we saw a guy just hitting a girl in the park—give her a couple of slaps— and me and my mates walked up to him and said, "look we don't like what you're doing to her and, like, she doesn't deserve it you know," and then he's just turned around and started swinging so we started swinging back. I've been a firm believer a woman doesn't deserve to be abused and nor raped so, yeah, I always give 'em respect and all that.

Ethical Intimacy

There was a range of ideas that explored the ways in which women and men of diverse sexualities could avoid violence and abuse. These centered on values and attitudes that both women and men need to develop to care for themselves and for others. These ideas meet the definition of sexual ethics or ethical intimacy, discussed in detail in chapter 6.

Respect for oneself and for the other person was a theme that participants mentioned frequently:

> Respect people if they want to have sex; if they don't want to have sex, don't judge them...like if they want to or they don't just, it's their right. No one else has any right to judge or say that's right or wrong for some other person's feelings or behavior.
>
> (Helen, aged 25, from a regional area)

This is also true for Alex, a 24-year-old gay man, from a regional center:

> I suppose...for me, um, sex should be about giving and taking and being really open to the other person's needs and boundaries. Um,

everyone has boundaries and we have to feel comfortable to express them when they're being encroached upon. I think that's really important and having mutual respect for the other person because, while you have boundaries, they have boundaries and you have to respect those things and be open about them...[sigh] and I think it's also about self-respect as well, you know.

For Doug, aged 22, from a regional area, these ideas about respect are something that he feels needs more attention in sexuality education:

[There are] a lot of young people who are just starting to form their own values and beliefs about how you respect and how you treat women. I guess the first thing would be to...to teach about women, especially for the males, how to honor women and how to protect women. I mean there's not enough of that going in, there's not, I don't think there's enough of that in education...um, also teaching women self-respect as well would be a good start, and men to respect themselves as well. I think, I guess, it's more of an ethical and a value thing, but it's important that young people are able to respect themselves and each other.

To develop self-respect requires a level of self-awareness that participants believed could be developed by a variety of strategies. These included considering what your expectations were of sexual intimacy and relationships, before you got into situations that were uncomfortable or damaging to your self-esteem. The process of self-reflection was seen as important:

I really think trying to encourage them, maybe, to even write down what their expectations are, or what their thoughts are, um, about what they expect from sex, what they expect from the person that they'll be with and everything, and even if they, I don't know, hang on to that. And so when their first time is sort of getting closer to happening...I mean obviously if you're drunk you're not going to whip out that piece of paper and have it right there and go, well, let me see what I'm talking about but...but at least you've got a clear idea and you've had that chance to look at it.

(Brenda, aged 22, from the city)

She suggests that this process of self-reflection could be done individually and in discussion groups divided by gender. She also reflects that what helped her gain some insight into her feelings was keeping a diary and looking back on it at times.

Karen, an 18-year-old Aboriginal woman from a regional town, believes that respect comes from self-worth. She describes a session

she attended given by an older Aboriginal woman and the approach
she took to get this message across:

> You are women, you have babies, you create the next generation, kind
> of, you know you need to have more respect for yourself, don't go
> throwing yourself around like you don't mean anything—you mean a
> lot. And that was like it helped them to have more confidence in them-
> selves, to not just ask questions but to ask questions and understand
> the answers.

Other strategies suggested by participants extended the concept of
self-reflection to understanding that we all have choices about who
and what we get involved with. This meant that people needed to
ask themselves: "What is right for me in this moment?"; "Am I
being respected or doing things just to please my partner or to gain
approval from my friends?"; "Is this what I want and how does this
impact on another?"; "Where will this take me?"; and "What are the
implications of my actions now and in the future?" There was recognition that "you need to look after yourself before you can look
after others." The need for being less trusting of people was also seen
as an important part of looking after oneself by Ellie, a 17-year-old
Aboriginal woman from a regional town:

> And there'd be like examples of some of those, be experiences on why
> you should take advice and then there should be experiences why you
> shouldn't trust everyone like the first time you meet them, why you
> shouldn't trust anyone going to parties and stuff, that kind of stuff.
> And the third one would be how to [be] aware of the situation, how to
> stay in control. Some kids wouldn't like it but you just do it.

Self-determination extends beyond your own individual feelings, as
Christine, aged 23, from the city, strongly argues:

> They [need to] know that it's not their church, it's not their partner,
> it's not their parents, it's not their own body [that] has a right to what
> happens, it's…it's their emotional and psychological process that has
> a right to say what does and doesn't happen.

Connected to these questions was also a call for young people to
understand their own limits and boundaries of what felt right for
them, especially when alcohol is involved:

> If you're going to go to a party and if you want to have fun, you
> drink, sometimes you drink too much. The real key is just don't drink.

You've got to be able to handle yourself, know your limitations, learn your limitations... 'cause when you learn your limitations you just you don't make a fool of yourself. I've learnt pretty quick; I had to learn the hard way though.

(Ellie, aged 17, from a regional area)

The pressure that young women, in particular, may feel to conform to pressure for sex from a partner should be resisted, as Mary, a South American Australian, aged 22, from the city indicates:

I'd say that they're developing the understanding that they should not give in to pressure. No matter how much he may say other people are doing it, we should do it too, that they need to be able to respect themselves enough to know that if they don't want to do it...so that you're not put in a position where you're like "oh no, what do I do? Do I have to because I'm in that situation or can I back off?" Just knowing where you stand first and being aware of, I wouldn't say your limitations, but just your boundaries.

The need to challenge particular forms of masculinity was also seen as needing some attention:

There are some wonderful things about that kind of male environment, and you know, male supportive environment, but there's a lot that's ugly and I would really like to see something implemented in football clubs, and not even men, with boys, with young boys, about respecting women and respecting boundaries and not giving into that pack mentality.

(Meryl, aged 22, from a regional area)

This had other meanings in relation to gay male sexuality for Rod, aged 20, from a regional area:

To be gay isn't having random sex with a lot of men. It's having feelings for people that you're attracted to and that's important. It doesn't matter if you're a person that does like to have these casual things but I don't want people to feel pressured by a stereotype to get themselves into situations because they think that's how they should act as a gay man.

Challenging Violence and Supporting Victims

Participants felt there was still a lack of knowledge about sexual assault and other forms of violence in relationships:

I think that maybe a lot of people, like younger kids from school and stuff like that, that when they think of violence they think of physical violence...maybe more education needs to be pushed towards the emotional issues and what you may feel the morning after as opposed to the night before talking about the fact that alcohol can remove inhibitions and things like that.

(Brenda, aged 22, from the city)

In particular, they felt there was little coverage of this in their school curricula, especially when applied to sexual assault between young people. For example, Carol, aged 21, from the city, said:

No one really addresses sexual assault while you're in high school and then by the time you get to university there's no sex education...unless you're taking a specific course.

There was a sense that people still do not understand that sexual assault and other forms of violence mainly occur between people known to each other, or that it does happen to young people. As one young woman said to me, "I thought it only happened to older women like you, Moira." Instead, there was a continuing belief that assault by a stranger was more common. Related to this was a lack of awareness of the various forms sexual assault can take:

Knowing what type of assault there is, because there are heaps of types of assaults—there's physical, there's sexual, like there's heaps of them—but have it in there so they know this is what sexual assault is...just have it simple as possible so guys and girls can read it and go, "oh, so that's what that is."

(Zoe, aged 19, from a regional town)

There was also a sense in which small communities need to be better informed and less blaming of victims of sexual assault. Gilda, aged 19, from a regional area, who experienced sexual assault, highlights the denial that still operates in small towns:

It's either very taboo or something that would happen to somebody else, but none of your neighbors or your friends or relatives or anything you know...or it's a hot goss[ip]-type situation that's pretty common, too, like small towns...so I think that's a big problem, because it then becomes the stigma and the blame and the "oh well, it wouldn't have happened to somebody else."

Awareness of support services for victims of sexual assault is not well known by young people. They may be reluctant to report, if they had been drinking at the time, or were not where they told their parents they were going. Zoe suggests that a bright and colorful wallet-sized card, with contact numbers of services, should be freely available so that:

> ...You can have [the card] in your pocket or in your purse and if you do come across somebody, like, it's just something that lays there in your bag and you forget about it and if you know it's still in there you should pull it out and give it to them, like, "here, ring this number," that type of thing.

Offering support to other women who have been assaulted was also seen as being important, not only for mutual support, but as a way of holding the perpetrator responsible and preventing further violence. For example:

> A lot of the times the rape happens I think it's because one woman won't speak up because she's terrified of what may happen...and then because one woman won't speak up another woman gets attacked and because both of them don't speak up a third gets attacked. Well, if all of those women got together and banded as a group then hopefully they would find strength in safety in numbers and, therefore, one person who's prone to raping women would, you know, would be in prison for a while and hopefully go through some sort of re-education program and it wouldn't happen again.
>
> (Melissa, aged 25, from a regional town)

Young people also considered that all forms of violence needed to be addressed including homophobia and violence in same-sex relationships. There was also some recognition that violence is not always perpetrated by men against women, as Roberta, a 19-year-old Aboriginal woman from a regional area, indicates:

> It's always about the guy hitting the girl. It'd be good to see things about the girl hitting the guy. I know a few people where the girls is [sic] definitely more dominant than the guy...they just focus on guys beating girls, but what about the girls beating the guys.

Another strategy suggested to challenge violence in the community was the need for role models for both women and men. Karen felt that, in the Aboriginal community in which she lives:

> The older girls can help educate young girls because young girls will listen; younger girls look up to you and you know it you know every single thing you drop out of your mouth they'll eat it up and believe every single word of it...some blokes just think it's okay, I mean they

haven't, you know they haven't had a specific person in their life say no you cannot do that.

Bobbie, a 17-year-old Torres Strait Islander man from a regional area, agrees:

> Someone closer to your age…Yeah, a footballer or like I don't know just someone in the community or something that's willing to speak out for what's right.

The parent-as-role-model was another area that participants felt needed improving. For some, their parents had a zero-tolerance approach to any form of violence and this was explicitly discussed and enforced. However, others felt that parents needed more education about relationships and violence in general, and that they needed to openly discuss these issues with their children:

> I think you just need to get the message out there that you're not going to be judged on it…people have got to stop making presumptions about people and I think that comes with general awareness, not just to 16–25-year-olds but to the older generations that actually, I think, are worse than the younger ones 'cause they don't realize the prevalence of sexual assault or domestic violence.
>
> (Sasha, aged 22, from a regional area)

The impact of a failure to address these issues had negative consequences for Rose, aged 19, from the city. When she was raped, she felt unable to tell her parents for a considerable period of time:

> But even then I guess it's something that you have to, maybe, you have to be taught at a young age, but also, I guess in the family as well…parents have to talk about it as well. It can't just be something that is external to the family environment; the family have to sit down and talk about it. I think that would've helped me a lot because, basically, I would've known that I could've gone to mum and dad if anything like this had happened

Delivery of Education

Participants felt that their personal development subjects at school had failed to adequately prepare them for the complexities of sexual intimacy and other relationships, or how to understand the possibility of abusive encounters and strategies for handling both. As indicated above, they felt there was a need for a much more detailed exploration of all forms of relationships and the skills to handle the complexities and anxieties they and other young people face.

Given the decreasing age of first sex found in this study, this preference for increased educational complexity would seem to be important in providing young people with knowledge and skills as they develop relationships. As discussed above, parents and school administration fear that an open discussion of sex results in a gap that will be filled often with inaccurate information from peers or the Internet.

Some people felt it would be good to have people visit schools who could talk about the impact of violence on their lives. Others thought role-playing of situations you might find yourself in and strategies to handle them would be useful:

> ...Like a play-type thing—if this happens, this is what we suggest you do or to this is what you shouldn't do or you know something like that, just so they can actually see what it's like. When you're told about it you don't really listen...you do to a certain extent but then you think, "well it won't happen to me, so I'll just carry on"...but actually see it and see that it can happen, then you kind of think about it more 'cause you've had that visual, or that's what I think, anyway.
>
> (Kelly, aged 25, from a regional area)

Another suggestion was for small group discussions that were separated by gender to allow free discussion:

> I would probably make sure that the sexes were separated during those classrooms because in school it's just embarrassing; you know you can't really talk about it.
>
> (Maureen, aged 21, from a regional area)

The way information was presented was also seen as important, especially for young Aboriginal women, as this could affect its impact. Karen, aged 18, explained:

> When you've got young girls and you need to tell them something, you have to watch how you say it 'cause if you make them shamed they're not going to listen.

Competing Discourses of Sexuality Education

The young people in this study are not alone in their criticisms of personal development or sexuality education. Canadian young people report that education is too focused on "plumbing" and often provided by teachers with whom they felt uncomfortable discussing sexual issues (Di Censo et al. 2001). In the United Kingdom, 16- and 17-year-old boys were asked what they wanted from sexuality and relationship education classes. The researchers found that boys were not being taught what they wanted to know. The areas of feelings and emotions, sexuality, and sexual techniques were some of the areas they felt were missing. They called for smaller classes, more active methods of teaching, and time away from the girls to express themselves without censure (Hilton 2007, 161). In Northern Ireland, a country underpinned by a particularly traditional and conservative strain of Christian morality, researchers asked young people, aged 14–25 years, their opinions about the sexuality education they received (Rolston, Schubotz, and Simpson 2005). Sexual feelings and emotions were not given priority or were presented in a negative way. If they were discussed at all, they were encouraged to delay or simply say no. In New Zealand, young people identified their sexuality education program as being concentrated on the dangers and risks of sexual intercourse, and that there was a failure to enhance the negotiation skills of students, or take into account the contexts in which sex occurs for many young people (Abel and Fitzgerald 2006, 105). Same-sex-attracted young people in Australia indicated the lack of usefulness of the sexuality education they received, as it did not acknowledge same-sex attraction and focused almost exclusively on heterosexual sex (Hillier and Mitchell 2008). Not addressing their needs failed to address the reality that, as a group, they are sexually active earlier than their opposite-sex-attracted friends. This placed them at increased risk of STIs and denied their sexual choice of same-sex partners. Information gathered by the International Planned Parenthood Federation (IPPF) European Network (2006) indicated that sex education in many Catholic countries in Europe was either nonexistent or was of a poor quality, although some of these countries may have reported having mandatory sex education programs (Kontula 2010).

Many young people surveyed by researchers from a range of countries are very clear and consistent about what they want to know and what is not discussed or is overemphasized. These include avoidance of discussion of emotional aspects of sexuality, a focus on reproduction, the absence of any discourse of desire, and a concentration on the dangers of sex for women such as pregnancy, abortion, and STIs. They also thought discussions limited sexuality to sexual intercourse. There was frequent avoidance of discussing same-sex desire, a failure to engage boys, and a focus on girls. They also were acutely aware of the awkwardness of teachers in answering difficult questions (Measor 2000, 123–124, as cited by Rolston, Schubotz, and Simpson 2005).

A more comprehensive approach to sexuality education is evident in the Netherlands. Ferguson, Vanwesenbeeck, and Knijn (2008) describe the context as "a sex positive environment" that accepts adolescent sexuality and teaches young people about sexual responsibility. Focusing on the Dutch experience, they highlight the comparisons with UK and US approaches. While UK and Dutch sexuality education cover similar topics, Dutch materials are more comprehensive and classroom discussions in the Netherlands are more open. Dutch materials generally present topics in a positive light, including the pleasurable aspects of sex and relationships, which also include lessons on the importance of masturbation in discovering your own body before you have sex with someone else. They argue that a defining characteristic of Dutch materials is that they don't tell young people what to do, but encourage them to think through what they want in advance, and develop the necessary skills to communicate and maintain those boundaries (Ibid., 99).

One Australian attempt to address gaps in sexuality education is the Sexual Health and Relationships Education (SHARE) project from South Australia. Implemented by SHine SA (a state-based sexual health service) as a three-year pilot project, it received funding from the Department of Health between 2003 and 2005. It involved young people in years eight, nine, and ten (aged 13–15 years), in 15 secondary state schools from metropolitan and rural South Australia, who volunteered to be involved and who had parental support (SHARE Newsletter, July 2006). The education program was developed after extensive consultation with parents, teachers, and students, and a review of Australian and international literature on sexual health and relationships. It involved several important components: a theoretical approach that was sex-positive, comprehensively interactive, and acknowledged students as sexual beings with specific social and cultural identities. They used a whole-of-school approach that included the development of resources for parents and young people and a detailed curriculum for teachers. Training and support was also provided for teachers while they implemented the program. The program included an impact-evaluation study conducted by Sue Dyson and Christopher Fox from La Trobe University in Victoria (another state to the one in which the program was run), in-depth interviews with key people involved in implementing the program by Professor Bruce Johnson from the University of South Australia, and SHine SA's own surveys of students, parents, and teachers. Between 2003 and 2005, the SHARE program was provided in 15 schools involving 14,000 students. Further, 314 teachers were trained and additional professional development was provided to 175 teachers and 100 student teachers (SHARE Newsletter, July 2006).

While the program was based on solid medical and health evidence that supported the need for a comprehensive sexuality program, its implementation was affected by an organized negative reaction from some groups. A socially conservative, pro-family, fundamentalist Christian coalition opposed the erosion of "traditional values" and promoted a moral panic (Johnson 2006, 17). This is consistent with the activities of the US Christian Right (Gibson 2007; Irvine 2002). As is common with many forms of moral panic, the claims about the content and intent of the program were grossly exaggerated and distorted, and public commentary was designed to create alarm and spread fear in the community. Claims were made that it centered on homosexuality, masturbation and the licking of body parts, and the use of sexual aids and mind/thought manipulation (Advocates for Survivors of Child Abuse, as cited by Johnson 2006, 16). The power of distortion and the associated fear generated reached the state legislature, resulting in the Minister for Education reversing a longstanding policy, where all students were included in sexuality education unless their parents withdrew them. Instead, all parents who wanted their children to participate in SHARE had to sign written consent forms. The vitriol and hostility by opponents was not only aired in media and parliamentary contexts, but individual SHARE staff—including teachers—were verbally harassed and threatened (Johnson 2006). Despite this concerted campaign, SHine SA stayed on target with their commitment and message around young people and sexual health. Parents stood by them, and 95–98 percent endorsed the quality and appropriateness of the program. Evaluation of the program by Johnson (2006) highlighted the comprehensive approach taken, and the positive responses from parents, teachers, and young people. He argued that it was an exemplary model of sexuality education and recommended further extension of the program.

Anti-sex Discourses

What we can see emerging from my study, and other studies internationally, is the gap between what young people want to know and what is being delivered to them via school curricula. This disjuncture taps into the heart of sexuality education debates. The above discussion of the SHARE program and the reaction to it highlights how sexuality education exposes some deeply felt beliefs by different groups of people in the community. Foucault (1990) reminds us that sex and children and adolescents have been subject to innumerable institutional devices and discursive strategies since the eighteenth century. Not only is the fear of adolescent sexuality evident here, but there is the fear of sex in all its diversity. The delivery of sexuality education is highly contested and there is ample evidence of competing discourses impacting on sexuality education, design, and delivery. On one hand, the reality that young people are sexual beings is often denied. It is overlaid by particular moral discourses that argue education undermines family values, promotes inappropriate sexual behavior, and that celibacy is preferable until after marriage, resulting in programs that promote abstinence (Dyson et al. 2003, 12). Sex is only (just) acceptable within the confines of heterosexual marriage and homosexuality remains the ultimate sin.

Abstinence-only education programs have been promoted by the federal government in the United States over the last decade and tied to school funding. While this is not as common in Australia, the US experience highlights how religious and moral issues can impact directly on the lives of young people. Fields (2008, 165) argues that abstinence-only programs institutionalize inequality through limiting access to education and free expression of sexuality. She argues it scapegoats the most vulnerable members of society—young people, people of color, low-income people, and lesbian women, gay men, bisexual, and transgendered and queer (LGBTQ) people.

The impact of "just say no" approaches to sex—either through abstinence models or as a public health strategy—reveals the lack of stability in, and transparency of, the meaning of sex (Gilbert 2004). Gilbert highlights how recent US research with 15- to 19-year-old boys reveals a shift to "non-coital behaviours" like anal and oral sex. She suggests, quoting Remez (2000), that this may be a reflection of the strong influence of abstinence programs in the United States. What is troubling about this finding is that anal and oral sex may not be understood by the boys as "sex," may even be viewed as abstinence, and, consequently those activities may be thought to be risk free. Gilbert (2004, 116) suggests this demonstrates an inspiring creativity by young people; they are not having unsafe sex because, according to their logic, they are not having sex.

A multi-country study compared pragmatic and sex-positive government policies in France, Australia, and the Netherlands to sexual abstinence based policy in the United States. It found the former had better sexual health-related outcomes (Weaver, Smith, and Kippax 2005). The authors argued that young people's reproductive and sexual health is best served when sex between young people is acknowledged, accepted, and regulated, rather than proscribed in all contexts outside marriage. Santelli and colleagues (2006) argue that abstinence-only programs undermine the ethical principles of informed consent and free choice in health care. They consider that these programs are inherently coercive, withhold information needed to make informed choices, promote questionable and inaccurate opinions, and, as such, violate human rights. They also indicate how these shifts have eroded comprehensive sexuality education: 96 percent of high schools were teaching abstinence as the best way to avoid pregnancy, human immunodeficiency virus (HIV) infection, and other STIs (CDC 2000). In addition, there is no room for sexual expression outside the confines of heterosexual monogamous marriage or acknowledgment of the range of activities possible within sexual intimacy.

Moving Toward an Alternative Curriculum

Sexuality education is one of the few places young people receive officially sanctioned messages about sex and sexuality. If young people receive the message from school that sexual activity is predominantly about danger, guilt, and risk, they know this isn't the full story. Elsewhere, in popular culture, in schoolyards, and in personal stories, it is promoted as involving fun, pleasure, and power. This results in sexuality education's warnings appearing didactic and boring (Allen 2005, 169). Hirst (2004, 125) indicates a pure focus on the "mechanics of sexual behavior" that can lead to it being de-contextualized in the lives of young people. Her research clearly indicates—supported by many other studies—that although the majority of young people today can explain risk prevention strategies, it does not mean they are taking up the behavior in their own sexual lives. Improving sexuality education is not purely about replacing limited abstinence-only approaches with comprehensive sex-positive discourses of education. Comprehensive programs need to ensure they do not replicate gender stereotypes and heterosexism by making invisible the diversity of sexual practices and sexual identities. Even in the progressive "free and equal sexual culture" of Norway, the absence of discussion about sexual practices and desire in sex education has been noted as an ongoing concern (Svendsen 2012).

Young people in my study and other studies have indicated to educators what it is they want from us in terms of sexuality and violence prevention education. They have made it clear what they think is missing. As Allen (2005) argues, there is often a complete disconnection or gap for young people between the formal curriculum and their own experiences and those of their friends. The challenge for us—as educators—is, therefore, to work out how we negotiate the competing discourses of education discussed earlier, community fear of young people and sex, and find new ways to address their concerns. The mere acquisition of knowledge about sexual matters will not result in increased skills of negotiation around sexual intimacy or a change in behavior. Any alternative discourses we may explore will need to consider that any knowledge gained from sexuality education will be applied in a context of shifting and complex gender relations (Allen 2005). As Louisa Allen argues, there is a need to transform social perceptions of young people and sexuality to see them as active sexual agents, and that their sexual activity is a normal part of growing up that brings with it responsibilities to them and to others. She goes further and argues "There needs to be greater recognition in sexuality education of the sexual pleasures of embodied sexual experience" (2005, 171). Without this, how can anyone make an informed decision about sexual activity?

Most of the discussion in this chapter has focused on the broader issues of sexuality education, as well as canvassing young people's ideas about how to improve both sexuality and violence prevention education. In chapter 5, I explore approaches to violence prevention education and their impact on young people.

Chapter 5

Sexual Assault Prevention Education—an International Overview

In the previous chapter, I discussed young people's understandings of the sexuality education they received at school and from parents, its limitations from their point of view, and what they thought should be changed. I argued, first, that we need to consider the breadth of sexual experience young people are involved in, and, second, that we need to hear what they tell us about their concerns and experiences. At the sharp end of their experiences are stories of pressured, coerced sex and sexual assault. If we are to embrace a holistic view of sexuality education, we need to consider the ethical and pleasurable, as well as the unethical and unwanted that manifests in sexual and other forms of gendered violence. This chapter, therefore, aims to add to a comprehensive approach to sexuality education by critically analyzing the emergence of gender-violence prevention education. Considerable research has emerged in the last decade on how to develop effective preventive education aimed at reducing violence against women. Research on effective sexuality programs suggests possibilities for improving the educational experiences of young people and contributing to more ethical and respectful relationships.

Preventing sexual violence against women and children continues to prove challenging to local communities, state, and national and international policymakers. Violence against women has been identified as a leading cause of injury, death, and disability to women globally (UN General Assembly 2006). A key strategy adopted by both industrialized and developing countries is the use of educational initiatives to reduce sexual and other forms of intimate violence. This chapter explores the issue from an international perspective. As such, it is a partial and incomplete picture, which nevertheless attempts to

provide insight into the complexity of the wide range of activities fall-
ing under the term "prevention education." The origins and reasons
for the sexual ethics approach taken in this book are cast within this
international body of research and practice that continues to evolve, as
nations struggle to find more effective ways to assist young people.

Educational programs are not neutral activities. They are underpinned by beliefs and attitudes, and they are particular forms of
knowledge or discourse. Discourse, following French philosopher
Michel Foucault, "refers to the historically variable ways of specify-
ing knowledge and truth—what it is possible to speak of at a given
moment" (as cited in Gordon 1980, 93). He argues that discourses
produce truth and, with this, particular configurations of power are
evident that render it fragile and open to challenge. Discourses may
have a number of components. There are the objects (the things they
study or produce), the operations, and the methods and techniques
or ways of treating the objects. In terms of prevention education,
this means we need to consider the diverse ways in which knowledge
about violence against women is presented, and how what is possible
to speak about at any given historical moment is open to change.
Discourse also constructs the subjects or objects of study and involves
a consideration of the techniques used to impart truths about violence
against women. Some discourses have more influence or power than
others at different historical moments. In the field of prevention education, there are a number of competing discourses evident. Whereas,
for ease of argument, I am presenting these separately, they are often
interwoven and inform each other. I begin by providing an overview
of the influence of feminist activism around violence against women
and how these discourses have impacted global recognition of gendered violence.

From Grassroots Feminist Activism to
Global Recognition

Persistent efforts since the 1970s, especially by feminists in Western
contexts, have aimed to render sexual violence a visible concern of the
public and the state by challenging the idea that it is a private matter
(Carmody 1992; Franzway, Connell, and Court 1989; Kelly 1988).
A plethora of activities aimed at reducing violence against women—
including sexual violence—have been promoted and implemented by
radical and liberal feminists over this time in many countries. Some of
these activities include law reform, development of support services,
introduction of school curricula; campaigns involving videos, films,

pamphlets, stickers, posters, and billboards; books, journal articles, and conferences; radio and television interviews, community education announcements, soap opera story lines; training of professional staff and students; direct action; public shaming; street marches such as "Reclaim the Night"; and tree-planting ceremonies. While much of this activity has provided an alternative discourse on sexual violence through public actions and declarations of antiviolence attitudes, what is unclear is whether it has prevented sexual violence (Carmody and Carrington 2000, 345).

These prevention efforts were located in a broader critique of society that reflected unequal and discriminatory legal and cultural practices, wherein sexual assault and rape were positioned as the inevitable end of patriarchy. Underpinning these interventions was a conceptualization of gender that initially denied the diversity of women's experience of sexual violence, and left unchallenged an assumption that sexual violence was inevitable—thus universalizing women as "victims" and men as "perpetrators." Identifying this was an important organizing principle to building links between women and challenging societal denial of the insidious and frequent incidence of sexual violence perpetrated by strangers and known offenders. As the campaigns continued, there was an increasing recognition of the diversity of women's experience of sexual and other forms of violence, and the need for different approaches to acknowledge differences as well as similarities between women. An increasing body of evidence has consistently indicated that the violence was most frequently committed by men who were known to the women (ABS Personal Safety Survey 2006; Black et al. 2011).

Four decades later, there is now a global recognition that violence against women—in all its forms—results in poor health outcomes and reduced opportunities for full citizenship and impacts significantly on individual women, their children, partners, families, and communities. Alongside feminist campaigns, there have been multiple international investigations into violence against women beginning in 1993 (World Bank 1993). The first multi-country study of 71 nations conducted by the World Health Organization (WHO 2005) on all forms of violence against women found that, on average, at least one woman in three is subjected to intimate partner violence in the course of her lifetime. Between 10 percent and 30 percent of women in other studies indicated that they had experienced sexual violence by an intimate partner (Heise, Ellsberg, and Gottemoeller 1999). In many cases, physical violence is accompanied by sexual violence. These findings made clear the endemic and wide-ranging extent and impact of gendered violence and the pressing need for determined and sustained preventive action.

In industrialized democracies, preventing violence against women has involved multiple strategies over many years such as legal reform, campaigns to increase community awareness and the commitment of resources for education, training of workers in the field, and designated support services for victims. In other countries, the prevention of violence against women occurs against a backdrop of poverty, cultural and religious barriers to women's full social participation, and political unrest and war. Despite these enormous challenges, there is evidence of community- and government-supported activity seeking to challenge violence against women. Following the World Health Organization's (WHO) release of the World Report on Violence and Health (Krug et al. 2002), there was renewed enthusiasm and hope that gendered violence could be prevented. This resulted from conceptualizing the primary prevention of violence against women using an ecological model. This model identifies risk factors for violence at each level of society—from the individual to the societal. It is frequently used in public health when planning and implementing health promotion interventions for a diversity of social health issues (Glanz, Rimer, and Viswanath 2008).

In relation to gendered violence, primary prevention can be defined as strategies, interventions, and programs that aim to prevent violence before it occurs (VicHealth 2007). Primary prevention is typically situated in relation to secondary and tertiary interventions that are understood to target those populations at high risk of violence against women and those already impacted by it. Primary prevention may include not only educational efforts but also social marketing campaigns, community mobilization, and policy changes that target the social determinants of health and behavior.

Post-Feminist Discourses

Over time as elements of greater gender equality have been entrenched in policy reform in industrialized countries, there has been less focus on understanding the issue through a gendered perspective. Instead, a public health framework has dominated the shaping of prevention activities as evident in the leading role of the Centers for Disease Control (CDC) in the United States and the Victorian Health Promotion Foundation in Australia (VicHealth). This is in spite of the increasing understanding of the far-reaching extent and lasting impact of violence against women and children from individual relationships through to institutionalized abuse within religious organizations and the military, most often committed by men. This contradiction is evident in the discourses underpinning some educational strategies for prevention.

In 2004, a UK review of educational programs addressing violence against women and girls was conducted in England, Northern Ireland, and Wales (Ellis 2004). Jane Ellis found that there had been a significant growth of programs between 2000 and 2003 that seems to have been driven by a combination of a Home Office focus on crime reduction and young people, a commitment to reduce domestic violence, and the creation of a children's fund, with a strong prevention agenda. Most of the programs were aimed at children and young people aged 3–25 years, had short-term funding, and were primarily delivered in school contexts. However, 38 percent were delivered in community contexts aimed at reaching marginalized and at-risk young people. Partnerships between teachers and community organizations, such as Women's Aid, delivered the programs. A gender analysis and feminist understandings of domestic violence and sexual assault were acknowledged by 66 percent of programs.

However, many programs seemed to think these were too controversial or not relevant and, therefore, reduced the discussion of the precursors to violence to interpersonal conflict. The influence of a public health discourse was evident in a focus of 42 percent of programs on healthy relationships from friendship to intimacy (Ellis 2004).

This concept of healthy relationships has global currency beyond the United Kingdom. I have a number of concerns about this approach. What exactly is a healthy relationship? It seems to me to reflect a medical discourse where we are constantly being asked to surveill our practices—from eating to sex—against some predetermined barometer of what is acceptable. One might ask to whom is it acceptable and what is regarded as acceptable? Is this a veiled acceptance of young people having sex as long as they comply with a heteronormative model of relating? What does this mean to young people who may form a connection to another person purely for sex? Is this considered healthy? Who determines this? Even more concerning is that, often, programs using a healthy relationship model focus on telling young people what isn't healthy. Jane Ellis found that although people in the UK programs said the aim was to identify positive and negative actions and feelings, the focus, in reality, was on telling young people about unhealthy relationships.

Obscured here is the complexity and diversity of gender, sexualities, and cultural and socioeconomic differences that impact differentially on the lives of young people. It also implies a static quality to relationships and sexual intimacy that is disturbing. The moral imperative here implies that, if young people understand the predetermined characteristics of a healthy relationship, this will result in self-governing and being better heteronormative citizens. Who decides what the characteristics of a healthy relationship are? Is it the teachers, the parents, the state, or young people themselves? How gender and sexuality are implicated in this model—and the possibilities of this being open to transformation and shifting subjectivities—is made invisible.

Knowledge about relationships is, therefore, constructed within a truth discourse of a binary of healthy/unhealthy. This reflects a particular form of power relations between the object of the knowledge (young people) and those who define how they should behave. I would suggest that the UK experience highlights the collision of competing discourses of prevention. This collision involves feminist concern to reduce violence against women and girls, the power of Home Office crime reduction policies targeting "the problem of youth," and the unacknowledged impact of prevention strategies utilizing public health discourse as the technology to impart a conservative moral and political agenda.

A further example of gender invisibility is evident in a Canadian review of violence prevention programs by RESOLVE Alberta, Calgary (2001, 14; cited in Tutty et al. 2005). They found that the majority of programs did not identify the fact that girls and young women were the most likely victims of many forms of intimate violence. A discourse of gender neutrality, therefore, obscures international data indicating the gendered nature of these crimes. These examples show how prevention work is deeply implicated in how we understand the communities in which we live and how women's experiences of sexual violence and other forms of violence are denied. The complexity is further exposed when we consider that, unwittingly, some feminist sexual assault prevention education has placed the focus on women managing the responsibility for sexual assault and its prevention. I will now consider the impact of this approach more fully.

Risk Avoidance Discourses

By the 1990s, in Western countries, there was evidence of an increasing reliance on neoliberal social policies focusing on the "at-risk" individual, and the exclusion from social/public support of those considered irresponsible in managing their risk (Culpitt 1999; Hogg and Brown 1998; O'Malley and Sutton 1997). Governmental solutions imagined from the new space of risk shifted the site for social intervention to personal responsibility (Hall 2004). Prevention strategies conceived within a neoliberal social policy framework have focused primarily on women taking action to avoid victimization. Key features of the risk avoidance discourse result in individualized approaches to sexual assault prevention, fostering fear in women, and a denial of gender—ignoring the broader aspects of violent societies—and focusing on stranger assaults and managing safety; for example, self-defense and verbal and physical resistance. This resulted in a paradox, in that women's agency is only possible through risk avoidance.

The United States leads the international field in published accounts of sexual assault prevention education. Interestingly, the origin of this response can be traced to Mary Koss's (1988) groundbreaking research on the high levels of "date rape" on university and college campuses. In the 1990s, many sexual assault education programs in the United States involved educational programs for women run on college campuses. The extent of this approach was indicated in Parrot's (1990) review of 26 US university programs that revealed 21 for women and only five programs aimed at changing men's behavior.

Since 1992, legislative amendments resulted in a requirement that every post-secondary educational institution receiving federal funds had to implement a sexual assault prevention program (Heppner et al. 1995). However, the legislative move did not spell out what kinds of programs were needed, how long they should be, or who should be involved. Other examples of the risk avoidance discourse in operation can be seen in drink-spiking awareness programs. We are expected to guard our drinks at all times and be responsible for managing the risk of being spiked. None of the programs I know about target the people who think drink spiking is an acceptable thing to do. The risk avoidance discourse is also evident in what Kitzinger and Firth (1999) call "refusal skills" being taught to young women as a strategy to manage consent; for example, "no means no."

One of the problems with the risk avoidance approach to prevention of sexual violence is its inability to address violence within relationships or between people known to each other that is the primary context for violence. It also fails to grapple with the social and cultural messages that impact on gender and relationships, and the broader normalization of violence in everyday life. This simplistic account fails to consider significant cultural and economic differences among women. Statistically speaking, not all women are equally at risk of sexual assault (Hall 2004). It shifts prevention and education that flows from it back to an individual woman's responsibility for managing risk, and leaves the broader structural issues of society unchallenged. Noticeably absent in this discourse of prevention is a conception of masculinity that moves beyond men as the problem, and seeks to involve them as part of the solution.

While industrialized countries continue to deal with the impact of neoliberal social policies and their impact on sexual assault prevention, there is another set of challenges facing developing countries. Alongside risk avoidance discourses, there has been an emergence of a human rights discourse to which I will now turn.

HumanR ightsD iscourse

The emergence of a human rights discourse challenged beliefs still held in many countries that violence against women was a family matter. While significant progress has been made in industrial democracies over the last decades, progress was somewhat slower in less developed countries, and is as recent as the mid-1990s. The WHO appointed Special Rapporteurs for the United Nations on violence against women, to report on progress in addressing these issues.

The shift to a human rights discourse did not come easily, and required concerted effort at an international level to challenge previous ways of understanding violence against women. For the World Conference on Human Rights in Vienna in 1993, women caucused and lobbied globally and regionally to redefine the contours of human rights law to include women's experience of violence. They presented conference delegates with almost half a million signatures from 128 countries demanding that such violence be recognized as a violation of women's human rights, and ran a global tribunal in which women's testimonies—including cases of violence from around the world—were presented in a human rights framework (UN In-depth Study 2006). This alternative discourse used the power of the United Nations to bring a sharp focus on the plight of millions of women. Advocates harnessed the power of international law to hold individual countries accountable for working toward eliminating violence against women in all its forms. This resulted in the declaration of a number of human rights treaties, regional conventions, charters, and protocols targeted globally. The particularity of violence against women and the breadth of women's exposure to violence were exposed. How it differed from men's experiences of violence was also revealed.

The strength of this discourse lies in a recognition that the conditions that enable violence against women are socially produced and, therefore, that the processes by which they are produced can be altered.

The 2006 report from the abovementioned UN Study acknowledges the need for an integrated and inclusive human rights approach that considers not only gender, but also race, ethnicity, class, sexual orientation, disability, religion, and culture. Here we can see how a feminist analysis of gender has not only impacted, but has also been extended, by a human rights discourse that also acknowledges men, the diversity of experience of gender including transgender people, and the links to violence. For many countries, human rights has been—and continues to be—a key organizing principle, as activists strive toward social justice, including gender equality for all of its citizens.

Public Health and Education As a Strategy for Behavioral and Cultural Change

Alongside the competing discourses of violence prevention, increasing focus since the mid-1990s has turned to questions of the effectiveness of education as a key strategy for prevention. Although governments and communities are often quick to suggest education as an answer to diverse social issues from global warming to reducing obesity, it is only recently that researchers have begun to address what works effectively. In response to this concern, a number of researchers have explored best practice principles to guide the field.

Nation and colleagues (2003) in the United States conducted a meta-evaluation of prevention literature across four areas of social concern (substance abuse, risky sexual behavior, school failure, and juvenile delinquency and violence) to ascertain factors associated with effective prevention programs. They found that the following factors were consistently associated with effective prevention programs: Programs were comprehensive, included varied teaching methods, provided sufficient dosage (amount of time), were theory driven, provided opportunities for positive relationships, were appropriately timed, were socioculturally relevant, included outcome evaluation, and involved well-trained staff. A few years later, Casey and Lindhorst (2009) conducted a wide-ranging review of successful, multilevel primary prevention approaches in other fields (e.g., HIV transmission). They identified six key elements for effective primary prevention: comprehensiveness; community engagement; contextualized programming; focus on structural contributors to the problem; sound theoretical rationales or frameworks; and an emphasis on positive development.

In Australia, the National Association of Services against Sexual Violence and the federal government commissioned a one-year project in 2008 to develop and trial a national Sexual Assault Prevention Education Framework to assist Australian services in evaluating and benchmarking their violence prevention education programs against best practice research. I led this research project. It involved extensive fieldwork across Australia and a detailed analysis of international best practice literature on effective prevention education. It resulted in six recommended national standards for sexual assault prevention education (Carmody et al. 2009). The standards have a number of similarities with both Nation et al.'s (2003) and Casey and Lindhorst's (2009) work, but were specifically focused on sexual assault prevention education.

Each standard is followed by a series of indicators. They are designed to be read and applied together in a dynamic and reflective process of prevention work. While many of the standards were seen as aspirational for prevention services across Australia at the time, they provide a framework to assess the potential effectiveness of existing programs, assist in the design of new programs, and provide guidance to policymakers on assessing funding applications. The six standards are briefly summarized below:

- *Using coherent conceptual approaches to program design.* Programs should endorse a clear framework for understanding why sexual violence occurs and how to reduce it.
- *Demonstrating the use of a theory of change.* Programs need to be based on models that facilitate attitude change, skills development, and behavioral change. This includes conceptual links between program content and the perceived change outcomes.
- *Undertaking inclusive, relevant, and culturally sensitive practice.* Program developers need to be aware of cultural aspects of program content and delivery and modify programs to ensure they are inclusive, sensitive, and relevant to all population groups.
- *Undertaking comprehensive program development and delivery.* Programs should aspire to integrate those whom the program is targeting; what the specific structure of activities are; where the program will be delivered (context and target group); and how long the program will be run.
- *Using effective evaluation strategies.* Evaluation strategies need to be accompanied by a clear identification of how program content relates to intended outcomes.
- *Supporting thorough training and professional development of educators.* The success and sustainability of a program is dependent on the expertise and skills of the educators involved. Programs should

provide educators with knowledge and skills to deliver the program, and adequately support participants (adapted from Carmody et al. 2009; Carmody et al. 2014.)

While standards indicate best practice goals, they also create space for new and emerging ideas of practice. No one program is suitable for all locations or with all groups, and it is necessary to create room for program development tailored to the needs of local population groups and the skills and interests of different educators. The standards aim to provide a method for the field to make informed judgments about the most potentially effective education programs in local settings.

Effectiveness of Educational Programs

Comprehensive discussions of evaluation models are strongly evident in the international literature on the effectiveness of violence prevention education in schools and other settings (Morrison et al. 2004; Schewe 2002; Tutty et al. 2005; Whitaker et al. 2006). Most educational programs include some basic attempts at evaluation, but rarely are their methods or results publicly available.

In the violence prevention field, process evaluations are commonly used to examine the links between program activities and program outcomes. However, customer or participant satisfaction surveys are most often used to gain an understanding of what participants liked or did not like about a training program. Verbal or written feedback at the end of an activity or day of training may also be used. These forms of evaluation are usually conducted by the service providing the education. Outcome evaluations to determine if the training made a difference to the skills of personnel involved or had any lasting impact, while recommended by the CDC, are—in my experience—much less common (see also Fisher et al. 2010).

Pressure for evidence-based practice is increasing, partly driven by the dominance of public health models and neoliberal managerial practices in public policy. Accountability for government or other sources of funding is a more than reasonable expectation. However, there are quite different views about the methods used to evaluate program effectiveness. In the United States, the CDC emphasizes the need for the science of evaluation to be taken more seriously, including the use of randomized controlled trials (RCTs). RCTs have often been seen as the gold standard in medical and health research. One of the downsides of the influence of the public health model is the expectation that RCT should be applied to a range of social or cultural interventions. Foubert (2011) has been very critical of the creeping expansion of RCTs into the evaluation of social issues. He argues that the evaluation of a rape prevention program is not like testing a vaccine. He states: "If we are studying complex social behavior where measured dependent variables cannot be assessed using a blood test, a broader range of assessment methods seem warranted" (Foubert 2011, 3394). Foubert also expresses concern about whether programs presented to groups should be evaluated at the group or individual level. These debates continue in relation to assessing the impact of educational input as part of gender violence primary prevention. An important additional consideration is lack of resources provided to agencies to design appropriate programs and conduct evaluations or a lack of expertise among educators to carry out effective evaluations (Tutty et al. 2005). This situation is further limited by the lack of any preparatory training of the personnel who deliver particular programs to others or any follow-up after delivery (see chapter 9 for a more detailed discussion of this issue). The enhanced development of the field needs these issues to be addressed to develop a stronger evidence base to inform future practice.

Despite the ongoing debates about methods of assessing educational effectiveness, new areas of practice are emerging. In particular, there is evidence of a paradigm shift—moving beyond a focus solely on women to actively engage men as allies in challenging sexual and other forms of gendered violence.

Promising Practices of Prevention Through Engaging Men As Allies

While many programs in Australia, the United Kingdom, Canada, and the United States continue to focus on awareness raising and attitude change as key strategies for prevention, there is some recent evidence in the literature of a shift in focus in the design and assumptions underpinning programs. This is most noticeable in work that is thinking beyond at-risk women, and constructively developing ways to challenge dominant masculinity practices by actively engaging men in programs and challenging cultural acceptance of male violence. Research and practice from the masculinities field has highlighted the importance of thinking beyond constructions of men that only focus on the effects of hegemonic masculinity following Connell and Messerschmidt (2005). They argue that the context of this work is, at the local level, defined as face-to-face interactions of families, organizations, and immediate communities. It is through this level of analysis that we can gain important insights into how men's relationships to each other and to women are realized and the consequences of particular performances of gender for them and others.

Alan Berkowitz (1994) from the United States was among the first to develop a protocol and program focusing on men's responsibility for preventing sexual assault. The program—now run as a required workshop for all men in their first year at a US college—was evaluated in 1996 and 2000. Both studies found a reduction in rape-supportive attitudes and increased understanding of the difference between consent and coercion directly on conclusion of the workshops. Unfortunately, this effect was not evident six weeks later (Berkowitz 2004, 185–186).

Jackson Katz (1995)—another pioneer in working with men—focused on reconstructing the masculinity of college athletes. Through the Mentors in Violence Prevention (MVP) project at Northeastern University in Boston, Massachusetts, Katz and his colleagues aimed to reduce men's violence against women by inspiring athletes, and other models of traditional masculine success, to challenge and reconstruct predominant male norms that equate strength in men with dominance over women (1995, 163). Katz (1995, 165) argues that few violence prevention programs foreground discussions of masculinity that he sees as highly problematic, given the high representation of males in violent crimes against women and men. He emphasizes the need to work with male students, rather than focus on men as actual or potential perpetrators. Instead, he builds their skills as active bystanders who can use their status as role models to intervene or prevent violence against women. By not acting, however, they are complicit in perpetrating violence. Similar approaches are being taken in the prevention of sexual violence in Australia that actively includes men (Flood 2006, 2011; Pease 1995, 2008).

A recently completed one-year study in Australia reviewed international best practice literature on effective ways to engage men and boys in gender violence prevention (Carmody, Salter, and Presterudstuen 2014). We found there were several approaches that have emerged over the last ten years that are particularly promising in their capacity to engage men and boys. These include: respectful relationship education; bystander strategies; whole of organization and community development approaches; infant and parenting programs; and social marketing (Carmody et al. 2014, 36). For the purpose of this discussion, I will focus on respectful relationship education and bystander interventions as they are key educational strategies. The following findings are summarized from Carmody et al. (2014, 36–38).

A shift away from program content based on discourses that assume men are inherently violent is evident in a shift toward the promotion of healthy, respectful, and ethical behaviors (Carmody 2003; 2009; Pease 2008). Rather than positioning men and boys as potential perpetrators of sexual violence, prevention programs are likely to focus on problem-solving tasks that encourage them to build respectful relationships with women.

This development has been very relevant in engaging men and boys in prevention programs. International evidence has repeatedly demonstrated that school-based approaches that help young people identify inappropriate sexual or violent behavior and shape their expectations and capacity to build and sustain respectful relationships are promising approaches to preventing violence against women (Harvey, Garcia-Moreno, and Butchart 2007).

This approach to prevention education is reflected in Outcome 2 (Relationships are successful) of the Australian National Plan to Reduce Violence against Women and their Children (2011). This Outcome included three strategies, one of which was to build on young people's capacity to develop respectful relationships—as a result, funding has been made available for respectful relationships education projects throughout Australia. The Sex & Ethics Program is one example of this new approach to prevention education and, indeed, received funding from this federal government initiative (see chapters 7 and 8 for detailed discussion of the impact of the program and young men's responses to it).

Another promising area of educational intervention is bystander approaches to prevention aimed at increasing participant willingness to act and speak out in the context of gender violence. A large-scale national survey of community attitudes undertaken by the Victorian Health Promotion Foundation (VicHealth 2009) in Australia found varying levels of capacity and confidence in the community to intervene in instances of violence against women and sexual harassment. The survey highlighted the potential contribution of bystander-intervention programs in building community skills in this area (Powell 2014). Drawing on social norms theory, this expanding area of men and boys' violence prevention looks at engaging men as social justice allies and encouraging bystander behaviors (Berkowitz 2004; Banyard 2004; VicHealth 2012). Research in this area suggests that men who take action to stop incidents of violence not only help lessen negative outcomes but also that their behavior fosters a sense of community responsibility for violence prevention.

The success of bystander-intervention programs has been attributed to their ability to mobilize young men in situations where they would have otherwise remained silent. Banyard (2008) found that education is important here; men and boys who have greater knowledge about gender-based violence (what it is as well as the consequences associated with it) were more likely to take up a role as active bystanders. The likelihood that a bystander will engage in pro-social helping behavior is increased if the person has an awareness of the problem and its negative impact on the victim; and if they are asked to help or make a commitment to help and feel they are partially responsible for solving the problem. Importantly, bystanders need to feel they possess the skills to intervene, have the opportunity to see individuals modeling the behavior, and have strategies to ensure their own safety (Banyard, Plante, and Moynihan 2004, 69). While positive outcomes are being reported in several studies using bystander approaches (Banyard et al. 2004; 2008; Carmody 2009; 2013), several key masculinities theorists and activists have warned against the dangers of men occupying a nonviolent ally position without challenging their own implication in perpetrating gender inequality (Pease 2008; Katz 2011).

Despite this concern, bystander programs have been developed for use in several settings including high schools, universities, and workplaces. One of the most well-known and rigorously evaluated bystander programs is the Bringing in the Bystander Program developed by Victoria Banyard and her colleagues from the University of New Hampshire (2004; 2005; 2008; 2011; 2015). The White House Task Force to Protect Students from Sexual Assault—created by President Obama on January 22, 2014—published its first report, *Not Alone: Protecting Students from Sexual Assault*, and its new website, NotAlone.gov, on April 29, 2014. In the associated press release, the Bringing in the Bystander Program is cited as one of the most promising prevention programs (White House 2014). The renewed recognition of the issue of sexual violence on college campuses also resulted in President Obama's renewed call to action and the creation of the Presidential Task Force on Sexual Violence in Higher Education to: "enact our best collective thinking to identify best practices in sexual violence prevention, to respond compassionately and effectively to those affected, and to rebuild the public trust" (White House 2014). Other bystander-training programs also find positive impacts on attitudes and a reported willingness to intervene in risky behaviors. (Coker et al. 2011; Gidycz, Orchowski, and Berkowitz 2011; Langhinrichsen-Rohling et al. 2011).

One of the strengths of the bystander model is that it moves beyond risk avoidance or targeting "at-risk" individuals (in this case, individual men) or groups to building community responsibility and capacity for preventing sexual violence. These findings have been incorporated into the Sex & Ethics Program, and their application and the response of young people to these ideas are discussed in chapter 8.

Reflecting On Primary Prevention Education Practice

This international overview of sexual assault prevention education indicates there are multiple forms of knowledge that inform educators and policymakers. Working to prevent sexual violence requires multilayered responses engaging all levels of community and government commitment. The CDC has concluded that direct participation programs such as education are unlikely to reduce the prevalence of violence against women in the absence of larger scale interventions (DeGue et al. 2012). Education is, therefore, only one part of a multisystem response. However, we need to constantly remember that education is not a value-free, objective truth. Rather, educational discourses in the prevention of sexual violence may have unintended consequences in reinforcing traditional gender and sexuality norms. They may easily retreat to risk avoidance strategies, with the result that women are seen as responsible for managing the risks associated with sexual violence and the prevention of it. Gender-neutral approaches also have hidden costs in obscuring the cultural and structural factors that foster interpersonal violence. Sexual assault and other forms of gender-based violence remain—with men overrepresented as offenders and with women, children, and other boys and men as victims.

Despite these difficulties, there is evidence of the emergence of alternative discourses, especially in the area of engaging men as part of the solution to sexual violence. The implications of these competing truths about violence prevention would suggest that what works in one community, or with different groups within it, may not work in another. The complexity of sexual violence requires us to develop diverse and innovative approaches that are well thought out, listen to the particular needs of the groups targeted, and are properly evaluated for their primary prevention impact. The emergence of national standards for sexual assault education in Australia (Carmody et al. 2009) and the reviews conducted by Nation et al. (2003) and, more recently, by Casey and Lindhorst (2009) provide important frameworks to guide the field to constantly work toward better educational outcomes and lasting cultural change in the attitudes and behaviors of women and men. As the above discussion highlights, education is not a value-free activity and we need to be vigilant about our practices. We need to be mindful to examine the implied or direct messages we convey through education about gender, sexuality, young people, and intimate relationships in general.

In Part II of this book, I present one approach to address some of these issues—combining knowledge gained from both the sexuality and violence prevention fields and working with young people.

Part II

Educating about Sexual Ethics

Chapter 6

Why Sexual Ethics?

In Part I of this book, I discussed the context and experiences of young people's experiences of sexual intimacy. I also highlighted the limitations of many sexuality and violence prevention education approaches. In this chapter, I discuss the sexual ethics approach I have developed and implemented with young people that attempts to address some of these questions. I begin with a reflective account of the evolution of my thinking on the sexual ethics approach I use and position it in relation to sex, violence prevention, and young people. From here, I move to consider the sexual ethics framework I developed based on French philosopher Michel Foucault's ideas about ethical sexual subjectivity. I then explore how these ideas have been applied in the Sex & Ethics Program as well as responses from young people and educators since its inception.

Reflecting On the Origins of the Ideas

In 1999, my colleague Kerry Carrington and I conducted a piece of research to investigate how effective government policy and community initiatives had been in preventing sexual violence. We critically evaluated feminist discourses of prevention, men's responses to preventing violence, public awareness campaigns, and community education initiatives in the United States and Australia (Carmody and Carrington 2000). Simply, we concluded there was much work still to be done. However, we suggested a way forward:

> Our proposition is that rape prevention strategies ought to be concerned with the promotion of a normative basis for the inculcation of sexual ethical conduct. This is not a simple task, but it is not impossible.

The task is to wed the psychosocial structures of sexual desire with mutually respectful and pleasurable forms of sexual practice. This requires policy and community responses that avoid universalizing frameworks (ie, all men are potential rapists), but actively inculcate ethical sexual practices that no longer tolerate intimate sexual violence as an expression of normal male sexuality. Developing ethical sexual practice will mean both women and men are required to re-evaluate their cultural expectations of each other in relation to intimate relations and to take explicit responsibility for their desires and practices (Ibid., 356).

This approach reflected a paradigm shift—both in relation to violence prevention research and practice and in sexuality research. It required a new way of thinking about gender, about sex, and about how these ideas could be reflected in education and other preventative strategies. While I subsequently became less comfortable with a normative approach to ethics, our position marked an important counterpoint to the "normality" of male violence and its acceptance by many as an inherent component of gender relations. Initial responses from some sections of the feminist refuge (or shelters as they are known in the United States) and sexual assault services were mixed. Some were extremely supportive, others not so. In one of my first speaking engagements on this approach at an international gender violence conference in Sydney in 2001, I was hissed at by some sections of the audience who took strong exception to my suggestion that men could indeed be ethical and that women could be unethical. This was dangerous talk as I challenged long-held views about the inevitability of sexual and other forms of gendered violence and suggested an alternative approach to explore. I found that sexuality researchers and educators, on the other hand, were extremely welcoming of this view. It spoke to emerging areas of work on self-care and cultures of care (see, e.g., Hurley [2002] and Race [2003, 2007] within human immunodeficiency virus (HIV) education. It provided ways for me to think about how the ideas could more actively engage men and also be used to reach out to lesbian, gay, bisexual, and transgender (LGBT) young people and adults.

My research continued to explore how the initial ideas about ethical sexual practice could be utilized more deeply. I extended the initial work on violence prevention strategies and argued they had been shaped by unarticulated discourses about sexuality focused primarily on women managing the risk of the unethical behavior of men. I have discussed this in more detail in chapter 5. Michel Foucault's ideas on ethics, sexuality, and power as productive and in a constant state of negotiation resonated with me. It provided a sense of hope and the possibility of individual and cultural change—not the pessimistic determinism of the inevitability of gender-based violence. I argued that all sexual encounters, regardless of the gender of the people involved, invite the possibility of ethical sexual behavior (Carmody 2003).

These conclusions were further extended by a study, with adult women and men of diverse sexualities, where I explored the multiple ways in which they negotiated sexual encounters (Carmody 2005). The women and men in the study demonstrated how they negotiated power in the context of shifting personal needs and desires. I argued that we needed to shift our thinking away from fixed notions of what is good/bad, natural/unnatural, and predetermined as pleasurable or dangerous. Rather, I suggested that the negotiation of pleasure and danger could be seen as dynamic, with the potential for developing ethical erotics. This erotics would involve care of the self, linked to care of the other, following Foucault. Without both being present, I argued, the balance would tip from mutual pleasure to dangerous sex—either physically or emotionally or oscillate between them.

As my ideas developed more deeply and my fieldwork with adults on sexual negotiation demonstrated the usefulness of sexual ethics as a theoretical approach, I turned my attention to the sexual lives of young people. In Part I of this book, I analyzed how difficult it is for young men and women to receive comprehensive sexuality education that speaks to their very embodied concerns. Education about sexual and other forms of gendered violence is also lacking. Discourses of risk, fear, danger, and social regulation dominate the lives of many young people as they begin to navigate their sexual lives. Children and young people's difference from the adult "norm" assumed of citizens in liberal models of citizenship result in overlooking their citizenship through constructing them as "not yet citizens" (Moosa-Mitha 2005). This is exacerbated by a recent return to the extension of the period that many young people remain dependent on their families (Furlong and Cartmel 2007). Despite this, they are often seen as a threat to citizenship and in need of retraining (Carrington 1993), ethical reconstruction, discipline, or protection by or from adults and the state (Bessant 2001). Young people are often subject to enhanced surveillance by institutions of the state (Kelly 2000). This is seen as essential to protect young people from sexual danger (Allen 2011) while young women remain subject to a gendered double standard, walking a fine line between being seen as "frigid" or as a slut if they are seen to be too knowing (Powell 2010).

As the research findings in chapters 2 and 3 indicate, young women and men have many thoughts, feelings, and ideas about the education they have received or not received and about their desires and dreams of what sex might bring them physically or emotionally. What they often didn't know was how to think about all of these issues and to balance their own needs against those of their friends, their family, their community, or their faith. This is where the three years of research from 2005 to 2008 began and resulted in the development of the Sex & Ethics Program (Carmody 2009b). In the following section, I provide a brief overview of some of the competing discourses within the literature on sexual ethics. I then present my approach to sexual ethics and how I have applied this in the Sex & Ethics Program.

Competing Discourses within Ethics

It is beyond this discussion to engage with the lengthy debates about morality/ethics (see MacIntyre 1998, for a detailed discussion). However, I will provide a few points to demonstrate the complexity of the territory. Sometimes, morals and ethics seem to be synonyms and, at other times, they are presented almost in binary opposition to each other. From my point of view, they are neither. Ethics is concerned with what is "right," "fair," "just," or "good." However, Weston (1997, 2) makes an important clarification when he argues that the point of ethics is not to moralize or dictate what is to be done. Rather, he suggests:

> Its point is to offer some tools for thinking about difficult matters...recognizing that the world is seldom so simple or clear cut. Struggle and uncertainty are part of ethics, as they are part of life.

It is some of the struggle and uncertainty that are part of life that I am concerned with in this book. In particular, I am interested in how ethics can assist us to think through the complexities associated with sexual intimacy, consent, violence prevention, and sexual pleasure and how this can assist young people who are beginning their sexual lives.

Lambeck (2010) suggests that the terms "ethics" and "morality" are not used consistently in either philosophy or social science. Sharon Lamb (2013), a US feminist psychologist concerned with the increasing sexualization of young women, invokes both morality and ethics in her recent sexual ethics curriculum for schools. In contrast, secular and religious ethicists often explicitly make distinctions between morality and ethics to try and indicate a different political stance from their counterparts. Continental ethical philosophers, for example, influenced by Nietzsche, including Foucault, tend to dismiss or move away from the term "morality" because of its long association with religion, duty, and its prescriptive demands, especially in relation to sexuality.

Claes and Reynolds (2013, 10) indicate the importance of bringing sexual ethics and politics explicitly into dialogue with each other, arguing that they are both at the core of how we understand and practice our sexual lives against a backdrop of sexual justice and emancipation. Cultural diversity renders impossible a single definition of ethics (Froese 2013, 1). In highlighting the difference between a Kantian focus on ethical decision making, Froese argues that Confucian philosophy places more emphasis on becoming an ethical person. She argues that "ethics is an art, and it requires practice and learning in order to acquire its skills" (Froese 2013, 3). There are, therefore, diverse ways in which people conceptualize and embody issues of morality or ethics, including examples of critique within religious voices. For example, Rabbi Laura Novak Winer (2011, 21) discusses the involvement of liberal Judaism in advocating for comprehensive sex education in US schools since the 1970s and, at the same time, condemning federal, state, and local funding for abstinence-only programs. She reports (Winer 2011, 24) on the development of the *Sacred Choices: Adolescent Relationships and Sexual Ethics* (2007, 2008) curriculum developed to respond to the ethical challenges young people are facing and to give a specifically Reform Jewish voice to those challenges. The lessons explore the Jewish texts and values that are relevant to what she calls "this crucial aspect of the human experience, sexual behavior, and relationships."

Further critique is evident from Marvin Ellison (2001, 4)—a Christian ethicist. He argues that the church has focused on dualisms in which "the morality of sexual acts has been judged on the basis of whether the sex has been marital (good), premarital (not good, but tolerated if the couple intends to marry), extramarital (bad), or same-sex (very bad)." He is critical of this approach:

> It is this patriarchal ordering of the sex/gender system, reinforced by compulsory heterosexuality that is now under critique inside and outside of faith communities. From many quarters, including the feminist and gay liberation movements, a resounding call has been issued for a sex-positive, comprehensive ethic of sexuality and human intimacy

that is not only woman-friendly and gay-friendly, but also attentive to sexual exploitation and abuse of power.

He argues for a break from "sexual fundamentalism" of a rigidly legalistic rule-based code for intimate relations and family life that does not address the diversity of experiences within the community. Rather, he calls for a sexual ethic based on difference and a sustained commitment to end power abuses within families and the church. He calls also for "a democratic, egalitarian ethic of sensuality and erotic delight, bodily integrity, and mutual empowerment."

There is much here to which sex-positive educators and researchers can relate. The difficulty for secular ethicists is the assumption that our sense of ethics is ultimately for the betterment of ourselves at the service of a transcendent power. Alongside these emerging positive narratives, there remain examples of regulatory moves to maintain sexual fundamentalism. The discussion in chapter 4 that highlighted an organized reaction from the religious Right to the Sexual Health Information, Networking and Education (SHARE) program in South Australia shows how morality discourses can be invoked in quite particular ways to justify repressive approaches to sexuality.

Broadly, my approach to ethics sits within the tradition of continental philosophy. This is concerned with determining the conditions for ethical exploration for different types of people, rather than establishing the borders of acceptable or unacceptable desires, thoughts, and actions. I extend the continental approach to include feminist conceptions of ethics, including a conception of gender that acknowledges the possibility of multiple forms of femininities and masculinities. Rather than assuming a fixed and stable feminine or masculine subject, a process of constantly becoming or performing gender, as Butler and Scott (1992) point out, is possible. Therefore, difference is acknowledged and ways how we can conform or resist dominant discourses of gender and sexuality are made possible.

These ideas provide hope of an alternative way of relating in intimate relationships that moves beyond deterministic views that see all women as potential victims of male violence, and all men as potential perpetrators of such violence toward women and other men. This is combined with an approach that takes seriously the material, the situated, and the contextual in working to live an ethical life. My approach to sexual ethics is, therefore, not about seeking new certainties in the sense of new moral codes. What I am interested in here is how notions of ethics can inform and foster possibilities. It is about devising new forms of personal existence, paying attention to the cultural, psychological, interpersonal, and emotional conditions of personal transformation that make ethical choices possible (Schroeder 2000).

In earlier chapters, I have discussed why I reject the idea that young people's sexuality is something to be controlled and managed purely through the lens of risk. I see young people as individually and collectively different, but shaped by their cultural and gendered positions, and as active sexual subjects, following Allen's central argument (2005). Developing a sense of sexual subjectivity—of being desired and desiring others—takes many forms throughout our lives. Our embodiment of desire(s) does not exist in a vacuum. As McClelland and Fine (2014, 12) argue, "bodies adhere with connective tissue to economic, political, historical and psychological landscapes." One way we can interrogate these issues and their application to working with young people as they begin to navigate their sexual lives is to consider how a consideration of sexual ethics may be of use.

Ethical Sexual Subjectivities

Building from this backdrop, I turn to the French philosopher Michel Foucault. He reminds us that there is a fluidity of ways in which individual subjects can produce a diversity of subjectivities (whether we are male, female, transgendered, or gender-queer) and that we can resist the power/knowledge discourses (as cited in Rabinow 1997). Foucault's work on ethical sexual subjectivities has particular relevance to thinking through alternate spaces and possibilities in working with young people. Despite his failure to conceptualize desiring subjects as anything but male, there are useful ideas to be drawn from his extensive histories of sexualities and power and how they are implicated in contemporary debates. A critique of modernist notions of the essential rational subject, the role of power/knowledge, and the subsequent social practices that flow from this have proved useful to poststructuralist feminists (see Bryson [1999]; Zalewski [2000], for detailed discussion of these issues).

In exploring ways of thinking through the role of ethics and sexuality, I have found it useful to consider Foucault's ideas on the development of the ethical subject and power relations. What I find useful in his ideas is the notion of mutuality and the constant state of reflection and renegotiation that we all require to assess and rework where we are in relation to living an ethical life. I will discuss this in more detail below.

Foucault invites us to consider that acts are the real behavior of people in relation to the moral code or prescriptions. The "code" tells us what is permitted or forbidden and determines the positive or negative value of different possible behaviors. This is clearly where laws about consent and community education come into play. The ability of laws and education to impact on regulating people's sexual behavior is, however, contested. While many individuals support and follow consent prohibitions, the high incidence of exploitative sexual encounters in most communities suggests that the threat of coercive power over individuals is not enough. Intimate relations between individuals are more complex than this. Individual subjects can't stand outside the discourses that shape them. Here, it is crucial that we understand how, historically, gender relations have shaped discourses about female and male sexualities.

Inherent in all relationships, as Foucault reminds us, are relations of power. His notion of power as mobile and productive and in a constant state of negotiation contrasts with grand narratives, such as radical feminism, in which power is always structurally defined by patriarchy (Card 1991). In this model, ethical behavior is to be achieved through gender equality or by regulation through laws and sexual conduct codes. The failure of these measures over the last four decades to prevent exploitative sexual relationships suggests we need to find creative alternatives to how we live and relate to others.

Foucault's work on ethics provides an alternative point of view, and to this I will now turn. Foucault's central argument about becoming an ethical person involves what he calls rapport à *soi*—the relationship you ought to have with yourself—which determines how an individual is supposed to constitute himself [sic] as a moral subject of his [sic] own actions (as cited in Rabinow 1997, 263). Others give this a slightly different inflection. It is the relationship one creates with oneself in interaction with others that forms one as an ethical subject. In that process, one engages with existing moral norms, refashioning as one goes. As Race (2009, xii) put it:

> [Foucault] wanted to conceive forms of care and relation that could pry themselves away from normative determinations where necessary, but retain some form of ethical stylization.

Foucault argues that care of the self is intimately linked with ethics and that ethics is, in a very practical sense, the considered form that freedom takes when it is informed by reflection (Ibid., 284). Care of the self is synonymous with living an ethical life, but it is not the Socratic admonition to "Know thyself," as if we can discover an essential self. The ethical adventure is not finding or revealing who we are, but the work involved when exploring the self in this or that cultural and historical lineage (Flaming 2006, 221). Rather, by critically reflecting about their self, a person is free to develop as a particular human being because they are free from the inhibiting normalizing or dominating discourses (Ibid). This is not a solo journey, rather: "The care of the self is ethical in itself: but it implies complex relationships with others insofar as this ethos of freedom is also a way of caring for others" (Rabinow 1997, 287).

We need to rely on other people's feedback when creating and engaging in technologies of the self (Flaming 2006, 222). Ethics is, therefore, always relational. The abuse of power manifested in exploitative sexual relations "exceeds the legitimate exercise of one's own power and imposes one's fantasies, appetites and desires on others" (as cited in Rabinow 1997, 288). Therefore, "one has not taken care of the self and has become a slave of one's desires" at the expense of another (Ibid). It is important here to remember that Foucault understood the subject or "the self" as constructed within discourse, as distinct from psychological processes; thus, he is arguing for a conception of subjectivity that avoids the modernist conception of an essential self.

A consideration of the development of the ethical sexual self requires an examination of how we can understand desire and the potential for pleasure. It is the anticipation of sexual pleasure that builds from desire. But while memory, fantasy, or experience may shape desire and acts, it can be argued that pleasure requires presence in the moment. So how do desire and acts become pleasure? Is pleasure a singular or mutual experience? Leaving solo masturbation aside, if there is an absence of mutual pleasure, does this mean the encounter was unethical? Foucault is helpful here in reminding us that care of the self (*rapport à soi*) implies complex relationships with others, and is also a way of caring for others. Being ethical is a way of being: being ethical is not something we do only occasionally (Flaming 2006, 224). This suggests that care of the self and the role of reflection in it require a consideration of the interrelationship among desire, acts, and pleasure and their impact on others. This challenges a singular focus on one aspect of sexual behavior alone. I want to suggest, therefore, that ethical sexual behavior becomes possible when we pay attention to all three aspects.

It is now more than 25 years since Michelle Fine (1988) spoke of the missing discourse of desire in American sex education. Her concerns initially focused on how school-based sexuality education operated to limit young women's sexual agency. Her arguments found support among many feminist scholars who wished to counter the discourse of women as passive sexual subjects disengaged from pleasure and desire (Rasmussen 2014, 155). With Sarah McClelland, Fine has extended her thinking to consider the concept of "thick desire." They describe this as "evoking the multifaceted 'nature' of sexual desire and desire as a product of intimate and social negotiation." Thick desire may be used to demonstrate how the dynamics of desire and cultural anxieties are mapped onto adolescent bodies and enacted in policy and research (McClelland and Fine 2014, 12). From the first emergence of the "missing discourse of desire" until relatively recently, much research has focused on globally uncovering the missing discourse or arguing for its importance as a key aspect of comprehensive sexuality education (Allen and Carmody 2012). Louisa Allen and I argued (2012) that the profusion of research and writing resulted in the unexpected inclusion of pleasure and desire in sexuality education despite it still being contentious in many quarters (Kiely 2005 for debates in Ireland). What followed the original flurry of activity was a period of reflexive pause influenced by Fine's (2005, 56) reflection on how desire had been "mediated and colonized by global capital, medicalization, privatization and the state."

As part of this reflexive pause, Louisa Allen and I (2012) worked together to interrogate our originally conceived intentions for pleasure in our work around quality sexuality education. We were keen to examine both the limitations and possibilities pleasure has. We argued (2012, 457) for the "continued importance of wedging open spaces for the possibility of ethical pleasures, in forms that are not pre-conceived, heteronormative or mandatory." Rather than merely wanting to insert pleasure back into sexuality education discourses, we argued for a more inclusive and expansive "discourse of erotics" (Allen 2011) and, in my case, an "ethical erotics" (Carmody 2005). Both of us, in our work, also aimed to extend the curriculum to actively include gay, lesbian, bisexual, transgendered, and young people with disabilities. The particular and different desires and pleasures of these groups had also been invisible in many curricula in relation to concepts of pleasure and desire. How these concepts were embodied by young women and men from diverse cultural and religious backgrounds was also of interest. More recent work by Allen et al. (2014) has questioned our collective hopes that the pursuit of desire and pleasure afforded greater possibilities, especially for young women's sexualities. Rather, they argue there is a need for a pause to interrogate the politics of pleasure in sexuality programs to open a space to consider the premises underpinning the hope pleasure would deliver. These are crucial components of further developing ideas around sexual ethics.

The Sex & Ethics Framework

The above discussion has canvassed, in some detail, the theoretical background to the sexual ethics approach I am taking. I would now like to turn to how I have adapted these theoretical arguments into a workable approach to sexual ethics that can be understood by young people and used by them in negotiating their desires, pleasures, and acts. This has been the focus of my work since 2006. The following framework is my attempt to bring theory and practice into a closer relationship.

With apologies to Foucault, I have taken several concepts from his work concerning how to build an ethical life in relation to sexuality and adapted them for use in this education program. The four concepts are care of the self, care of the other, negotiation (which I have added), and reflection. I will describe what I mean by each of these in turn, but they are interrelated—as the plus signs indicate in Table 6.1. I would suggest that the combination of these dynamic processes enhances the possibility of ethical sex. This process of ethical reflection is not intended to be a one-off reflection, but dynamic, open to constant change, and context specific. Indeed, it may even be used many times within one encounter.

The first component of encouraging young people and others to think about how they can be ethical in their sexual encounters or

Table 6.1   The Sex & Ethics Framework.

What is the Sex & Ethics Framework?
Caring for myself
+
Being aware of my desires and wants and the possible impact on the other person
+
Negotiating and 'asking'
+
Reflection

©Carmody,M (2009b).

relationships is: Caring for myself. By this I mean asking questions of one's self such as:

- "Am I doing what I really want to do?"
- "What is the best and worst thing that can happen to me if I do this?"
- "Am I safe emotionally and physically?"
- "Does anyone know where I am and who I'm with?"
- "Have I done something like this before and felt bad afterwards?"
- "How do I know that the other person will treat me with respect and concern?"
- "Have I thought about safe sex?"

This first part of the reflective process encourages awareness of one's own feelings and thoughts in contrast to just complying with someone else's desires. This is particularly important for young women who may be subject to a traditional gender discourse of compliance to another's needs, particularly opposite-gender partners.

Being aware of the other person is the second component. This involves being aware of our own desires and wants and the possible impact of them on the other person. Reflection in this part of ethical negotiation invites the following considerations:

- "Just because I feel or want something doesn't mean I can assume the other person wants it too;
- "They may want to be close but not necessarily have sex in the way I am imagining it in my mind. I need to know what they are imagining also".
- "I need to be aware that sometimes we start to go along with something and then we are unsure and don't know how to stop it. I need to be on the lookout for these signs and take responsibility for getting more information to know if the other person feels okay with what is happening. How do I know they want to do this? Am I okay with it too?"

These reflective questions involve being aware of nonverbal as well as verbal communication. Awareness of the other person in a sexual encounter encourages greater mutuality between those involved, and attempts to avoid and prevent sexual encounters that are pressured or coerced. Without this awareness, the sexual encounter becomes focused on the needs of one person alone, and the partner's needs are ignored or denied. A denial of the other person's humanity and a lack of empathy for how your own desires and acts may impact on them is, I would suggest, unethical, and can contribute to sexual assault and unwanted and coerced sex. This awareness of the other's needs is particularly important for young men who may be more focused on performance issues than on mutual exploration that meets both partners' needs. The question now becomes how can each person work out the balance between their needs and the other person's needs?

Negotiating and asking is the third component of the framework. Much communication in sexual contexts is nonverbal. As discussed in chapter 3, speaking about sex is often very hard to do, either because we don't have the language or experience to be able to speak about sex easily, or we feel constrained by gender or other social determinants such as education, class, or culture/race that may inhibit frank discussion. It may also be that words are irrelevant because we know "what that look means." While I recognize the pleasure associated with sexual anticipation, not speaking can have significant negative consequences, as the young people in this study have indicated. It may result in one person's needs dictating what happens, without regard for the other, but it may also mean that opportunities for exploration of unimagined possibilities are lost. Therefore, in this program, young people are encouraged to work out what both partners want from the sexual encounter, and this involves teaching them skills in both verbal and nonverbal communication. I suggest that better communication—whether it is verbal or reading nonverbal signs accurately—has the potential to lead to better quality sex for both partners. It also ensures that both are freely consenting. Every part of the process discussed so far has reflection intertwined through it. Reflection is the fourth step introduced to young people in the sexual ethics program. I will now explain how I use this term.

Reflection or thinking through issues in their complexity can involve thinking as we act ("reflection-in-action") or after an event as we try to understand the events that happened ("reflection-on-action") (Payne 2002). Reflection allows us to experiment with alternative approaches and to try them out. It provides an opportunity to consider our real-life experiences and try to make sense of them. Reid (as cited in Payne 2002, 126) uses a reflective cycle to describe the process involved. Reid argues that we begin with moving from description (what happened?) to feelings (what were you thinking and feeling?) and evaluation (what was "good" or "bad" about the experience?) to analysis (how can you make sense of what happened?). We then move to conclusions (what were the alternatives?) and an action plan (what would you do if it happened again?). These steps are similar to ones used in the Sex & Ethics

Program, with some important additions. The above description is context neutral and, on its own, could imply a purely individual and internal process. I think we need to extend this concept to take a more reflexive stance on how we are situated in our lives and how age, ability, gender, sexuality, culture, and faith, for example, may impact on our ethics and the possibilities we are able to imagine. A consideration of these additional factors moves beyond individual musing to locate these very musings within a historical, cultural, and gendered context.

This process of reflection was a new idea for many young people who took part in the groups of the Sex & Ethics Program. As part of explaining the sexual ethics framework to them in the second week, they are also introduced to the Sunlight Test. Often associated with former US Supreme Court Judge Justice Brandeis, the Sunlight Test asks a person to imagine how they might feel knowing that the decision they made was going to be made public and questioned in the full light of public scrutiny. More importantly, how would you feel if the people you most admire knew about the proposed course of action (St James Ethics Centre 1997)? In the program, the following questions are put to them to consider as part of the ethical framework.

- "Would my behavior stand up to being exposed in the light of day to those people whose opinion of me is most important?"
- "Would I like to see what happened written about or filmed and put on social media or in the newspaper?"

This form of ethical questioning extends individual personal reflection into a broader context: it recognizes that each of us is part of a community, in which we are subject to the positive and negative sanctions that members closest to us deliver. The Sunlight Test has limitations. This is a concern, especially if sexual pressure or other forms of abuse are seen as acceptable to the individual's friendship group. However, it still provides an opportunity to challenge this kind of belief and to confront its acceptance by asking if they would want someone they care about to be treated in that way. There are also some difficulties if the people you most care about (e.g., your parents) disapprove of sex outside marriage or same-sex relationships. Same-sex, gender diverse, queer, and transgender-identified young people face particular hurdles in terms of familial, friendship group, and community discrimination. The ethical challenge they face requires understanding the values of others, but developing their own sense of an ethical stance that provides them with the space to explore and still care for themselves. The Sunlight Test was a concept that grabbed the attention of many participants, and was frequently mentioned in written and verbal feedback during and after activities and in the six-month follow-up.

Opportunities for reflection were built into the program design beyond just being one component of the framework. Spaces were provided for individual private reflection within and outside the groups and the participants were encouraged to use a journal to record their thoughts and feelings. Group reflection on activities was part of group discussion, as was using artwork to display their reflections on content. Each session began with a reflection on the previous session, providing opportunities for young people to share additional insights they had gained between sessions. I discuss this in more detail in chapter 7. Educators also reflected on group process after each session, and recorded notes on their observations, feelings on how things had gone, and what they needed to do for the next session. They also completed an end-of-group reflection individually that they used as the basis for a reflection with their co-educator on how they worked together, and their overall sense of how the group had progressed.

Revisiting the Sex & Ethics Framework

Introducing an explicit conceptual framework into comprehensive sexuality and violence prevention education program is, in my experience, quite rare. Often, the content is delivered with embedded messages concerning gender and sexuality and an undeclared ethical stance. We can see this in programs from across the political spectrum framed within a risk discourse that works from a public health–harm minimization position, and in programs that aim to prevent sexual violence by focusing only on how to say no to sex and abstinence programs that convey morality messages about sex outside of marriage. These '"truth" claims tell young people what they should do. In contrast to this, the Sex & Ethics Framework provides a way of thinking reflectively and reflexively about sexual decision making. It, therefore, creates space for a multiplicity of responses to working out what feels ethical for that person, at that time, and in a particular context.

When the framework is introduced to young people and educators in education groups, it may at first feel a bit mechanistic. The framework is introduced in Week Two and is consistently applied to real-life scenarios, activities, and reflections; so, it potentially becomes part of considering everyday experiences and how to make sense of them from an alternative position. One educator found her mixed gender group of 16- to 18-year-olds seemed to be having trouble grasping what felt like abstract ideas. Using the metaphor of learning how to drive, she explained the framework as being aware of what you needed to do to be safe on the road for yourself and that you also had responsibilities to other road users. This use of metaphor allowed them to embody the ideas with a reference point most of them understood. As one young man commented at the end of group reflection: "The L plate idea was good to explain the framework; it helps so we are fully licensed before going out on the road of love." Others commented at the end of the six-week group that "it was easily applied to real life" and "very important to understand what you and the other person wants."

When I developed the Sex & Ethics Framework, I had many hopes it would be useful but I had no idea if it would work. It was grounded in a sound evidence base that indicated quality programs require a coherent theoretical underpinning (Nation et al. 2003). It was also based on a theoretical approach to ethics that recognizes the variability and dynamic nature of power and the importance of self-care and care of others and a constant process of negotiation. In particular, I wanted an approach that was dynamic, easy to grasp, inviting to both men and women, created possibilities, and helped young people develop skills in ethical sexual decision making to reduce pressured, coerced sex and sexual assault. I wanted them to feel able to say yes to sex if they wanted to but also to be able to decline and for this to be respected. I hoped they would find pleasures and that they would realize their potential as ethical sexual citizens. On reflection, it was a rather ambitious demand to place on four small steps in a framework.

Since the framework was introduced to the pilot training group of educators and the first groups with young people in 2007, it has been unanimously well received. Some groups resist the dynamic and fluid potential the framework offers and speak about it as a set of rules for living an ethical life. While this was hardly my intention, if it helped them to have a set of tools to guide their decisions, is it my place to correct them? Two young women from a rural area told their educator that they had made a poster of the framework that they put on their bedroom wall and consulted each weekend before they went out. They took it very seriously—that is, they reflected, and more importantly they found it helpful.

As the empirical data show in the following chapters, the framework resulted in tangible changes in behavior by both women and men in relation to self-care and care of their partners. These changes were maintained over time. Consistently, end-of-program evaluations from young people and educators demonstrate that one of the most significant things they got out of their program was the Sex & Ethics framework. Not only did it make sense to them, it demystified ethics and it helped them with a set of tools to think about sexual negotiation and broader life issues. I wondered if the framework would receive the same response from culturally diverse young people and, over time, have found nothing to suggest it didn't. For some cultural groups, the ideas used in the framework applied to responsibility for preventing gendered violence through becoming an active bystander tapped into the importance of collective responsibility—a core value in their communities.

The framework is the backbone of the Sex & Ethics Program and from these concepts the structured six-week program invites participants to reflect on their current understandings about gender, sexuality, sexual practices, communication, and preventing sexual violence. They are offered the opportunity to develop skills in ethical negotiation that they can use in everyday situations. What they decide is ethical is not predetermined apart from condemning abuse or coercion in sexual and other intimate matters. This approach recognizes and respects young women and men's agency and their ability to embody ethical sexuality and practices as an ongoing journey.

In chapter 7, I discuss the details of the Sex & Ethics Program and the application of the framework to the six sessions of activities. In chapter 8, I provide the findings of outcome evaluations of the program since 2008 in Australia and New Zealand. The final substantive chapter 9 provides an evaluation of educators' responses to the training they received prior to running the program with young people.

Chapter 7

The Sex & Ethics Education Program

In this chapter, I explain the Sex & Ethics Program I developed in 2007 that continues to run in Australia and New Zealand. There has also been interest from researchers and educators in the United States, United Kingdom, and Canada. I outline the values that underpin the program, structure, and philosophy and provide an overview of the six-session interactive format. It explores how the issues raised by young people in interviews and discussed in chapters 2 and 4 have been incorporated into the program content and activities to provide "real life" situations that speak to the concerns of young women and men.

As discussed in chapter 4, current approaches to sexuality education are failing young people by focusing almost exclusively on "risky sex." Moral panic is often associated with sex and young people, and results in approaches that try to impose particular ethical positions on them, denying their own embodied experience, and minimizing their competence in decision making. This discourse of sexual anxiety results in a focus on the negative consequences of sex—whether that involves sexually transmitted infections, unwanted pregnancy, pressured sex, or sexual assault. The impact of this approach denies the potential emotional and physical pleasure of sexual intimacy. Violence prevention education is also dominated by risk discourses, as discussed in chapter 5. As a result of these approaches to sexuality and violence prevention education, much research is focused on identifying what doesn't work in relation to both.

The Sex & Ethics Program moves beyond this critique and, instead, offers a method of making sexual intimacy "work better," acknowledging both pleasure and danger. It aims to reduce unwanted and pressured sex, but not at the expense of the positive experiences sex can provide. This alternative approach sees young people as having agency and the ability to negotiate ethical sexual lives. The program offers them the opportunity to practice or develop knowledge and skills to realize this potential more fully. It also moves away from a purely risk focus, and offers an opportunity to explore both pleasure and potential danger from an ethical stance.

There are a number of values that underpin the program. These reflect my own ethical stance in relation to this work. It is a stance informed by many years of policy and practice work at a state and national level on women and sexual assault prevention (1983–1995) as well as by my research and education work nationally and internationally (1995–2014). These values may differ from those of others who work in this field. However, I consider it is important for others to understand what has informed the decisions I have made that are reflected in the program philosophy, design, and structure. These values include the following beliefs:

- Most of us have the potential to make ethical decisions.
- Both women and men can consider the impact of their gender conditioning and make active choices to comply with dominant forms of masculinity or femininity or resist them.
- Sexual intimacy is only one aspect of the multiple ways in which women and men can relate.
- Young people need spaces in which they feel safe and can be encouraged to explore the complexity of sexual intimacy.
- Sexual intimacy has the potential to be pleasurable and, at times, dangerous.
- Sexual identity is not fixed for many people and can change over time.
- Sexual assault impacts both heterosexual and same-sex-attracted young people.
- Manipulating, physically coercing, or demanding sexual activity from another person by either gender is unacceptable, and is, in fact, a crime under many legal codes.
- Young people have lots of very worthwhile ideas about sexuality and sexual assault prevention, but they are often told what to do and what to think, and are condemned if they make the "wrong" decision.
- An ethical framework focuses on the process of decision making and is not about prescribing what any person should think or do in any given situation. It involves providing knowledge and skills to assist in the decision-making process and exploring the implications of the decision for oneself and others.

- Ethical reflection is a dynamic, lifelong process.
- Active reflection on who we are and how we operate in the world is beneficial and necessary for ethical relations.
- Safety and support for educators and young people dealing with sexuality and sexual assault issues is a key component of ethical educational programs.
- Gaining skills in ethical relating will not protect against all sexual assault, but it may assist people to understand when situations or relationships are emotionally or physically dangerous and what they cand oa bouti t.

In the following section, I discuss the structure of the program and provide an overview of the activities and ideas presented to young people who have taken part in the program since 2007.

Structure of the Program

The program is based on six weekly sessions of two to three hours. The rationale for this is based on best practice research from the United States regarding sexual assault prevention education and sexuality research internationally (see Schewe 2004, for a comprehensive analysis of sexual assault prevention education and DeGue et al. 2012 for a review of the Centers for Disease Control's work on sexual violence prevention). The research indicates that, the longer the program runs, the more likelihood there is of sustained outcomes of change. A compressed mode of delivery, on the other hand, inhibits the reflective process on the issues that may emerge between sessions. The program allows for a high level of small-group work in dyads or triads and whole-group discussions with personal time for reflection. The differences between young people are acknowledged throughout the program so that genders, cultural diversity, differences in age and sexuality, and recognition of the importance of friendship and peer groups are present in the case studies, and also in the questions to guide discussion. We used a range of activities including written, verbal, drawn, and visual approaches to take into account different learning styles.

The Sex & Ethics Program has been run with single-gender and mixed-gender groups. It has been suggested by some researchers that single-gender programs effect greater behavioral change compared to mixed-gender groups (Vladutiu, Martin, and Macy 2011). Sexuality researchers have also indicated that mixed gender groups are less willing to discuss issues freely (Halstead and Waite 2002). However, the research on this variable is still very unclear (Piccigallo et al. 2012).

Involvement in the Sex & Ethics Program has included single male gender (footballers and also young gay men), single female gender (young lesbians), and mixed-gender groups. I found there to be no significant differences in responses or impact of the program as a result of this configuration. Rather, what has been more important is the credibility and skill of the workers who recruited them into the program.

The Sex & Ethics Program structure is a flexible one, and activities can be adapted to different subpopulations. While case studies and scenarios used in the activities include both women and men from diverse cultural and sexual backgrounds, specific tailoring of the program has occurred. For example, a number of case studies were refined to reflect the particular needs of same-sex-attracted and queer young women and men to ensure there was a better fit with a wider range of contexts where they may find themselves such as large dance parties or sex parties held in public or private premises. Similarly, with male football groups, the characters and locations of events were adapted to include locker room conversations, club tours at the end of the season, or managing issues in public spaces when they may be well known. For participants living in university/college residences, there were further refinements to reflect particular issues in that setting such as increased personal freedom and invitations to engage in high levels of casual sex and drinking alcohol to excess. In New Zealand, specific adaptations were made to address the needs of Maori and Pacific Islander young people from a youth center and with a university-based queer group.

The focus in weeks one and six is on the social construction of sexuality and relationships. In Week One, this aims to help participants to understand the differences between young people and their views and experiences of sexual relationships. Weeks two to five focus on skill development in relation to negotiating sexual intimacy ethically for oneself and others. In the final week, the focus shifts to the wider community and teaches young people how the sexual ethics framework is helpful in making ethical choices to either stand by and let abuse happen or safely challenge attitudes and behaviors that promote and condone sexual exploitation. In this way, the program ends by skilling participants to be ethical bystanders in their communities and stand up against sexual violence.

Sessions of three hours are recommended for community organizations that work with young people; however, in some settings, this may cause some organizational difficulties, so sessions may need to be halved and run over 12 weeks instead of six. While it is possible to carry out each session in two hours, educators have found that three hours worked better to allow for setup time and finishing off the session and breaks at relevant points in the session. The six sessions are:

- Getting to know each other: how we learn about sexuality and gender
- What are sexual ethics?
- Understanding other people's desires and needs
- Ethical consent
- Is this relationship working for me?
- Standing up against sexual violence

In the following section, I will describe the focus of each of the weekly sessions, and summarize the purpose of the activities and the responses of the young people to these activities. A full description of the activities in each session is available in Carmody (2009b). The few quotes from young people in the descriptions are not credited to a person by name, as their responses were drawn from educators' notes of the sessions, and were recorded anonymously during sessions.

Learning about Sexuality and Gender

The first week focuses on helping the group members get to know each other, establishes group rules, and provides a context for the exploration of gender and sexuality and negotiation skills in the weeks to come. The key activity is a role-play using characters drawn from the research interviews. A group of young people meets to discuss their different views about sexuality. There are seven characters made up of three males and four females—representing the diversity of young people's feelings and beliefs about sex. They are culturally and sexually diverse and come from both urban and rural areas. They consist of Doug, a committed Christian, who is holding out until he is married to have sex; Louise, a lesbian who is struggling around issues to do with her Catholic upbringing and how you consent to sex; Dianne, who believes in knowing someone well before you get sexually involved; Don, who describes picking up for casual sex; Marion, who has had 22 sexual partners and never uses safe sex, as she is usually drunk; Simone, who is in a committed relationship based on equality and talking about sex with her partner; and Bill, who is strongly opposed to violence against women and committed to negotiating sex with his partner. The role-play encourages participants to identify the different values held by each character, and to discuss gender attitudes about young women and men and sex. The influence of peer pressure on developing attitudes to sexuality and gender was a key element of their discussions. Interestingly, quite a few groups reported how surprised they were that there were so many different approaches to sexuality. As one young woman commented, "I thought everyone thought the same as me and my friends." This comment underlies the importance of opening up space for young people to hear about other young people's experiences, and realize there are many ways to think about and do sex. This session, therefore, provided a broader social context for discussions and activities that would occur in the following weeks.

A principle of reinforcing learning outside sessions was established in Week One by encouraging participants to do a take-home activity. In Week One, it involved a discussion with their friends about their views on sexuality. In future weeks, it included discussion with friends about alcohol and sex or the best ways to breakup with someone and rewriting a situation from an ethical point of view or writing in their journal. These were aimed at encouraging ongoing reflection and keeping the issues alive for young people between groups. Not all participants took up this opportunity, but a number of them did, and this enlivened the conversations at the beginning of the new session.

What Are Sexual Ethics?

The sexual ethics framework that informs this program seeks to translate these ideas into an accessible and productive alternative education experience. Young people are, therefore, seen as active agents in their own lives and they are not told how they should behave. Through a carefully sequenced series of exercises, role-plays, and discussions, they begin to see how they can use sexual ethics to help them decide what will work for them and their partners at that particular moment. In Week Two of the program, young people are introduced to the sexual ethics framework. For a detailed discussion of the theory behind the framework, see chapter 6. Simply put, this framework involves four interconnected steps:

1. Caring for myself—is this what I want, am I safe?
2. Being aware of the other person's needs—how do my desires and needs impact on the other person, how do I know what they want?
3. Negotiating and asking using both verbal and nonverbal skills to explore what both people want, and
4. Reflecting during and after the sexual encounter—what am I doing or what happened and how could it be different, what was my role in this and what was the other person's role?

Once the framework has been introduced and discussed, the subsequent activities in weeks two to six provide opportunities to apply the framework to real-life situations facing young people, taken from research interviews. This helps them to see how it can apply to their own lives. In the following weeks, activities are, therefore, focused on building knowledge and skills related to sexual ethics.

In a sexual experience survey that participants completed in Week Three, the issue of pressured sex was raised as a direct question to find out if they had experienced it, and whether they had talked to anyone about it. A high proportion—35% of the women who participated in groups—indicated they had experienced pressured sex, with significantly lower numbers from men. This is consistent with the recent findings of the 5th National Survey of Secondary Student and Sexual Health conducted in Australia (Mitchell et al. 2013). If the women spoke to anyone about this issue, it was only to their friends. This finding suggests the importance of considering pressured sex in the lives of young people, and teaching them the skills to feel more confident in resisting this pressure or pressuring a partner. In Week Two, following the introduction of the sexual ethics framework, participants considered a case study taken from the interview research, in which a young woman discusses her confused feelings about a verbally abusive relationship, which included great sex. She found it hard to work out what was going on, and the young people considered the range of feelings and how the sexual ethics framework may have helped her. Through this example, they could see how knowledge of the sexual ethics framework would have provided her with some skills to work out what she wanted from the relationship, how it would have helped her partner to take some responsibility for his actions, and to reflect on the impact of his actions on his partner.

The second activity was centered on one person inviting another person to come along to see a band they really like for a once-only performance the next night. A complicating factor for the person being invited is that it is their mother's birthday and the whole family is taking her out for dinner on the same night. This activity is designed to provide an opportunity to feel pressure from another person whose friends are also present to add weight to the pressuring. There were varied responses across the group as to who agreed to go and who resisted. Some found a compromise—to go for dinner and then on to see the band—while others flatly refused. Some said yes "just to get the pressure off," "to not offend the other person," or because they felt they had no choice. They felt the pressure was intense and increased by the person who made the invitation teaming up with a friend, and the persistence made it hard for some of them to resist. One person indicated: "I can recognize now when I have been manipulative and used guilt trips to get someone to do something I want and that isn't very nice." Another realized that the persuader was completely ignoring the nonverbal signals of discomfort of the person they were asking. In the discussion following the activity, the young people explored whether it was easier or harder to resist someone they knew, compared to a stranger. They were able to see that this could create more opportunities to negotiate, but others felt they would be less mindful of self-caring, as their guard was down. Participants readily identified links to sexual contexts. Discussion indicated that some of them had already begun to use the sexual ethics framework to care for the self in the face of significant pressure, and others indicated they had used skills of negotiating and asking to try to convince the other person to come to see the band.

Understanding Other People's Desires and Needs

Week Three focused on understanding other people's desires and needs through activities based around nonverbal communication and alcohol, drugs, and sex.

Nonverbal Communication Skills

Nonverbal communication is a key feature of the young people's stories about sexual intimacy, as discussed in the previous chapter. The difficulty in relying solely on nonverbal communication to indicate your own desires—and to ascertain the desires of your partner—is interpreting them accurately. Young women and men who took part in the education groups were aware of the importance of nonverbal communication, but hadn't realized that it can be quite difficult to do it accurately. An exercise involving communicating food preferences nonverbally highlighted for them the difficulties in being sure they had read the signals correctly. They explored the experience of this activity and the links to sexual situations. All participants in groups identified the different ways in which women and men communicate and the significant variation between people and contexts. For example, a woman kissing a man she has just met could be interpreted as meaning that she is interested sexually in him, when it may be a group custom in her friendship group that you kiss people when you meet, and it is no more than a friendly gesture of greeting. Cultural background can affect how actions are interpreted or misinterpreted. They, therefore, suggested it was unwise to make assumptions based on first signals alone, and that more time is needed to clarify what is happening.

The activity highlighted, for some, how you can get so focused on what you are doing that you don't pay enough attention to the other person's response. This is clearly an issue in sex when one person is not paying attention to the other person. Participants explored the barriers to people paying attention to another's nonverbal cues and why they got it so wrong sometimes. They felt this was due to a number of possibilities: only seeing what you want to see, being drunk, focusing on your own needs, receiving conflicting messages, being dishonest, being too polite, not being assertive enough, or gender (as one young man said, "guys get excited by everything") and personality differences. The connection was made between how our food preferences change from day to day, and how this translates to changes in what people want sexually from day to day, or even within one encounter. Another fascinating insight into negotiation was raised by this exercise in relation to preferences. While they found they could quite accurately work out the strong feelings of like and dislike of food items on the menu, they felt it was much harder to interpret the middle ground. This raises an interesting point about sexual activities that are acceptable to the partners, but not especially desired. How does one communicate this middle ground? Participants in all the groups were very clear on the need to talk to the other person to clarify what they wanted, and to ensure their interpretation of the other person's needs and wants. They felt this was hard to do, but to fail to attempt to do this could result in confusion, unwanted sexual activity, non-consent, and resentment. One young woman spoke about how her cultural background resulted in her and her boyfriend having different needs and expectations. She felt he did not pick up on her nonverbal cues, resulting in confusion and her responding aggressively to him. They were unable to speak about the situation, and this resulted in them breaking up. She reflected in the group that she felt this situation resulted because of her lack of knowledge and skills about how to talk about their relationship and their different needs.

Alcohol, Drugs, and Sex

Issues around alcohol, drugs, and sex were explored in another activity using a continuum line. Alcohol was the main focus, as this is what most young people in the interviews indicated was their main drug of use. This activity involved reading out a range of situations, and participants locating themselves along a line, depending on how ethical they thought the activity was. For example: "Having sex with someone who is really drunk"; "Going home with someone who you find attractive when you have shared a couple of drinks with them"; "Flirting with someone at a club but not going home with them"; or "Going home with someone you have just met when you are really drunk." The idea here was to provide the young person with an opportunity to reflect on self-caring and to consider how ethical it was to have sex with someone who was not really able to make informed judgments. It was not aimed at denying opportunities for drinking alcohol and having sex but rather, to raise their awareness of how putting alcohol into the mix could impact on their decision making or lack of it.

The discussions that followed highlighted how common alcohol is in many young people's lives, and how they had not necessarily thought too much previously about how this might impact on their ability to have ethical sex, including giving informed consent. In locating themselves along the continuum, from ethical to unethical, the differences between participants became visible to each of them. In a traditional risk-management program, this may be just left as revealing differences or the values of the educator are imposed on the participants. This also has the potential for people to feel group pressure to conform or to be hostile to the position of others. Educators carefully redirected this by employing strategic questioning, bringing the group back to asking how the ethical framework could assist in understanding such differences. This allowed them to understand that one person's ethical stance may not be the same as another's. This underscores a key element of the program: that ethical reflection and actions are not about what one should do. Rather, it invites us to consider the implications of the actions and beliefs we hold. Through discussion, there was recognition that they needed to be more mindful of the messages they could give to other people, of the need to look out for each other, and to have a safety plan, such as letting your friends know who you were with and where you were going. It also involved learning your own limits in terms of alcohol consumption, how this impacts and, depending on what else is going on, how much you have eaten and how quickly you drink.

Ethical Consent

The session in Week Four on ethical consent began with providing information on the legal definitions of sexual consent and sexual assault. In Australia, the term sexual assault has replaced the legal term rape in most jurisdictions since the 1980s. Most participants were unaware of these definitions and they were very interested in knowing more. An activity followed that presented a case study of a male and female couple—Phil and Cindy. The story is presented from the two different points of view of the partners. The male partner, Phil, interpreted the fact that his girlfriend, Cindy, had dressed up for a party and had then retreated to an upstairs bedroom as an invitation for sex. Phil then proceeds to have sex with Cindy, despite her attempts to fight him off. He now can't understand why she won't talk to him. Cindy, on the other hand, felt trapped and unable to get away. He was too strong and she was too embarrassed to scream, as they were at a party. Participants are asked to consider what was happening, and at what point either could have done something differently. Discussions within the groups demonstrated that the participants could apply the sexual ethics framework and identify how Phil failed to accurately read Cindy's nonverbal communication, did not negotiate, and was focused on his own needs, and, therefore, not on ensuring they both were in agreement. The majority identified this situation as a clear example of sexual assault.

Participants who were 16–18 years of age began their initial discussions of this scenario with reflections on traditional gender norms and victim blaming. However, when challenged to consider the situation using the sexual ethics framework, they were able to set these aside and consider the situation from a different perspective. The take-home activity for this session invited them to rewrite the story from an ethical point of view, where both had fun. Several participants, including several young men, pursued this activity energetically. The purpose of this was to move beyond identifying an abusive and criminal act, by helping them explore how an ethical focus could still result in pleasure and avoid one person's needs, especially those of the male, dominating, with him failing to understand or pay attention to his partner's nonverbal responses. This scenario was also presented with same-gender couples for lesbian, gay, bisexual, transgender, intersex, and questioning (LGBTIQ) groups, and, for opposite-gender participants, one of the questions in discussions focused on asking them to consider how similar of different the situation would be if the scenario included same-gender couples.

A further activity focused on consent by participants working in pairs to develop a poster on ethical consent. Different instructions were given to each. One person was briefed to demonstrate nonverbal discomfort about the direction the poster design was taking after approximately five minutes. If the partner picked up on this, they then proceeded to negotiate on changes together. If the person who wasn't briefed didn't pick up the nonverbal cues, the partner was instructed to say, "No I don't think this is okay." If the other person doesn't stop at this point and negotiate, the partner needs to become more forceful and say, "I really mean it, I don't want to do this." This was a challenging exercise for participants because they found it really hard to speak up about changing things, with some just going along with the stronger partner. Others had difficulty paying full attention to someone else having a different point of view. As one person said, "I just went ahead when she said no because I wanted to do something myself." They found it frustrating, confusing, and puzzling when things went wrong. In the discussion afterwards, some participants were embarrassed. One said, for example, "Before this exercise I assumed that I would be good at picking up on non-verbal cues, but in this exercise, I missed them; this is confronting." Others made the point that we need to know what it is we want before we can agree or disagree. The links to what happens in negotiating in sex became very apparent to participants in this exercise. They were able to see how you need to persist in getting it clear as to what both people want, that you need to avoid assuming you know what someone else wants, unless it is negotiated, and that, if there is still uncertainty, you need to reconsider. This session ended with young people identifying the skills they thought were necessary for ethical sexual consent, which ones they felt comfortable with, which ones they felt less confident in doing, and what would make it easier for them to improve on those skills. Some examples of skills they found hard to pick up were saying no, being able to refuse something in an awkward situation, and asserting and negotiating their own needs. Ideas about improving their skills included not making assumptions across situations and contexts, being more aware of what it is you are trying to communicate, and being mindful of the balance between your own needs and the other person's. This activity reflects the specific approach used throughout the program. Not only are problems identified, but also there is an exploration of other possibilities and skills needed to resolve difficulties or doing things differently.

Negotiating Conflicting Desires and Needs in Sex and Relationships

This session explores issues of negotiation in relation to conflicting needs and desires within sex or a relationship. It begins with a private reflection on what participants want out of a relationship, how they want to be treated, and how they would treat their partner. This is extended to reflect on previous relationships—either sexual or other close relationships—and their experience in them. Two case studies are then presented for discussion. The first involves Marty and Chris, whose gender is deliberately unclear, and concerns Marty's dissatisfaction with the sex—it is too fast and there is no time to explore. Marty doesn't want to hurt Chris, but there is little pleasure in the current way things are going. Participants' practiced role-playing being Marty and telling Chris about their feelings. This aims to provide experience in both telling someone you care for that something isn't okay and being the receiver of this news. Challenges raised by this activity highlighted how hard it was to speak about what goes on in sex—especially when there is a mismatch—and how hard it is to really hear the other person without getting defensive. Female participants demonstrated a particularly gendered response and struggled with not wanting to offend the male partner. They felt it would be more ethical to highlight what you did want and be proactive about it, rather than focusing on the negatives. The naming of the protagonists with ambiguous gender created the opportunity for participants to imagine whoever it is that they have sex with or would like to. It also proved useful in challenging heteronormative assumptions within the group if everyone automatically assumed Marty and Chris were heterosexual.

The second scenario involves John and Kate, and reflects a verbally abusive relationship in which John denigrates Kate in front of friends, and has increasingly become controlling around her. Participants were quick to identify this as an abusive relationship that potentially could escalate to other forms of violence. Skills development focused on Kate telling John she is unhappy, John being angry and defensive and then actively listening, and the couple trying to resolve the issues, including the option of Kate leaving John.

The final activity in this session focused on issues around how to breakup with someone ethically. The young people really loved this activity and were readily able to come up with a long list of ways people breakup. They were challenged to consider how this felt for the other person, whether they would like to have it happen that way to them, and whether there were more ethical ways of doing it. Several groups felt that using text messaging, getting your friends or even your parents to tell them, just going out with someone else, or not saying anything were all "gutless" (cowardly) actions and failed to consider the other person. They felt the length of the relationship might dictate the most ethical way to breakup. Generally, there was agreement that, despite a face-to-face break-up being difficult, it was more ethical.

Standing Up Against Sexual Violence—Developing
Skills As an Ethical Bystander

As indicated in chapter 5, one of the promising areas of sexual assault prevention education is work focusing on how to increase the role of community members as active bystanders in challenging the social norms that promote and condone sexual violence. The concept of bystander skills aims to intervene in and reshape social or cultural norms that promote or condone gendered violence. Social norm theories highlight the ways that the majority culture or normative environment can support beliefs and attitudes held by an individual (Dyson and Flood 2008). Building from these theories, violence prevention researchers and educators have increasingly been focusing on bystander behavior. This approach seeks to mobilize community members from purely witnessing an event to intervening safely in situations of violence, discrimination, or other unacceptable or offensive behavior (Powell 2011). The research on pro-social bystander interventions suggests positive engagement by members of communities that previously felt issues such as violence against women were private matters (see Banyard et al. 2004, 2007, 2008, 2009a, and 2009). It has proved a particularly engaging strategy to involve men in promoting nonviolent forms of masculinity (Berkowitz 2004, Banyard et al. 2004, 2007, and 2008). Central to men's engagement in programs is the notion that men may be particularly effective in challenging violence-supportive behavior or speech among their male peers (Flood 2006).

The work done by Victoria Banyard, Elizabethe Plante, and Mary Moynihan (2004, 2007, 2008, 2009a, and 2009b) in the United States is particularly interesting. They argue that one of the many problems hampering prevention efforts to date has been too strong a focus on individual change and a failure to grasp ways in which we can—as a whole community—challenge sexual violence. Using concepts from community psychology, they highlight ways in which communities become ready to change, and argue that we need to understand this to enhance prevention efforts. They suggest we need to build community competence in the face of sexual violence and more fully engage all community members in the process of sexual violence prevention. Banyard and colleagues (2004, 68) hypothesize that, as the skill level of bystanders is crucial to intervention, building the capacity of, for example, college students will increase the likelihood that they will intervene with regard to rape, attempted rape, sexual violence, and intimate-partner violence incidents within their college campus. Their aim is to build competent communities wherein a shared responsibility for preventing sexual violence becomes the alternative social norm. They sought to build competent allies for survivors and to work with others to de-escalate risky situations. The program they developed and evaluated confirmed their proposition, with improvements in attitudes, knowledge, and behavior at four and 12 months for both women and men who participated (see Banyard, Plante, and Moynihan 2007, for a detailed discussion).

My approach extends the work of Banyard, Plante, and Moynihan in several ways. While my goal is to provide an alternative form of sexual assault prevention education, it locates the program more broadly within sexuality and intimacy issues in relationships. Banyard and colleagues seek to build allies for survivors and to de-escalate risky situations through a model based on the mobilization of pro-social behavior on the part of potential bystanders (2004). However, their model has little to say about how elements of empathy, respect, mutuality, and the negotiation of sexual needs are to be worked out between people known to each other. For me, the concept of developing ethical responsibility is, therefore, more relevant to my research and practice focus. As such, the heart of my work is more on women and men of a younger age, as well as college or university students. Despite these differences, it was important—in terms of the approach I took to the program—that I moved beyond individual intimate situations and encouraged young people to develop skills as competent and ethical friends and citizens in their communities. Not only is this important to their role as members of the wider community, who can carry sexual assault prevention efforts wherever they go, but also as they are a key resource to their friends. This is particularly important, as my research interviews showed how young people relied on their friends as a source of norms in relation to gender and sexual experience and of advice on what to do if they experienced problems with their parents, partners, or other friends. Many victims of sexual violence do not report coerced sex or even necessarily realize that what occurred in a dating context meets the definition of a crime (Gavey 2005). Therefore, in terms of education, young people need: first, to understand the complexity and subtlety of sexual violence in all its forms; second, to have an opportunity to learn the skills of being an ethical bystander to prevent sexual violence before it occurs; and third, to challenge the privatized hell that many unsupported survivors experience.

These issues are taken up in the final session of the six-week program by introducing participants to the real-life tragedy of Dianne Brimble—an Australian woman found naked and dead on a P&O

cruise ship in September 2002. This real-life situation received a large amount of media coverage in Australia for a number of years as the various court cases unfolded and most participants in the program were aware of the case (Brown 2006; Fleming 2006; King 2006; Lauder 2006; McMahon and Jacobsen 2006; Welch 2008). There was much discussion in the media as to why people failed to intervene on Mrs. Brimble's behalf, even when they personally saw her lying unconscious and naked on the cabin floor. Apart from the unethical behavior of the men involved, her death raised questions about a failure to act by other individuals, and called into question the behavior of the police, the cruise ship's failure to meet their duty of care to passengers, and the criminal justice system. This example highlights many of the elements that help explain why bystanders fail to act. We can see, in this story, elements of "diffusion of responsibility" among individuals and representatives of systems who are supposed to have some sanctioned responsibility for others. This is the idea that other people will take responsibility and not you. There is also evidence that some people who saw Dianne felt the situation was ambiguous, as the passengers were all consenting adults and assumptions were made that she was "just drunk," and, therefore, could be seen to be responsible for the situation she was in and dealing with the consequences.

The importance of context is also relevant here. A cruise ship is marketed as a place to have fun, to let your hair down, and have a good time. Drinking and meeting up with new people are all part of the social norms of this context. However, the darker side of these activities, and the associated risks for passengers, is not uppermost in people's minds, and this can create a context in which the social and cultural norms of home have the potential to be replaced by anything goes. This has the potential to impact on other people's responses to the events and actions they observe among other passengers, and to intervene may result in them being seen as a wowser [puritan] or a spoilsport [party pooper].

The Dianne Brimble story is a powerful, real-life introduction to the topic of bystander behavior. It is confronting and distressing, and drives home the point that people often find themselves in situations that go beyond what they had anticipated. In the absence of friends, we rely on a wider social sense of care and concern for others to assist us. It challenges the privatized nature of what is happening to others who may or may not be our friends in social situations. It also provides an opportunity for program participants to reflect on how they would feel if this happened to them or someone they cared about, and no one did anything. As such, it begins the process of developing ethical bystander skills by attempting to invoke empathy and ideas about community responsibility and ethics.

Participants moved from this story to a more general discussion about bystander behavior, considering examples from their own lives when they did or didn't intervene, when they saw someone else intervene or someone intervened on their behalf, and some of the barriers to intervening. They then moved through considering the steps to safe intervention developed by Banyard and colleagues (2005a, 2005b). This allowed them to see that there are issues to consider in making a decision to act, and how they can do this safely, without putting themselves at risk. Five case studies were used in small group work to explore a range of situations. Participants were required to consider their role as ethical bystanders. The case studies are, once again, drawn from real-life situations. They include: challenging victim blaming and sexist language about a woman who was raped; receiving a cell phone video message of a woman giving oral sex to a guy that has been circulated to everyone at school, except the woman on the video phone; finding a group of men hassling a woman on her way home by blocking her path and pulling at her clothes; providing support to a friend who calls to report being raped by a hook-up she met at a bar; and observing drink spiking happening. Each of the situations is explored in small groups with a focus on getting participants to consider what the safe steps to intervening might be, working out a plan, considering the implications of non-action, and practicing challenging the behavior through a mini role-play.

In chapter 8, I discuss the responses of young women and men to the Sex & Ethics Program and the impact on their lives following the group's completion.

Chapter 8

Sex & Ethics in the Lives of Young Women and Men

Sexuality and violence prevention education programs have been developed and implemented in most Western countries for many decades, as indicated in chapters 4 and 5. However, it is only since the 1990s that serious attention has focused on questions around the effectiveness of the programs and their lasting impact. A growing body of evidence has developed in the United States since 1994, when Congress passed the Violence against Women Act, and in 1995 mandated rape prevention efforts on campuses that receive federal funds (Carmody and Carrington 2000). Much of this important work has centered on the efficacy of education programs that have involved college students and has excluded wider discussions of the impact of programs with broader population groups. Very little work assesses impact beyond the life of the program or educational activity. These factors played a significant part in shaping my commitment to including a formal evaluation of the Sex & Ethics Program from its inception. This chapter begins with a short reflection on the original research findings published in 2009 (Carmody 2009a). The primary focus of the chapter, however, is on program development and outcome evaluations since the initial pilot.

As discussed in chapter 1, the results of the original 2007 pilot of the Sex & Ethics Program (Carmody 2009a) were based on a three-part outcome/impact evaluation. This included administering surveys prior to the group commencing (pre-test), at the end of the six-week program (post-test), and repeated again at four to six months after the groups ended. The findings indicated there was a substantial increase in self-knowledge from the start of the program (pre-test), based on their responses at the end of the six-week program (post-test). There was an additional small increase in self-knowledge or confidence levels six months later. At the six-month follow up, 63 percent indicated mutuality as a primary concern for them in negotiating sex. This suggests there was a shift from self-focus to an increased awareness of the need to negotiate with partner(s) and also consider their needs.

These findings indicate that, not only did their self-knowledge and confidence levels improve over the life of the program, but also they held onto these gains and slightly improved on them over a significant time period post the group. Overall, 82 percent of young people reported using sexual ethics ideas since the group had ended, and 74 percent had used skills learnt in the groups. For people beginning relationships or thinking about having sex, the education program gave them the confidence to work out what was right for them, for example:

> It really helped me as I am just starting to enter a relationship. It gave me a good base to start…to know what I need and want and what my other half [partner] needs and wants.
>
> (Jane, aged 17, from the city) (Carmody 2009a, 136)

While these findings were very promising, the sample was very small and there was a need to assess whether similar findings would result from larger more diverse samples collected over time.

Since this promising start, the Sex & Ethics Program has continued to grow and been refined for particular population groups and implemented across several states in Australia and in Wellington, New Zealand. Three-phase data collection from participants in the program has continued where funding has been obtained to conduct the formal evaluation. In some areas, funding has not been provided, and this has meant that educators have collected only end-of-group process-evaluation feedback or customer satisfaction data on the program structure and activities. The following section, therefore, presents data collected from two sources. The first part details the findings of the formal, three-part outcome evaluation collected from participants who took part in groups from 2009 to 2011. The second part of the chapter discusses data sourced from one specific site—a university residential college that runs an adaptation of the Sex & Ethics Program with senior residents who act as mentors and advisors to other students living in university housing. The university has made an ongoing commitment to run the program as compulsory training for its student advisors. The data they have kindly provided to me are drawn from anonymous group feedback sheets collected in 2013 and 2014.

It is provided here to demonstrate the ongoing uptake and impact of the program despite lack of formal evaluation funding and as a case study of how the program can be used effectively with students living in university/college housing.

The Impact of the Sex & Ethics Program, 2009–2011

Young people were recruited into the Sex and Ethics Program primarily through professional staff, such as youth workers, who worked directly with young people. Access to young people was obtained from a variety of different settings such as generic and specialist youth services, schools, university residential colleges, football clubs, and university student associations during 2009–2011. They were located in rural, regional, and urban areas in New South Wales (NSW), Queensland, Western Australia, and Wellington, New Zealand. The young people were sexually, geographically, economically, culturally, and gender diverse, varying in age from 16 to 26 years. Approval from Human Ethics Committees or Institutional Review Boards (IRBs) in the United States was obtained from the University of Western Sydney in NSW, Australia, and also from the Health Service in New Zealand to collect evaluation impact data. Written consent was obtained from all participants and parental consent was also obtained for 16- to 18-year-old participants unless they were legally recognized as independent young adults living away from their family of origin.

The data that follow are based on survey responses from a total of 153 young women ($n = 71$) and men ($n = 81$), aged between 16 and 26 years (mean age = 19.4 years). Of the total sample, 81 participants or 52.94 percent were men. Participants self-reported 35 different cultural and ethnic backgrounds. The largest were Anglo-Australian (26.2 percent), Pākehā-New Zealander (20 percent; non-Maori New Zealander), and Samoan (7.8 percent). Participants also identified with a range of sexualities, including gay (9.8 percent), queer (6.5 percent), bisexual (5.9 percent), and lesbian (3.3 percent), with the largest group identifying as heterosexual (66 percent).

The method of data collection involved administering a short standardised survey at three time periods. The first baseline data was collected at the first group meeting (pre-group survey); it was repeated again at six weeks in the final session of the program (post-group survey). A further email survey was administered four to six [1] months following completion of the education groups (follow-up survey). There were 153 participants who completed the pre-group survey in Week One and again in Week Six (post-survey). At the follow-up email survey stage, 94 participants (61.4 percent of the original sample) completed the web-based survey. Of this remaining group, 52 participants (55 percent) were male, and 42 (45 percent) were female. The attrition rate across the post-group and follow-up survey was 38.6 percent. This rate is to be expected, but is lower than anticipated given the online mode of delivery and the lapse in time between the end of the program and the follow-up surveys.

I developed the survey for the original pilot study in 2006 (Carmody 2009a). It included two specific survey items to determine what impact, if any, the program had on young people's behavior and sexual relationships, and whether this was maintained six weeks and four or six months later. It also included knowledge about sexual assault and the most important factors in negotiating sex. Dr Georgia Ovenden, my research associate who was involved in the project evaluation for a number of years, and I jointly carried out the data analysis. The five-point Likert scale used in the survey asked participants to identify their level of agreement with the statement: "I know how to work out what I want from a sexual experience." The second item aimed to determine participant understanding of their partner's needs in sexual experiences: "I know how to work out what someone else wants from a sexual experience or relationship with me." This focus on self-care and care of the other reflects the approach to sexual ethics underpinning the program and is discussed in detail in chapter 6. The following section addresses statistical research results concerning these questions and is followed by a discussion of the qualitative findings.

StatisticalR esults

A paired samples t-test was conducted to compare participant scores from pre-group to post-group, and from pre-group to follow-up. The results from the data analyses indicated a statistically significant increase (from pre-group to post-group surveys; and from pre-group to follow-up surveys; $p < 0.001$) in their understanding of their own needs and their partner's needs in sexual relationships after they had completed the Sex & Ethics Program. These results indicate a significant increase in participants' understanding of themselves and their partners in negotiating sexual relationships (see Carmody and Ovenden 2013 for more detail).

The follow-up email survey results indicated that the increases achieved by the end of the Week Six session were maintained a number of months after the program had ended. We found that four to six months after the program was completed, 88 percent of young people reported using the ideas and 87 percent reported using the skills they had learnt in the program, as well as using ethical bystander skills as discussed in chapter 7.

Differences Between Young Women and Men

The statistical data revealed that both young women and young men reported a significant increase in their understanding of their own needs and their partner's needs in the time between the pre-group to post-group evaluation. Young women showed the largest increase in mean score observed across the pre-group and post-group surveys for "understanding of *own needs* in sexual relationships." For young men, the largest increase in mean score across the pre-group and post-group surveys was observed in their "understanding of their *partners needs* in sexual relationships." These patterns in the data are promising when we consider gender differences in sexual relationships in the broader cultural context. For example, previous research suggests that young women are likely to take on their partner's—rather than their own—needs in sexual relationships (Holland et al. 1998).

Qualitative Findings and Analysis

The qualitative results add a depth of understanding to how young women and men used the program ideas and skills in their real-life situations. Their responses provide insight into the process of developing their identities as ethical sexual subjects and citizens. The extended response questions were analyzed using thematic decomposition—an approach outlined by Braun and Clarke (2006). The following section describes some specific examples from the follow-up survey. It begins with responses from young women, and this is followed by the responses from young men. No real names have been used.

Responses of Young Women

Young women embodied increased understanding of their own needs as the following examples highlight. For a number of young women who participated in the program, considering their own needs, and the needs of their partners, represented an entirely new way of thinking about sex. For example, one young woman suggested that the program "opened up a path" for her to talk and think about things that she had not considered previously. This opening up was reflected by several young women and took a number of different forms. For example: one young woman suggested that the program had given her confidence to "be straight forward about what (she) wanted" rather than assuming that her partner will "just know" and "being confident to say no to things, to ask for what I wanted without feeling insecure." For another, it involved skills in communicating more effectively, to "have the courage and skills to check things out verbally" that she felt was often quite difficult with a casual partner. For another, the program "taught me how to avoid unwanted situations, like someone trying to push me into something I didn't want to do."

These examples highlight the complex processes of negotiation that are required before and during sexual intimacy and how the young women felt the program equipped them with more skills to tackle the sensitive negotiation required. Without these skills, women are vulnerable and at risk of unwanted sex. The following example highlights how Tess, aged 21, renegotiated her own needs and desires during sexual activities:

> I had sex with someone I knew. During sex I did not enjoy it and felt that it was something not for me. I stopped and explained to the person that this is not something I want to do, and that I wanted to talk about what else to do instead of sex, as I was not ready and felt uncomfortable. It felt good. Usually I would either hide away or would let the person have their way without them knowing what I was going through or thinking.

Her ability to halt the process and renegotiate indicates a high level of self-care and, as she herself said, "usually I would either hide away or would let the person have their way." This is a challenge to sexual compliance and feeling pressured to continue sex despite feeling uncomfortable. In addition, she demonstrates a sense of responsibility to her partner in making it clear that she was not enjoying what was happening. Her ability to do this and that her partner respected her wishes highlight the importance of understanding that sexual consent is a *process* of mutual negotiation rather than a one-off agreement that may have been communicated verbally or nonverbally before sex began.

Given the consistent findings from the Australian studies of secondary students (Mitchell et al. 2014) about the high levels of unwanted sex experienced by young women due to being drunk, the following comment from Barb, aged 18, indicated how the program helped her take better care of herself when she was drinking:

> Meeting a person I was attracted to whilst drinking, I found that my perspective on what was healthy for myself and them sexually was a

lot different and I felt like I considered the decision much more in depth...Afterwards, I felt like I'd considered my own welfare much more than I would have before the course.

The above examples demonstrate some of the multiple ways in which women who participated in the Sex & Ethics Program increased their levels of self-care and, in the process, refashioned traditional expectations and the power operating around gender and sex. This is particularly important for women whose needs are often seen as secondary in the context of heterosexual intimacy.

Responses of Young Men

The research findings indicate that, not only are heterosexual women reshaping their expectations about sexual intimacy, young men are also restyling their own traditional gender performances. As indicated in chapter 4, successfully engaging men in sexuality and violence prevention programs is relatively recent. The following qualitative data indicates how young men responded to this opportunity.

Men were asked to indicate the three most important things for them in negotiating sex. There was a strong recognition of the need for clear, honest, verbal, and nonverbal communication. However, participants also recognized the need to ensure their own physical safety. They were particularly being mindful of how being drunk could negatively impact on their decision making and ability to negotiate consent. Recognition of the importance of mutual consent was evident in many of the comments made, for example: "ensuring that both of us really want to do it"; "respecting the other person's decision"; "both parties know what the others intentions and feelings are"; and "it's important to check in with the other person to clarify each other's expectations."

While men did demonstrate some evidence of increased self-care, for example, "The Program taught me how to be open about what I like and dislike," the most important finding demonstrates an increased recognition of their partner's needs. For example: "I gained a better understanding of body language and how to read it and how easily signals can be misinterpreted." There was also an increased awareness of the need to communicate clearly to ensure "we were both understanding each other to ensure that neither of us got into a situation that we did not want."

For a number of young men who participated in the program, the examples they raised underlined their understanding of the importance of negotiated consent, and making sure it was established before they engaged in casual sex or sex with their regular partners. For example, one participant indicated he decided not to have sex because his partner "was too drunk." This is both an important ethical decision and also reflects recent legal amendments across Australia on sexual consent that indicates consent cannot be freely and voluntarily given if the person is too intoxicated (e.g., Crimes Act 1900 [NSW]). For other young men, their responses focused on the importance of negotiating sex when their partners were ready and making sure (they) both agreed.

Other young men extended this knowledge of a dynamic approach to consent, demonstrating an increased recognition of considering his partner's needs:

> I would always ask for consent and not assume that they want to do it. I would also ask questions on what they prefer and like in sex rather than just thinking about what I want and my satisfaction.
>
> (Bill, Sydney)

Some men articulated very clearly their views on sexual assault following the end of the program. Rick, from New Zealand, highlighted the importance of consent in both casual and ongoing relationships:

> It doesn't matter if you are together or not, you may be a couple that regularly has sex, but there has to be consent made. If you are too drunk, you are not in a position to give consent.

Two other men, Barry and Chuck, who were footballers, were more succinct about sexual assault and how to prevent it: "ask questions; don't assume or go to jail"; and "don't do it."

John, a gay man from Sydney, indicated the importance of negotiation of expectations and how it can go wrong without this:

> I learned the importance of clarifying each other's expectations when negotiating sex, and how easily a partner's intentions can be misinterpreted when communication breaks down.

For others, an awareness of the impact of their desires on another was demonstrated by stepping back from a traditional male aggressive pursuit of a woman in whom they were interested. For example, Darren, aged 18, said:

> The other night I was out, met a girl, she wasn't giving me good signs. So I knew to walk away.

A number of men talked through how the ideas and skills they learnt in the program helped them in negotiating sexual situations and working out what each person wanted. Tony, a Pacific Islander living in New Zealand:

> I've used the framework from the Program with my girlfriend all the time when negotiating sex. (The) framework was a huge help in regards to sex.

Several men echoed this view. They used the Sex & Ethics framework to negotiate with existing or new sexual partners. For Matt, a young footballer, it involved using his increased listening skills to understand how his girlfriend was feeling before they became sexual:

> My girlfriend has had a bad experience with sex before and just said that she needed me to understand her situation and fears before initiating sex. I felt that talking to her about her issues and how she feels about the situation has brought us closer together as I can understand her feelings and concerns.

This response not only avoided any harm or trauma for the young woman, but Matt could see the benefit of his approach in caring for her needs and how it brought them closer together. Vic from New Zealand, who identified as queer, commented on an increased level of confidence in articulating what he needed in order to care for himself while also paying attention to his partner's needs:

> Being intimate with somebody and being able to confidently ask what they liked, and being confident to say no to things without feeling insecure and also being able to ask for things or say yes to things without feeling insecure.

These findings indicate that young women and, indeed, men are actively participating in diverse subject-positions that resist and reshape gender relating in intimate sexual encounters. The evaluations at the end of the six-week program and four to six month post group surveys reveal ongoing evidence of women and men using knowledge and "skills to deal with everyday real life situations." While this sample of young people was diverse on many criteria, a larger sample would be needed before results could be generalized to wider populations of young people.

These qualitative data indicate that women and men have reworked issues around communication, consent, interpreting body language, finding a voice to set limits on specific sexual activities and speaking up about their desires for pleasure, and challenging potentially sexually coercive situations. Young women learnt new ways of caring for themselves, including the possibility of an active sexuality. By doing so, they demonstrate an active resistance to traditional gender norms and developing a clearer "voice" to express their needs and desires within sexual contexts. The findings from young men indicate evidence of counter-discourses to dominant traditional views of male gender performance and sexuality. They disrupt biological essentialist assumptions of men as unable to control their sexual desires prior to and during sexual situations. This suggests that, for young men, the program has assisted them to reflect on their attitudes and behavior and recognize that ethical relationships require recognition of a partner's needs as well as their own. Through ethical reflection, gaining an understanding of the impact of sexual scripts on others, and learning new skills in negotiation, both women and men embodied a different kind of gender performance based on ethical mutual concern. They were fashioning new identities as ethical sexual citizens.

The Sex & Ethics Program in University Colleges

Background and Context

The transition from secondary school to tertiary education can constitute a time of increased freedom, exploration, and expansion. Students may experience new opportunities and increased pressures to negotiate complex sexual and social relationships with fellow students (Lindgren et al. 2009). The problematic aspects of housing cultures within university life have focused around a number of key issues: initiation rites or hazing, as it is known in the United States; alcohol- and other drug-fuelled violence; sexual harassment and sexual assault; and racial vilification and physical violence. The relative abundance of US-based hazing data can be attributed, in part, to the centrality of initiation rites in fraternity and sorority cultures in US tertiary institutions; for example: being publicly humiliated, tied up and confined to small spaces, drinking large amounts of alcohol to the point of passing out or getting sick, being forced to watch live sex acts, and being made to perform sex acts with same gender (Allan and Madden 2008, 9–10).Certain of these initiation rites have garnered negative attention for their capacity to inflict harm upon participants—in some cases, even resulting in death. Links are made also to the persistence of these practices within both university and wider public sporting cultures (see, e.g., Johnson and Holman, 2002; Lipkins, 2006).

As with hazing, data surrounding the prevalence and nature of inci-
dences of sexual assault, harassment, and discrimination in residential
colleges is primarily US-based (see, e.g., Payne (2008); Palmer et al.
(2010); Fisher, Cullen, and Turner (2000)). The relative availability
of data surrounding the sexual victimization of college women in the
United States can be attributed, in part, to the interest of Congress in
campus crime issues. This interest has been reflected in the passing of
the *The Jeanne Clery Disclosure of Campus Security Policy and Campus
Crime Statistics Act* or the *Clery Act* of 1990. The bill was named
for Jeanne Clery, who was raped and murdered in her dorm room at
Lehigh University, Pennsylvania, in 1986.This act was amended to
include the Campus Sexual Assault Victims' Bill of Rights in 1992
that requires colleges and universities to develop and publish policies and programs regarding the awareness and prevention of sexual
assault, and to afford basic rights to sexual assault victims. In 1998,
this legislative framework was further amended to include additional
reporting obligations and campus security-related provisions, as well as
the requirement for colleges/universities to keep a daily public crime
log (e.g., see Oregon State University Cascades (2014)).

Australia, also, has state and federal legislative requirements for
public educational institutions, and administrators of residential
housing, including universities, to protect their students from sexual
assault and discrimination according to sex, disability, age, or race.
The NSW Anti-Discrimination Act 1977 provides further provisions
against sexual harassment, discrimination, or vilification on the basis
of race, homosexuality, transgender, and human immunodeficiency
virus (HIV)/acquired immune deficiency syndrome (AIDS) status.
While these acts require that universities and colleges do not discrim-
inate on the aforementioned grounds, they do not impose specific
requirements for policies protecting students as per the US campus
security legislation or reporting publicly on crime figures or incidents.
In fact, in recent years, there have been a series of incidents involving
students at prestigious universities that resulted in student's requiring
hospitalizations as a result of being forced to drink copious amounts
of alcohol as well as alleged sexual assaults. Universities have been
publicly condemned for their failure to act to provide safety for all
students and a failure to act on allegations of serious misconduct and
a lack of transparency on any actions taken claiming privacy concerns.
For examples, see SMH (2009) and 9 News (2014).

The incidence of sexual assault is of major concern in relation to university locations. As early as 1986, the Federal Bureau of Investigation
(FBI) found that young adults, especially those in colleges and

universities, constitute a large portion of those individuals affected by date rape (FBI in Gross et al. 2006, 288). These results have been corroborated, and enlarged, by the National College Women Sexual Victimization Survey (NCWSV) (Fisher, Cullen, and Turner 2000). The study found that 35 out of 1,000 college students are raped each year (Fisher, Cullen, and Turner 2000). Since the results of this study were released, one further large-scale examination of sexual violence against female campus students has been conducted by Gross et al. (2006), who surveyed unwanted sexual experiences encountered by 935 undergraduate female college students enrolled at a state university in the southeastern United States. Results of this study indicated that, since enrolling at university, 27 percent of the sample respondents had experienced unwanted sexual contact; more than one third (37 percent) of these victims reported multiple forced sexual experiences.

These findings indicate the importance of developing appropriate, high-quality, evidence-based interventions to try to prevent gender-based and other forms of violence on campus as one key setting that involves large numbers of young people.

Engaging With Student Residential College Advisors

Alongside the findings from the formal outcome evaluation studies discussed above, additional data has been collected from one university, in Australia, in 2013 and 2014. This resulted from a research project in 2011–2013 with colleagues Kath Albury, Peter Bansel, and Georgia Ovenden. The project focused on working with a large metropolitan university to assess community climate and develop policy and education strategies for enhancing cultures of respect and leadership within student housing. Student housing in this university provides services to over 1,000 students in multiple locations. The student population is diverse, with 31 percent from a culturally and linguistically diverse background, with 46 percent born outside Australia. This included local students and a high proportion of international students from diverse countries and regions such as the United States, Asia, and the Middle East.

An educator-training program was run in 2012 for 12 staff from the university drawn from counseling services, housing, and the diversity unit. The *Building Cultures of Respect and Safety in Student Housing Education Program* was adapted from the original Sex & Ethics Program to more explicitly incorporate wider issues of gender and cultural differences. This was to address the high level of international students and the competing understandings of gender and sexuality that emerged from research with students and staff. The theoretical approach based on building student's skills in ethical relationships was maintained. However, changes were made to case studies and settings that incorporated data obtained from the research project.

Following the training of the university staff, the *Cultures of Respect and Safety Program* was implemented with two student groups in 2013 and one group in 2014. Forty-eight student advisors took part in a revised format of four sessions over three weeks. These student advisors play a significant role in the day-to-day running or management of the student residences. They provide orientation for new residents, pass-on information regarding policies and procedures, and are charged with the responsibility for building social relationships. By far, the most significant aspect of their networking responsibilities is the building of social relationships and community, which is a critical aspect of managing both the residences and the residents. They are, most significantly, in charge of building community. They build relationships at the whole residence, floor, and room level by engaging residents in socialization and entertainment activities, and managing (and reporting on, where appropriate) disputes, tensions, or conflicts in the rooms. This means that the advisors are fulfilling key leadership roles in shaping both the formal and informal cultures of the residences. A comprehensive induction is held for the advisors at the beginning of their term. Ongoing meetings and additional input on specific topics supplement the induction.

Feedback from Student Residential College Advisors

The participants in the program expressed positive views about how the program was run, the range of activities, and their practical nature. For example: "The activities were from real life experiences and made us think about aspects we don't usually consider"; "a very useful program to solve real situations"; "activities encouraged me to think from different aspects of views"; "what to do in difficult situations"; "fantastic"; and "eye opening, interesting, mind changing."

There was strong evidence in the comments demonstrating that they embodied key aspects of the ethical framework. For example, several participants showed they understood and had learnt to think more about self-care: "[I] look at my own practices and reflect on my own behavior"; "I can be the one who makes changes and how to do this"; and "be careful with what impression I am giving or receiving." Other participants recognized the interplay between care of the self and care of the other person or people: "I am very glad I got to take part in it. It's made me think a lot about my place in my community and how to take care of myself and others."

The ethical framework was well received by participants who indicated that they found it: "very practical and applied"; " it helps keep you and your friends safe"; "a necessary tool which helps us not be regretful of our behavior"; and "a frame to help make good decisions for *ourselves and* others." It also assisted them in their role as student advisors: "as an advisor to stick to the framework and maintain order" and "it is transferable to all kinds of situations not just sex."

Advisors were drawn from diverse cultural backgrounds and several of them commented on how useful the program had been in increasing their knowledge and understanding of Australian law and customs:

- "I would tell my friends do it as soon as possible";
- "More activities needed like this for Asian students who don't understand the framework";
- "What you really need to know and understand";
- "Being from a completely different culture this was an eye opener for me with regards sex and other cultures and potential problems";
- "I was impressed to learn about the law and sexual assault as the law is not strong in my country and I learnt that the situations I thought were normal can be a sexual assault."

Given the role advisors are expected to take in building and maintaining cultures of safety and respect within student housing, it was not surprising that many participants identified the session on learning about how to be an effective bystander as the one most important for them: "Being an effective bystander"; "I feel like I could do more than being passive"; "I can influence situations"; and "I learnt how to prevent and act when it is necessary."

One of the educators who ran the training told me about the immediate impact the program had on one student advisor. He was in one of the residences in the evening after the program session on pressured sex and alcohol. He became aware that one of the women who lived on the floor was very drunk and was being led into a bedroom by a male who did not live in the residence. He intervened in the situation and got the guy to leave the premises. The next day, the young woman approached him and thanked him for his help and indicated that she had only recently arrived in Australia and was unused to being able to drink freely under the age of 21 (the legal age for drinking in Australia is 18). She was not used to the effects of easy access to alcohol and was unable to make it clear to the guy who was taking her into the bedroom that she did not want to have sex with him. The advisor successfully intervened in a potential sexual assault and the young woman learned a valuable lesson about needing to pay more attention to her own self-care and safety. The young man, hopefully, was challenged to rethink his own behavior when challenged by another man.

The feedback from the student advisors demonstrates the ongoing effectiveness of the program in this specific setting. Their responses indicate an embodiment of key principles of the ethical framework that underpins the program, as evidenced in their comments about the importance of self-care and understanding the impact of their desires on another. Beyond the personal insights they gained by reflecting on their own ethical behavior, they also understood the power of intervening in unsafe or risky situations as ethical bystanders. This was an important and useful skill for them to use in their role as student advisors to promote cultures of respect and safety in student housing.

Conclusion

The formal outcome evaluation of the Sex & Ethics Program demonstrates the significant changes that occurred in the lives of the young people who took part. These changes were found to be statistically significant. Additional insights into how they embodied these changes were revealed in the participants' qualitative responses. The finding that 88 percent of both women and men were still using ideas and skills they learnt in the program six months after it ended suggests the ongoing relevance of the program to their everyday lives. The adaptation of the original program for the university student-housing context reflects the flexibility of the program to be adapted for particular sub-populations and settings. Their positive response on the usefulness of the program to enhance their leadership is a finding that would be interesting to see tested in multiple similar settings.

Note

1. The difference in length of time was determined by when the follow-up time period occurred. For example, if the follow-up date fell at six months in December or January, the chances of securing meaningful return rates would have dropped considerably due to summer holidays in Australia and New Zealand. Therefore, some groups were followed up earlier at four months.

Chapter 9

Becoming a Sex & Ethics Program Educator

In this chapter, I reflect on my experience of training educators to deliver the Sex & Ethics Program. The conceptual approaches underpinning training are discussed as are theories of change utilized in training. International sexuality education literature often focuses on the philosophies underpinning programs, and/or an analysis of the politics of competing views about sexuality education or the content of particular programs (Jones 2011; Ferguson, Vanwesenbeeck, and Knijn 2008). Less attention is given to how sexuality educators are actually prepared to deliver sexuality education and if it involves organized training, and what beliefs, values, and skills underpin the actual training. The difficulty of accessing adequately trained professionals in the field of violence prevention has also been identified as a key challenge (Carmona 2005). This chapter draws on my experience training educators from diverse backgrounds between 2008 and 2012 and delivering the Sex and Ethics Program over six weeks to young people (Carmody 2009a, b).

The following discussion is primarily reflective, drawing on multiple data sources: a review of themes emerging from end-of-training-process evaluations; diary entries on training and personal reflections of the challenges I face in doing this work; and conversations with my co-facilitators, and data from semi-structured interviews with 12 Sex & Ethics educators that were conducted by an independent researcher in 2011 (Hercus and Carmody 2011). My hope is that the issues that have emerged in this project may be useful for other sexuality and violence prevention educators preparing professionals in college and university as well as in agency and community settings. I also want to encourage other sexuality educators to publish more reflective accounts of the process of educator training.

Contextual Factors Influencing Program Delivery

The development of the Sex & Ethics Program, like all education, occurred within a larger political and social context. The contested nature of sexuality research and practice reflects multiple beliefs and attitudes not only about sexuality but sexual practices, relationships, gender, and other variables such as faith, class, and cultural background. This work is never value neutral. These factors operate alongside public health research on the risks of sexually transmitted infections, unplanned pregnancies, and intimate partner violence and sexual assault. Both community expectations and governmental policies will impact directly on the resourcing allocated to sexuality and violence prevention education. Funding tied to specific beliefs on sexuality—as evident in school funding and abstinence education in the United States—is a case in point. The careful and considered preparation of personnel who will deliver sexuality education in all its complexity is, therefore, crucial.

Debates in the literature suggest that professional groups who are most often assumed to be the most suitable to deliver sexuality or violence prevention messages are not always the most appropriate. While some professions include sexuality as one aspect of the curriculum, this is often very rudimentary and does not address the specific skills needed to deliver sexuality education competently to diverse groups of people. Ambuel, Hamberger, and Lahti (1998), for example, found problems associated with training health practitioners in prevention because they are prone to using a pathology model that individualizes problems and can lead to victim blaming by health workers. Schoolteachers are often charged with the responsibility of delivering sexuality education. Research with young people has found that their experience of school-based education indicates it is at best focused mainly on "plumbing" and often overlaid by negative messages focused on the risks of sexual activity (Hilton 2007; Rolston et al. 2005; UNESCO 2009). Addressing the ethics and values of potential educators, therefore, becomes crucial to ensuring that effective programs are implemented. Despite the fact that sexuality education is saturated in values debates, research suggests that very few programs seriously attempt to provide opportunities for critical reflection on educator values. Where it seems most common is in the human immunodeficiency virus (HIV) education area (James-Traore et al. 2004; Kaaya et al. 2002; Mukoma et al. 2009).

Concerns about the suitability of particular professional groups providing education have led to increasing interest in using peer education models. This model of program delivery is based on the premise that peers are a significant influence on behavior and that program participants are more likely to accept the message if the people who are presenting it are more like themselves (Wissink 2004). Peer education can be as simple as informal conversations with young people at a nightclub or sports club around risky health behaviour, or via more formal presentations, workshops, distribution of pamphlets, and theater productions, for example (Sriranganathan et al. 2010). Peer educators are most often assumed to be drawn from young people sharing similar backgrounds and life experiences, but the term is used widely and can also include people across a spread of ages from 14 to 25 years of age. Ellis (2008) comments that, while youth peer education is an increasingly popular approach, there is little evidence suggesting this model enhances program effectiveness. Harden et al. (2001) found that most peer-delivered health promotion programs are evaluated qualitatively for process rather than outcome and there are very few high-quality outcome evaluations of peer education programs. Therefore, it cannot be simply assumed that peer education will significantly impact on behavior). The key to increasing educator effectiveness is providing a comprehensive program of screening, recruitment, intensive training, and ongoing support. These provisions are required to ensure high-quality program delivery and that peer educators remain on target with health promotion messages.

The need for comprehensive training and ongoing support is one that applies to both peer education models as well as other forms of education in the sexuality and violence prevention field. For a comprehensive analysis of a peer education program focused on recruiting and training male peer educators in a sexual health program, see Cupples et al. (2010). Without a conscious planned process of preparing educators prior to program delivery, the potential for negative unforeseen consequences is high. Educators may consciously or unconsciously impose a particular set of values on their audience. This may result in reinforcing gender and sexuality stereotypes and presenting sex, primarily, as an activity laden by risk and danger. The potential for pleasure can disappear in a discourse dominated by sexually transmitted infections and unplanned pregnancy. Heteronormative assumptions may silence same-sex desire within the group context and may not even be discussed as part of the diversity of sexual practices within the community. The tension between sex-positive and sex-negative beliefs is, therefore, very high and needs explicit discussion. This transparency will then allow the matching of particular approaches to specific population groups. For example, faith-based communities may be less willing for a comprehensive sex-positive sexuality program to be delivered, but an educator needs to know this and to make their own ethical decision about the type of education they are willing to deliver. Not all educators are suitable for all audiences. Decisions will need to be made based on pragmatic as well as ethical grounds. Educators will need to make a judgment about whether some education is better than no education or whether to engage on restricted grounds violates the principle of do no harm. There are some benefits in trying to find a way to work in these settings even if it is not possible to provide a fully comprehensive program. These include building a working relationship between the program provider and the host location, raising participants' awareness of the nature of sexual assault (especially legal definitions and where to go for help), and being one small action toward the long-term goal of preventing sexual violence (Carmody et al. 2009, 46).

Apart from addressing values underpinning sexuality training and the context of delivery, educators also need to understand that how people learn varies, and a diverse approach to how they facilitate is necessary to reach all members with whom they speak. Effective training programs also provide opportunities for educators to practice new skills in delivering activities and to receive feedback on how they can improve. These principles all informed the development of the educator training that I developed to support the implementation of the Sex & Ethics Program discussed below.

Working With Educators Around Sexual Ethics

Provision of comprehensive training for educators prior to delivering a sexuality program is rare in Australia. In the violence prevention field, it is even scarcer. In response to these gaps, I developed a five-day training program for educators who could then deliver the Sex & Ethics Program in their communities and evaluate its effectiveness. The educators from this project were all employed by government-funded state or community agencies or universities that worked specifically with young men and women aged 16–25 years of age. Training was conducted in several states within Australia and in New Zealand. Group size was capped at a maximum of 20 and a minimum of 12. Two facilitators ran all training sessions. I have primarily worked as a co-facilitator with Karen Willis from Rape and Domestic Violence Services, Australia, whose organization was my industry partner on the original research. Over time I also worked with other skilled facilitators, Kath Albury (from the University of New South Wales in Sydney) and Clif Evers (currently at the University of Nottingham in Ningbo, China). Both are gender, cultural, and media scholars but also have a strong commitment and involvement to community-engaged practice. The principle of always having two group leaders is designed to share the responsibilities of holding the group dynamics effectively over five full days of work. It also is central to our own ability to reflect on the work as it unfolds with each new group of educators and to monitor our own responses to the group and refine as necessary.

Personnel who want to be trained as Sex & Ethics Program educators were provided with information at the recruitment stage that indicated they would be participating in the same program they would subsequently deliver to young people. They were advised it would be experiential and require them to actively participate in structured skill-based activities, group and individual discussion, and to practice presenting an activity from the program to the group. This meant that, for the first three days, participants were involved in experiencing all the activities in the program. On Day One, they completed weeks one and two of the program; on Day Two, weeks three and four; and on Day Three, weeks five and six. Day Four was for group presentations and Day Five was included for groups who wished to take part in the formal research evaluation and needed briefing on how to complete the surveys with young people.

This structure resulted in them rapidly gaining an understanding of the activities and also the ethical issues they raise as well as their own personal responses to the material. Ample time was provided for this process to unfold and to guide educators to then consider how this would impact on their program delivery. This experiential focus aimed at increasing self-understanding but also reflected an ethical stance of not asking young people to reflect on their ethics without a similar commitment from educators in their own training program. I discuss this in more detail below.

Before we move into that discussion, there are a number of other theoretical principles that underpinned my approach to this educator training. These include conceptual or theoretical underpinnings of the program, linking sexuality and violence prevention education, the understandings used to work with young people, and strategies to achieve attitudinal and behavioral change. I will consider each of these in turn, being mindful that they link together to provide one model of working around sexual ethics. The first area I consider is the conceptual approaches that underpinned the program.

Conceptual Underpinnings of Educator Training

Prevention programs rarely articulate an explicit theory or conceptual base and this absence has been critiqued (Morrison et al. 2004). A failure to be explicit about the foundations that underpin the conceptual frameworks used may result in confused objectives, alienating certain populations, and also in a lack of coherence within the program and across activities. My response to this more general critique seen in the research literature was to be very transparent about my approach. The theoretical underpinning of the Sex & Ethics Program is based on a particular theoretical approach to sexual ethics. As discussed in chapter 6, it is concerned with determining the conditions of ethical exploration for different types of people, rather than with establishing the borders of acceptable or unacceptable desires, thoughts, and actions. I include feminist conceptions of ethics; including a conception of gender that acknowledges the possibility of the many ways it is possible to be female or male (Carmody 2003, 2006, 2009a). As previously indicated, I have found that the French philosopher Foucault's work on ethical sexual subjectivities has particular relevance to thinking through alternate spaces and possibilities in working with young people. Drawing on Foucault, Kane Race put it this way (2009, 108):

> Ethics involve taking up a position in relation to others...embodied capacities are intricately entwined with social location and historically formed...it makes no sense to enter a discussion of agency, responsibility, responsiveness or resistance, without also considering the historical and social specificity through which particular capacities, attributes, and possibilities are embodied.

The conceptual or theoretical approach to sexual ethics is introduced in the second session of the program. The ethical framework focuses on the *process* of decision-making and is not about prescribing what any person should think or do in any given situation. The four elements of the framework—caring for myself; being aware of my desires and wants; their possible impact on another; and, negotiating, asking, and reflection—are a method of critical reflection to consider the implications of actions for oneself and others. I argue, ethical reflection is a dynamic and ongoing process and can be used several times before, during, and after sex with another person. The framework needs to be understood as dynamic and fluid and it needs to be grasped that the focus may shift between and across elements.

A detailed description is provided to participants and, then, a case study drawn from an interview with a young woman is used to demonstrate how the framework can shift discussion about a complex and abusive relationship from who is right or wrong to consider the ethics of the actions taken by the woman and the man in the example. This is often a crucially important learning moment as people move beyond their existing frames of reference and understand complexity more fully. Throughout the remaining sessions of the program, the framework is constantly referred to and is displayed on a poster in the meeting room. Participants are encouraged to critically examine their own ethical stances in relation to diverse sexualities, to young people, and to gender-based violence.

Conceptually, I also have attempted to bridge the gap between sexuality education and violence prevention education. These are often seen as separate fields of study and involve different kinds of staff and agencies. However, real life is not so compartmentalized. A sexual encounter or relationship can run the gamut of a continuum from pleasure to fear and pain and everything in between. Education that fails to provide ways of negotiating this continuum seems to me to be lacking and leaves young people, in particular, extremely vulnerable (see Carmody 2006; 2009a for detailed discussion).

The third element in the conceptual frame underpinning my approach to training relates to how I understand young people. Rather than seeing them as one undistinguishable group, I recognize their diversity in all its forms. As discussed previously, I also see them as active sexual citizens who can—and do—shape their own embodied experiences of sexuality and sexual practices (Carmody and Ovenden 2013a; 2009a; Allen 2011). This is in contrast to views that see young people through a universalizing lens as victims of a sexualized culture or seeks to control and surveill their practices and their relationships around sexuality. Alongside these frames of reference is recognition that sexual and other forms of gendered violence can result in short- and long-term trauma. The high incidence of gender-based violence in our communities also suggests that some group members will either have worked directly with victim/survivors, have personally experienced these crimes, or know family or friends who have. Creating a safe and supportive respectful climate for working as a group, therefore, is crucial with this group of educators. It is these conceptual lenses of sexual ethics, sex as both pleasure and danger, young people as active sexual citizens, and a trauma awareness that underpin the program with young people and that I invite educators to consider in their training.

Becoming a Reflexive Educator

The key objective of the Sex & Ethics Program is to foster attitudinal and behavioral change and contribute to new cultural norms of nonviolence and ethical relating for women and men. This requires a clear theory of individual behavior change, of how to maximize the likelihood of achieving this objective educationally. To achieve this change, educators are provided with multiple opportunities to reflect on attitudes and values about sexuality, relationships, and gendered violence. The structured learning activities within the program have specific learning objectives and a rationale documented in the program manual, *Sex and Ethics: The Sexual Ethics Education Program for Young People* (Carmody 2009b). While these are important, they are primarily a vehicle to open up a dialogue within the group about specific aspects of sexual ethics such as negotiating consent, how gender expectations impact on sexual decision making, and standing up to abuse.

It is through the observation of self and other, reflection, and discussion of how people respond to the activities that competing views about sexual ethics emerge. Power is central to all relationships, and the abuse of power is fundamental to gendered violence. Brookfield (2009, 294), a leading author in adult education, highlights the importance of critical reflection as a method to interrogate power:

> ...Critical reflection calls into question the power relationships that allow, or promote, one particular set of practices over others. What also makes reflection critical is its foregrounding of power dynamics and relationships and its determination to uncover hegemonic dimensions to practice.

While reflection is important, there also needs to be opportunities for educators to become reflexive. As Patton (2002, 65) argues that reflexivity provides a level of consciousness of "cultural, political, social, linguistic and ideologic origins of one's own, and others' voice and perspective." Critical reflection, therefore, becomes a strategy to increase our understanding of the link between the personal and the structural to create reflexive and reflective educators. This approach is utilized in the program through structured activities and, most importantly, a dialogue around ethics that occurs as part of the individual and group reflection. Educators are, therefore, asked to consider not only their own personal response to material raised by activities but also how this reflects another level of complexity and understanding when located in the broader social and political context. How this plays out will become clearer by discussing the response of educators to the training considered in the following section.

In addition to a focus on the educators' values and reflection, opportunities are provided within the training to refine or learn specific skills they can use in delivering the program to achieve its objectives. To successfully achieve these goals, individual and group learning models are utilized, including social norm and bystander-intervention models (Bandura 2004; Banyard et al. 2004; Breinbauer and Maddaleno 2005). Adult education models are also central to the approach used. This approach recognizes adults need to feel autonomous and self-directed in learning situations that deliver practical, goal-directed knowledge that seems immediately relevant to their experience (Knowles 1973).

People learn differently and this was incorporated into both the Sex & Ethics Program and the training of educators. A mixture of learning strategies was used including: mini-presentations where factual knowledge was imparted concerning the law, for example; dyad and small-group structured activities; observation of and feedback to others practicing a skill; large-group discussion; creation of art work or collages; anonymous question box drop; private reflection and journal keeping; and "homework" activities and video. The training sessions were very active, the energy was high, and there was much laughter and, sometimes, tears.

Educator Recruitment Into the Sex & Ethics Program

In 2009–2010, I provided four different Sex & Ethics educator-training programs for 59 participants. All but one of these programs received funding from either the Australian or New Zealand governments to support targeted staff to attend, to deliver programs, and to evaluate the outcomes of the groups run with young people. We put in place a written selection process for all applicants to ensure they had relevant baseline qualifications and expertise and were in key positions to influence program development and delivery in their local areas.

In April 2009, funding was obtained from the Respectful Relationships Program in the federal Department of Families, Housing, Community Services and Indigenous Affairs to implement the *Sex & Ethics Violence Prevention Program* in New South Wales (NSW). In May 2009, 13 educators were drawn from the inner city of Sydney, the Central Coast, Armidale, and outer Sydney (Campbelltown and Wollondilly). These sites included populations drawn from diverse socioeconomic and culturally diverse communities, urban and outer-urban areas, and one rural regional town. They were targeted with the intention of increasing the number of trained facilitators in these areas, thereby increasing the capacity for future sustainability of the program. Participants were recruited from community organizations, area health services, youth services, university counseling services, and sexual assault services. Additional funding was provided in late 2009 for the Sex & Ethics Program to be refined specifically for 16- to 18-year-old National Rugby League trainees in Queensland. The training involved 17 current and former players and was run over two consecutive weekends. For the first time, the educators were all male, except for one female welfare officer.

Funding from the New Zealand Ministry of Justice provided further funding in 2009–2010. This resulted in 15 educators being selected based on their skills and background experience working with young people from diverse cultural and sexual backgrounds. These educators delivered training to eight groups with young people in 2010.

Further training programs were run in 2010 and 2012. Training was offered on the basis of popular demand and differed from the previous educator training in that it was not supported by government funding. Educators enrolling in this course did so based on a fee-for-service basis—paid either by their organizations or themselves. The 34 educators came from the Australian Capital Territory, Western Australia and Sydney, and NSW.

Educator Reflections on Sex & Ethics Educator Training

In 2011, I employed a researcher who had had no prior involvement in the research or education program to carry out some follow-up work with educators who had taken part in training from 2008 to 2010 (Hercus and Carmody 2011). I was keen to investigate the various ways that educators had used their training. Overall, 59 educators completed a training program from 2008 to 2010. From this total number, 39 of the educators supplied their email address at the time of their training. An invitation to participate in the research was sent out to all 39 email addresses, with ten email addresses being identified as no longer active, resulting in 13 interview volunteers. The group who participated in interviews included seven women and five men. They were drawn from several states in Australia and New Zealand, and represented diverse organizations including youth services, universities, sexual assault services, and sexual health organizations. They came from a diversity of disciplinary backgrounds including nursing, social work and social welfare, psychology, and teaching. They varied in age from 30 to 55 and were also sexually diverse. The cultural background of the majority was Anglo-Australian.

Themes that emerged from the research interviews included reflections on the actual training, the philosophy of the program, alternative uses of the skills they learnt, successful experiences of implementing the program, ideas for program modification, organizational barriers and challenges, support needs for educators, and future directions for program delivery. I will address only the first three here: their reflections on the training program, the philosophy of the program, and alternative uses of the skills they learnt. A detailed discussion of the organizational barriers and challenges in providing sexual assault prevention education is available in Carmody (2015).

Many of the educators interviewed for this research were motivated to participate in the Sex & Ethics educators training as they saw a clear need for a new approach to violence prevention education. As one educator said:

> We've been looking at that area of sexual assault for a long time and not been very effective in it. We need to get our head around what is actually happening here and this program looked good, especially because it was heavily researched based.

Participants found the experiential focus of the training quite different from other courses they had attended:

> [The] Sex & Ethics program and the training around Sex & Ethics are a bit of a revelatory approach really. Doing the program as a participant I think pushes you to acknowledge quite how revelatory it is. Instead of talking about the theory about why ethical relating would have a consequence of sexual violence and intimate partner violence not being possible, when you're actually examining that the framework, the Sex and Ethics framework in the context of your own sexual decision making – and you're being pushed into quite uncomfortable placesIt hink.

For another participant, it helped understand how people might react when they ran groups:

> I think the idea of actually working your way through the actual program is genius. It's absolutely brilliant. It just prepares people for being

in the facilitator's seat really effectively for having been through the process as a participant. There's plenty in it that I think even if you are familiar with the content and the issue that is really confronting. So I think it's necessary to actually put people through that experience of being in the room as a participant before they're, to whatever degree, bringing their expertise as the group coordinator or facilitator

Another educator who came from a sexual health background reflected on the skills he felt would be useful with young people:

> Even though I knew Sex & Ethics was based in [the] prevention of sexual violence, I felt like at least it was trying to provide young people with skills to negotiate…That's what I got out of the training. I got inspired by these opportunities to provide the training for young people or do a course and after it would give them skills.

The Sex & Ethics educator's training did not cover skills training in group facilitation. In the application process, educators were required to demonstrate their previous experience in group facilitation. When asked to reflect on this element of the educator's program design, responses were mixed. One experienced educator said:

> I think that your experience of the training would depend on how familiar you were with that kind of training and also with that kind of group work delivery. I don't see it's their [the lead facilitators for the program] job to train people in group-facilitation – these are skills that are expected to come with people.

Another educator shared a different view:

> I think they could have spent more time focusing on group facilitation- some of the discussion we wanted to have was moving from being in the activity to talking about facilitating. If you had people in the room that hadn't got a lot of facilitation under their belt, well then they'd need to spend more time on that perhaps than the program allowed.

This example highlights some of the challenges in running a training program with staff drawn from different disciplines and levels of experience and expertise. The issue of prior knowledge was one that also emerged in regard to knowledge about sexual and other forms of gendered violence. One organization identified skilled potential educators around sexuality issues but they lacked sexual violence knowledge. They developed a one-day seminar that educators were required to attend prior to the Sex & Ethics Program. They recognized:

We knew that we weren't going to get people who could be Rape Crisis advocates by doing one day's work with them, but we wanted them to be coming with at least an understanding of how gendered sexual violence is in terms of reported sexual assaults and at least an understanding of the double standard around being sexually active for women.

Through this process of training, educators often find themselves confronted by issues within their own personal lives or their professional practices and, thus, uncomfortable. Comfort in dealing with sensitive issues as a group facilitator takes some time and practice as indicated by this educator:

I understood the activities. I understood how to do it. But what it's like to be the person asking people to undertake those forms of personal reflection and personal engagement and probably my own place in relation to their reflections and their engagement, I think only doing it can help with that.

One educator recounted the impact of a group discussion on one of the other educators that emerged in the training group he attended:

… There was certainly one incident where there was a very significant impact on one of the participants…that came out of left field for everyone. But it was a really effective reminder that the content can be incredibly personal, even in most unexpected ways. As trainers, we have to be incredibly careful how we let the talk in the room evolve, if that makes sense…I think the space was as well prepared as possible. I think people were – people didn't know the content beforehand. But I think there was a sense of, please, this is personal stuff. Be aware of it. That was kind of reinforced all the way through.

Clear guidelines were established at the beginning of the group to encourage participants to be mindful of how they responded to others in the group and to monitor their own responses to material or activities and have in place self-care management. All participants were provided with support service information at the beginning of the group and reminded of it during the program. Group facilitators closely monitored responses by participants to ensure safety and the ongoing work of the group.

Over the years I have been running the program, there have been people who have needed to step out of a session for some time. Others have reviewed their personal relationships with a fresh eye and considered whether they felt their needs were being met or whether their partner was consuming all the relationship space. Some have found new resolve to end relationships, others have begun them, and even others have reported practicing the ethical sex framework during sex with a partner after hours during the training program! Other educators have faced different challenges. Some find the idea of stepping back from an expert role of educator challenging. Often, they have only received training consisting primarily of how to implement knowledge transfer. This conception of education denies any prior knowledge or expertise of participants—viewing them as empty vessels to be filled up with knowledge by an educator. Therefore, training that is purely content driven or knowledge transfer leaves unexamined the embedded values and concepts underpinning the content and the attitudes and beliefs of the educators. Alternatively, in this program, the Sex & Ethics educators were being invited to consider working alongside young people who would take part in the program and to assist them to explore and articulate their own ethical stance(s).

Reactions to the Philosophy of the Training Program

The conceptual underpinnings of the program are based on a particular form of sexual ethics as discussed previously. The training program also brings together research and skills around sex-positive sexuality and violence prevention work. All of those interviewed expressed support for this approach to sexual ethics. For one educator who had a background in the field of sexual violence prevention but now worked in a sexual health setting:

> I think the philosophy is outstanding because, for me, it actually brings together two things that were sitting in isolation from one another. One is a real recognition and engagement with the experience of sexual victimization, but in the context of a sex positive, diversity-affirming framework. It wasn't trying to teach the right answer. It was about teaching a process.

The ethical framework was designed as a method to assist in sexual decision making and not to be prescriptive of any specific ethical stance except to condemn pressured and coerced sex. This approach was recognized and valued by many educators. For example:

> In fact, it's clear in the outlining of the ethical framework. It's like this is not a checklist; it's a process. You're trying to describe the dot

points. [They] are to help facilitate understanding, not to be used as a tick-a-box.

Program Modifications

A number of themes emerged during the interviews about ways in which educators' had modified the Sex & Ethics Program to meet the needs of specific groups. The strongest theme to emerge was the need for some program modification to suit specific cultural groups. Examples of such modifications included using culturally appropriate language, as illustrated by one educator when she said:

> I'd like to utilize Wiradjuri [a local Aboriginal language] language in the actual program. We found that we had to modify words like families, instead of saying "family"; we said "the mob" and "grog" instead of "alcohol."

Another educator highlighted the importance of selecting the right educators when delivering to specific cultural groups:

> So one of the things we did around that was that we made sure we had at least one ethnicity-matched educator delivering those contexts.

One educator recognized the need to make adaptations to the program based on cultural norms around gender and sexuality. This was highlighted when she said:

> There was some particular gender stuff around working with Pacifica [people born in the Pacific Islands and New Zealand] young people that we took advice from our two Pacifica educators around – essentially it was just that talking about sexual relationships for Pacifica is not culturally done at all, having any kind of conversation around it. One of the things that made delivery around that easier was to have gender-separate space, so we would often start out exercising the gender-separate space, do that groundwork together and then come together to talk about it afterwards and let the young people direct how much they wanted to share of what they had done.

Several educators discussed the need to recognize specific cultural norms around the discussion of sexuality and how the Sex & Ethics Program might challenge those norms. A number of educators recognized the need for consultation and engagement with parents ahead of running the program to secure buy-in and establish safety. One experienced educator shared the way in which she addressed this issue in the lead up to running a Sex & Ethics Program with young Maori Pacifica people in New Zealand:

> With some of the groups that we ran, we ran an introductory session to name that, to name that we were doing something that was unusual. The way we tried to open up that space was to put it as a gentle challenge to young people…We don't get many places to try and do this, so if you want to accept that challenge. I don't think we ever ran an intro session where everyone who came didn't come to the program. That worked really, really well. It's just literally that kind of bridging session. I guess for us was really important, with that particular cultural group.

Another educator highlighted the need type of modifications necessary for audiences with low levels of literacy:

> We needed to be more verbal. That was one of the main things, because there were a few kids there that were illiterate. It's not the framework that's a problem; it's how you get the framework across to them. It needs to be simplified a bit, ask the same questions in a more simplified way. It just seemed a bit heavy at times for them.

Further refinements were done to fine tune the program to meet the needs of a same-sex-attracted group of young people:

> When we ran the all queer program here we queered almost all of the activities, because our thinking was, actually we want these young people to be thinking about this in their context and [same sex] and opposite sex for some of them as well. Those are the sexual opportunities we talked about needing to negotiate so that's what we'll do, except for the ethical bystander session. We didn't do it for that one because we felt strongly that people need to be able to intervene in situations where things are different from what they might be doing. That worked really well.

In discussing the modifications made to the program, the majority of educators confirmed that the types of adaptations made were a necessary part of ensuring the program had relevance for their target audience; however, they constituted only a superficial change. None of the educators interviewed in this sample, who ran Sex and Ethics Programs with young people subsequent to the educator training, reported making any change to the sequence, structure, or delivery time recommended in their training.

While educators unanimously agreed there was, on occasion, a need to make program modifications to bring relevance to specific audiences, one educator shared her views about the potential risks this can have on the program's efficacy:

> I feel really strongly that this needs to be sitting with sexual violence specialist knowledge, because I think if you don't have that you can quite easily get diverted into doing something that is not really about how we negotiate healthy sexual encounters at all, but might turn out to be about something very different. I still think there needs to be some kind of checking mechanism to make sure that the integrity of the issues the program's trying to address are still being addressed; that we haven't watered it down to something that's not going to be as useful for people.

The need for what is known in the prevention education field as program "fidelity" is an important one to ensure that replicating a program in a different context is not deleterious to program effectiveness (Elliott and Mihalic 2004).

Wider Applications of the Ideas and Skills Learnt From the Sex & Ethics Program

Other educators commented on the applicability of the conceptual approach of the program to other areas of their work, for example:

> I think it should be applied in private [clinical] work, in schools, with culturally diverse people; all that needs to be developed moving forward. The beauty of this program is that it's not saying this is the right way. It's not based on a set of moral principles pertaining to some religion or to [politicians] or whoever; it can be used by anyone.

Educators' endorsement of the value gained through the Sex & Ethics educator training is evident, with 75 percent of the educators indicating they had continued to use the skills gained in other areas of their work with young people. As one educator reported:

> The educators talk about this program in the other parts of their lives. We've got one guy who works with sex offenders for corrections here. We've got some youth workers. We've got advocates that work in a local refuge [shelter]. We've got counselors who work in different counseling sessions, so we've got quite a lot of people in different kinds of roles. I think probably all of them at one time or another has

talked about this work as part of their other work, so there is kind of a sense of – and I guess that's the community development approach – that violence prevention and the ethics framework is central to what we do.

A further 34 percent of respondents reported using elements of the Sex & Ethics Program in the design of other programs. As one educator reported:

I do face to face sex education training for teachers. So a lot of what I discovered [through the Sex & Ethics Educator's training] is more about, not so much the nuts and bolts of sexuality education but around the relationships, the ethics, the negotiations. I put more of that information, more of that discussion, into the training that I was doing and the work that I was doing.

A significant 42 percent of the sample reported using the skills gained through the Sex & Ethics educators' training in their counseling work with individuals. For example:

Even though I haven't run a [Sex & Ethics] group since 2009, I refer back to the framework in my one on one work with clients quite often because we have a lot of students who are discovering their own sexual needs, they are living in this domestic college environment and trying to figure out what's the relationship, what are my needs, what's the person's needs, so I walk people through the framework.

Two other educators discussed the use of the Sex & Ethics Program as a professional development strategy with a group of youth workers. They were faced with a situation where youth workers in a particular setting reported high levels of underage sex (16 is the age of consent for all genders in most states in Australia). They conducted a local needs assessment and determined that the youth workers were lacking in skills and confidence in how to broach concerns about pressured and unprotected sex and consent with the young women and men in their area. The educators felt that it was premature to train these youth workers to deliver the Sex & Ethics Program as they were concerned they did not have the background knowledge or skills to deal with the complex situations that might arise. Rather, they used the program:

…as a professional development for those youth workers so that they could engage with young people in a new and different way. Maybe have some new skills to talk about these issues that they were alarmed about.

They followed up the youth workers some months later, and received very positive feedback:

> We had a lot of good feedback that it gave people more confidence in talking to young people around their sexual health. They gave them more skills and more options in their tool kit I guess to deal with difficult situations.

Conclusion

Working with personnel who come from such diverse disciplinary backgrounds and varying levels of experience is challenging as an educator, but it also brings rewards. Providing a safe, supportive, and fun space in which to explore complex issues of sexual ethics is a reward in itself. Working with people as they grapple with new ideas and alternative ways of thinking about sexuality, violence prevention, gender, and the lives of young people and their own role in this work can be inspiring.

My reflections on the content and process of providing training for educators from a sexual ethics perspective suggest that a number of issues impact on the effectiveness of training and the sustainability of skills learnt. There is a need for greater leadership by communities, agencies, government, and academic researchers to recognize and advocate for funding to provide high-quality educator training and to evaluate its outcomes. Often, it is assumed that this is already in place when the reality is that there is no organized and consistent system of training educators in these fields. Professional training in Australian and New Zealand that is carried out in universities rarely addresses these issues. Training is often ad hoc, if it exists, and varies across states and across the country. In some community settings, staff are merely handed a manual and told to go ahead and run programs in schools and other settings. There is no equivalent in Australia and New Zealand to the US Centers for Disease Control, their training guides, and their funding for gender-based violence prevention services (Fisher et al. 2010). The ability of community-based agencies to play an active role in the provision of sexuality and violence prevention education is directly impacted by the wider context of program delivery and funding priorities. This needs to be understood as it impacts on program sustainability.

Evidence has been growing over the last 15 years that sexuality and violence prevention programs need clear conceptual frameworks and a theory of change to be effective (Schewe 2002). In addition, demonstrating competency about content does not indicate an ability to deal with the complexity of values or lead to behavioral change in participants (Hilton et al. 1998; Banyard et al. 2005). Transformative education is centered on providing opportunities for critical reflection and developing an ethical stance to education (Mezirow 2009). I have found that the most effective facilitators have an ongoing commitment to their own reflexive practice, a sense of humor, and flexibility in addition to content knowledge and effective facilitation skills. This includes needing to understand the different learning styles of groups of educators.

An example will highlight how knowledge of different learning styles needs to be translated into the training room. The male football educators I worked with were very engaged in all the small-group activities within the training program but were less engaged when we attempted to bring them into a whole-group discussion. As Albury et al. (2011, 345) point out: "the majority of learning about what it means to be a professional footballer is accomplished through doing." They didn't see the need to discuss in detail the issues that emerged from the activities in the larger group. This was in contrast to previous training experiences where educators were drawn from the health and welfare sectors and were primarily female. The mixed-gender health and welfare educators wanted to tease out the issues in some detail and, often, we were required to limit discussion time on some topics. This experience suggests both differences based on professional background and context and how gender may impact on learning styles. We quickly learnt that the allocated times for discussion needed to be reduced with the male footballers and we needed to keep the program moving. For Clif Evers—my co-facilitator—and myself, it meant we needed to be quick on our feet to readjust our timings and to find alternative strategies to keep the educators engaged.

After completing training, educators worked in their communities with the structured program as originally designed but were also mindful of the need to make adjustments to case studies and scenarios to reflect the specific population groups with whom they worked. These adaptations were applied to reflect the needs of specific cultural groups, for same-sex-identified and queer groups and also with footballers. Educators working with groups of young people with lower levels of literacy used more verbal descriptions of activities to reduce the need for people to read case studies. A subsequent project in 2012 initiated by Kay Humphreys—a long-term educator and sexual assault prevention advocate from rural NSW—resulted in providing us with funding to develop a detailed refinement of the program to meet the particular needs of Aboriginal and Torres Strait Islander young people (Wright and Carmody 2012).

The educators, who have taken part in the educator training to date, found that the Sex & Ethics framework assisted them to move beyond entrenched ideas about gender, sexualities, sexual assault, and young people. They found it useful in both individual counseling work and in multiple settings and situations beyond the life of its original conceptualization. These findings suggest that the Sex & Ethics Program is having an impact beyond its original purpose. It is contributing to ongoing dialogue about sexual ethics and how these ideas can be incorporated into other areas of practice with young people. Another key finding is the benefit of following up educators who take part in training programs to assess the impact of the training on their professional practice and how they have refined and adapted the concepts and skills to meet local needs. This information is important to contribute to the development of the evidence base on effective sexuality and violence prevention programs. Having obtained feedback from educators, it is then up to more program developers and implementers to publish reflective accounts of the *process* of delivering these programs. It is from this knowledge that we gain more insight into how to provide high-quality educator training that promotes comprehensive sexuality and violence prevention education.

Chapter 10

Building Ethical Communities

When I began to focus my specific attention on the effectiveness of education for the prevention of sexual violence in 1999, I had no idea where it would lead me. One of the pleasures of being an academic researcher is that I have the privilege of stepping back from my practice and having time to reflect. I am acutely aware that many front-line workers do not have this luxury, and I know I didn't in the decades where this was the sole focus of my work. Many of the approaches I have critiqued in this book are ones that I had been involved in developing and delivering. I was often left with a sense of unease after delivering an awareness program in schools or with professional groups. I now know why. It was, at best, a partial picture of the complexity of relationships; it did not seriously address ways of preventing sexual violence before it occurred. And like my schoolgirl experience of sexuality education, thoughts and feelings about the messiness of sexuality and violence in intimate relationships were submerged. Boys and young men were excluded from these discussions and, in many violence prevention programs, they still are. With the best intentions in the world, I had ended up mainly talking to women about how to avoid sexual assault and pressured sex.

In this book, I have held my own and others' good intentions up to scrutiny. However, I have attempted to do more than this by providing an alternative form of prevention education that draws much from sexuality education. Like many researchers across the globe, I have listened to what young women and men have told me about their experiences of sexuality education. This is less common in the violence prevention field and, therefore, this research redresses this oversight by locating young people at the heart of its design and implementation. I have heard their stories of trying to work out how to balance the demands of fitting into their friendship groups, balancing their emerging desires for sex and intimacy, and the pleasure and the pain this has caused them. The people I met had a hunger to talk about these issues, to reflect on their experiences, and were pleased that their experiences and views were being heard. This was not purely a self-reflective experience. They wanted me to pay attention to their stories and make this public, to try to improve the ways in which we currently *do* both sexuality and violence prevention education. They were a diverse selection of young people. They were of both genders; of varying ages, cultural backgrounds, and sexualities; and were both rural and urban young people. Some had much sexual experience, others had none. Some were high achievers academically, others were not. Unlike many studies, a significant number were recruited beyond the school and university gates. This allowed a broader sample of young people than those usually recruited within universities. Young people in one country town, for example, were part of a youth employment scheme, having left school earlier than other participants.

The young people who took part in the Sex & Ethics education groups appear, from the very positive results, to have gained much from the sexual ethics approach. They grasped the Sex & Ethics theoretical framework quickly and readily, and could see how it related to the activities discussed within the groups. More importantly, they found it had meaning in their lives as shown by their use of the program framework and the skills some six months later. My interpretation of this finding is that the program was based on issues that had relevance to them, was skills focused, and acknowledged them as active sexual agents in their own lives. It provided a safe space to explore the confusions and complexities of sexual intimacy that was missing in many of their experiences of sexuality education at schools and at home. The groups were run by well-trained, experienced educators—not by teachers who are often thrown into this work with little support. Most importantly, it didn't tell them what they should do, but rather gave them the knowledge and skills to reflect and make ethical decisions that were "right" for them and their partners. They also had fun discussing the issues and trying out new skills. The impact of gender on their sexual decision making was held up to scrutiny in a way that allowed for multiple ways to be a woman or a man, and allowed an exploration of multiple sexualities.

Educator' reflections on their training indicated a high level of acceptance of the philosophies underpinning the program and the activities and skills they learnt. Many of these skilled practitioners operate in community-based settings where resources are restricted and demands on services are high. In some agencies such as sexual assault and domestic violence services, demand for counseling of victims is the primary focus of funding and skill of the staff. A commitment in time and philosophy to primary prevention is a hurdle for some, balanced against the immediate needs of a recent victim of sexual or domestic violence. However, without this commitment, gender-based violence will continue unchecked. They also need to be skilful in managing relationships with schools, parents, and other community members who may hold quite divergent views on issues of sexuality and violence prevention education. We ask a lot of both government educators in schools and community settings. They are in need of much more support and resources from government and other sources of funding to provide training, supervision, and skills in evaluating their practice so they can more effectively carry out their work on the front line.

The ideas developed during the Sex & Ethics research and education projects have resonated in ways beyond the original idea of developing an education program for young people. Counselors have used the Sex & Ethics Framework in individual counseling with survivors of sexual assault and intimate partner violence and with young offenders engaging in sexually risky behavior. One worker is working individually through the program with a young woman with an intellectual disability to assist her in learning about respectful relationships while others incorporate it into their sexual health consultations. The program has also been run as a staff personal development activity to increase youth workers' skills in feeling at ease with raising or addressing sexuality and violence issues with their clients or as a method to highlight primary prevention activities for counselors who work directly with recent and past sexual assault survivors. Elements of the program have been incorporated with my agreement into other respectful relationship and sexuality program manuals and in online resources. The Australian National Rugby League uses the Sex & Ethics framework to underpin their Respectful Relationships Welfare Program. In university/college residential halls, the ideas from the program have been incorporated into induction and training programs for senior students in mentoring roles. In another research project with Kerry Robinson and Sue Dyson, we worked with ideas about sexual ethics and explored how they may be useful in working with young children and their parents around developing concepts of respect and sexual knowledge. Currently, the program concepts are also being adapted to an ethical leadership program focusing on preventing gender-based violence in workplaces.

These findings suggest the flexibility of the program and tap into wider conversations about the importance of ethical leadership in public and private life as corporations, religious orders, sporting codes, the military, and other organizations face up to endemic and longstanding abuses of power including sexual, physical, and emotional abuse. There is recognition by some that conversations about ethics need to begin early in life. In my home state of New South Wales, ethics classes are now offered in some state government schools for 5- to 12-year-olds of families who do not want their children taking part in religious scripture classes but are keen for their children to learn about ethical behavior.

For professionals working daily with others, it requires an understanding that "ethics in the professional context engages with elements of human virtue in all its complexity, as expressed through the nuances of attitudes, intentions, words and actions" Campbell (2003, 9). This is the challenge we face—not only in professional life but also in how we treat others in our private and intimate relationships. The young women and men who took part in this research were encouraged to hold their attitudes, intentions, words, and actions up to scrutiny. It is not reasonable to ask them to do this unless we are also willing to open ourselves up to this kind of ethical reflection and mindfulness about our own practices. I think we need to be honest with them about the complexity of living an ethical life and that, often, life is not simple or clear-cut. The Sex & Ethics Program engages with this complexity and uncertainty and offers one way to think and feel through this complexity

One area that has not been covered in this book is the issue of how to engage parents in a dialogue about ethical intimacy, and how they can support young people as they begin their sexual lives. While parents have been consulted in some sexuality research studies (e.g., Dyson and Smith 2012; Walsh, Parker, and Cushing 1999), this is less common in violence prevention work—an area that needs much more research.

Education is one aspect of a response to preventing sexual and other forms of intimate partner violence. The Sex & Ethics Program alone will not bring about the eradication of sexual violence. As I have discussed in chapter 5, we need to ensure that multisectoral responses to violence form the basis for community-wide responses to gendered violence. This involves an ongoing sustained commitment from governments at all levels, corporate and philanthropic funds, and from settings that work with the whole population and targeted programs for those most " at risk." Sexuality researchers such as Louisa Allen (2005, 2012, 2014), Anastasia Powell (2007a, 2007b,), Julia Hirst (2004), Pam Alldred and Miriam David (2007), and others have called for a more embodied approach to sexuality education. They have recognized the limits of an education that denies the complexity of young people's lives and fails to address what it is they want to know about sex and relationships. As I have argued throughout this book, there is much to be learnt from this for violence prevention education, especially in relation to young people's lives. A more embodied approach to sexuality education can only enhance our violence prevention work. The Sex & Ethics Program attempts to do this within the context of young people's emerging sexual lives. The merging of work from the sexuality field, with an alternative approach to sexual assault prevention, reflects an emerging discourse of ethical erotics.

We need to be mindful that any educational programs that we develop pays attention to the lessons gained from program evaluations conducted locally and internationally. There also needs to be a recognition that not all programs work in every context or country or with all groups of young people. While there are promising results emerging from new work to more actively engage men in violence prevention work, there is a need to ensure we critically evaluate this work. It is not as simple as adding men to the mix of program offerings and assuming this will result in cultural change. As Pini and Pease (2013) point out, the study of men and masculinities is connected to political imperatives of social equality and justice. They argue the importance of interrogating research in this area to ensure that it doesn't reproduce disadvantage and discrimination. We, therefore, need to be much more sophisticated in developing well-researched programs that recognize and address the political nature of education work and address the needs of diverse populations of young people. Funding bodies need to recognize that short-term pilot projects that do not provide funding or time for longer term evaluations will not build a body of knowledge about preventive education. Raising awareness of the problems is not enough to bring about the cultural change we need to prevent sexual and other forms of gender-based violence before they occur. We also need to consider the differential social and political contexts within cities, across regions and nations, and ensure there are policies and strategies designed to increase gender equality and reduce socioeconomic disadvantage.

The field of sexuality and prevention education is growing and changing rapidly, as we begin to understand the complexity of sexual and other forms of gendered violence and the need for diverse and creative responses. The increasing involvement of social media and web-based technology in all our lives has grown expediently over the last ten years. It will continue to develop and, with it, bring new challenges in educational design as well as new forms of ethical negotiation as new generations come of age with higher levels of technological literacy at younger ages. The current punitive approach of legal codes in some jurisdictions and the use of digital self-representation (sexting) and its conflation with child pornography provides another example of the gap between young peoples' sexual cultures and institutions of the state (Albury et al. 2013). Conversations about ethical use of this technology are now an important part of any educational programs with young people. There will be other issues that we have not yet imagined.

There is, therefore, much more to be done. Diversity of sexuality, culture, age, sexual experience, and settings was reflected in the Sex & Ethics research and education projects. However, there is a need for wider application of the ideas with larger groups and in different countries and with specific sub-populations to assess wider efficacy. The ideas presented here are one small contribution to international research and education to prevent gendered violence and to promote comprehensive sexuality education. The challenge we all face is working out what kind of communities we want to live in and the ethics of public and private relationships. While my focus on this book has been on young women and men, there is much we can all learn from their experiences. I welcome feedback and discussion with people wanting to explore these ideas in their own research or professional educational practice. It is through dialogue in text and in person that we can build ethical communities.

References

Abbey, A, Ross, LT, and McDuffie, D, "Alcohol and dating risk factors for sexual assault among college women." *Psychology of Women Quarterly,* 20(1): 147–169, 1996.

Abel, G and Fitzgerald, L, "'When you come to it you feel like a dork asking a guy to put a condom on': Is sex education addressing young people's understandings of risk?" *Sex Education: Sexuality, Society and Learning,* 6(2): 105–119, 2006.

Albury, K, Carmody, M, Evers, C, and Lumby, C, "Playing by the rules: Researching, teaching and learning sexual ethics with young men in the Australian National Rugby League." *Sex Education: Sexuality, Society and Learning,*11(3): 339–351, 2011.

Albury, K, Crawford, K, Byron, P, and Mathews, B, *Young People and Sexting in Australia: Ethics, Representation and the Law.* ARC Centre for Creative Industries and Innovation/Journalism and Media Research Centre, University of New South Wales, Australia, April 2013.

Allan, E and Madden, M, Hazing in View: College Students at Risk. Available at http://www.hazingstudy.org/publications/national_hazing_study_pilot_web.pdf 2008.

Alldred, P and David, ME, *Get Real About Sex: The Politics and Practice of Sex Education.* Open University Press, Maidenhead, UK, 2007.

Allen, L, "Girls want sex, boys want love: Resisting dominant discourses of (hetero)sexuality." *Sexualities,* 6(2): 215–236, 2003.

Allen, L, *Sexual Subjects: Young People, Sexuality and Education.* Palgrave Macmillan, Basingstoke, 2005.

Allen, L, *Young People and Sexuality Education: Rethinking Key Debates.* Palgrave Macmillan, Basingstoke, 2011.

Allen, L and Carmody, M, "'Pleasure has no passport': Re-visiting the potential of pleasure in sexuality education." *Sex Education: Sexuality, Society and Learning,* 12(4): 455–468, 2012.

Allen, L, Rasmussen, ML, and Quinlivan, K (eds), *The Politics of Pleasure in Sexuality Education: Pleasure Bound.* Routledge, New York, 2014.

Ambuel, B, Hamberger, LK, and Lahti, J, "The Family Peace Project." *Journal of Aggression, Maltreatment & Trauma,* 1(2): 55–81, 1998.

Attwood, F and Smith, C, "Investigating young people's sexual cultures: An introduction." *Sex Education: Sexuality, Society and Learning, 11*(3): 235–242, 2011.

Australian Bureau of Statistics *Census of Population and Housing: Australia's Youth*, cat. no. 2059.0. ABS, Canberra, pp. 17–18, 2001.

Australian Bureau of Statistics, *Sexual Assault in Australia: A Statistical Overview*, cat. no. 4523.0. Australian Bureau of Statistics, Canberra, 2004.

Australian Bureau of Statistics, *Personal Safety Survey Catalogue*, cat. no. 4906.0. Australian Bureau of Statistics, Canberra, 2006.

Bandura, A, "Health promotion by social cognitive means." *Health Education and Behavior, 31*(2): 143–164, 2004.

Banyard, VL, Plante, EG, and Moynihan, MM, "Bystander education: Bringing a broader community perspective to sexual violence prevention." *Journal of Community Psychology, 32*(1): 61–79, 2004.

Banyard, VL, Plante, EG, and Moynihan, MM, "Sexual violence prevention through bystander education: An experimental evaluation." *Journal of Community Psychology, 35*(4): 463–481, 2007.

Banyard, VL, "Measurement and correlates of prosocial bystander behavior: The case of interpersonal violence." *Violence and Victims, 23*(1): 83–97, 2008.

Banyard, VL, Moynihan, MM, Crossman, MT, "Reducing sexual violence on campus: The role of student leaders as empowered bystanders." *Journal of College Student Development, 50*(4): 446–457, 2009.

Beres, MA, Herold, E, and Maitland, SB, "Sexual consent behaviors in same-sex relationships." *Archives of Sexual Behavior, 33*(5): 475–486, 2004.

Beres, MA, "Spontaneous' sexual consent: An analysis of sexual consent literature." *Feminism & Psychology, 17*(1):93–108,2 007.

Beres, MA, "Rethinking the concept of consent for anti-sexual violence activism and education." *Feminism & Psychology, 24*(3): 373–389, 2014.

Berkowitz, A (ed.), *Men and Rape: Theory, Research and Prevention Programs in Higher Education.* Jossey-Bass, San Francisco, CA, 1994.

Berkowitz, A, "Fostering men's responsibility for preventing sexual assault" in Schewe, P (ed.), *Preventing Violence in Relationships: Interventions Across the Life Span.* American Psychological Association, Washington, DC, 2004.

Bessant, J, "From sociology of deviance to sociology of risk: Youth homelessness and the problem of empiricism." *Journal of Criminal Justice, 29*(1): 31–43, 2001.

Black, MC, Basile, KC, Breiding, MJ, Smith, SG, Walters, ML, Merrick, MT, Chen, J, and Stevens, MR, *The National Intimate Partner and Sexual Violence Survey (NISVS): 2010 Summary Report.* National Center for Injury Prevention and Control, Centers for Disease Control and Prevention, Atlanta, GA, 2011.

Board of Studies, New South Wales *Syllabus: Personal Development, Health and Physical Education Years 7–10.* NSW Board of Studies, Sydney, 2003.

Bolger, A, *Aboriginal Women and Violence in Australia.* Northern Territory University, Darwin, 1991.

Bourdieu, P, Chamboredon, JC, and Passeron, JC, *The Craft of Sociology: Epistemological Preliminaries*, de Gruyter, Berlin, 1991.

Braun, V and Clarke, VL, "Using thematic analysis in psychology." *Qualitative Research in Psychology*, 3: 77–101, 2006.

Breinbauer, C and Maddaleno, M, *Youth: Choices and Change: Promoting Healthy Behaviors in Adolescents*. Pan American Health Organization, Washington, DC, 2005.

Brookfield, S, "The concept of critical reflection: Promises and contradictions." *European Journal of Social Work*, 12(3): 293–304, 2009.

Brown, M, "Sex, drugs and naked man in corridor." *Sydney Morning Herald*, p. 1, March 15, 2006.

Bryson, V, *Feminist Debates: Issues of Theory and Practice*. New York University Press, New York, 1999.

Butler, J and Scott, JW (eds), *Feminists Theorize the Political*. Routledge, London, 1992.

Cameron-Lewis, V and Allen, L, "Teaching pleasure and danger in sexuality education." *Sex Education: Sexuality, Society and Learning*, 13(2): 121–132, 2013.

Card, C (ed.), *Feminist Ethics*. University Press of Kansas, Lawrence, 1991.

Carmody, M, "Uniting all women: A historical look at attitudes to rape" in Breckenridge, J and Carmody, M (eds), *Crimes of Violence: Australian Responses to Rape and Child Sexual Assault*. Allen & Unwin, Sydney, pp. 7–17, 1992.

Carmody, M and Carrington, K, "Preventing sexual violence?" *Australian and New Zealand Journal of Criminology*, 33(3): 341–361, 2000.

Carmody, M, "Sexual ethics and violence prevention." *Social and Legal Studies: An International Journal*, 12(2): 199–216, 2003.

Carmody, M, "Sexual ethics and the erotics of consent" in Cowling, M and Reynolds, P (eds), *Making Sense of Sexual Consent*. Ashgate, Aldershot, pp. 45–56, 2004.

Carmody, M, "Ethical erotics: Reconceptualizing anti-rape education." *Sexualities: Journal of Culture and Society*, 8(4): 465–480, 2005.

Carmody, M and Willis, K, *Developing Ethical Sexual Lives: Young People, Sex and Sexual Assault Prevention*. Social Justice Social Change Research Centre, University of Western Sydney, Sydney, 2006.

Carmody, M, "Preventing adult sexual violence through education?" *Current Issues in Criminal Justice*, 18(2): 342–356, 2006.

Carmody, M, *Sex and Ethics: Young People and Ethical Sex*. Palgrave Macmillan, Melbourne, 2009a.

Carmody, M, *Sex and Ethics: The Sexual Ethics Education Program for Young People*. Palgrave Macmillan, Melbourne, 2009b.

Carmody, M Evans, S Krogh, C, Flood, M, Heenan, M, and Ovenden, G, *Framing best practice: National Standards for the primary prevention of sexual assault through education, National Sexual Assault Prevention Education Project for NASASV*. University of Western Sydney, Australia, 2009c.

Carmody, M, "Young men, sexual ethics and sexual negotiation," *Sociological Research Online*, 2013, forthcoming http://www.socresonline.org.uk/May.

Carmody, M and Ovenden, G, "Putting ethical sex into practice: Sexual negotiation, gender and citizenship in the lives of young women and men." *Journal of Youth Studies*, 16(6): 792–807, 2013.

Carmody, M, Salter, M, and Presterudstuen, GH, *Less to Lose and More to Gain? Men and Boys Violence Prevention Research Project Final Report*, University of Western Sydney, Australia, 2014.

Carmody, M, "Sexual violence prevention educator training opportunities and challenges" in Henry, N and Powell, A (eds), *Preventing Sexual Violence: Interdisciplinary Approaches to Overcoming a Rape Culture*. Palgrave Macmillan, UK, pp. 150–169, 2015.

Carmona, RH, "Health professional training in youth violence prevention: A commentary by the Surgeon General." *American Journal of Preventive Medicine*, 29(5): 173–174, 2005.

Carpenter, LM, "Gender and the meaning and experience of virginity loss in the contemporary United States." *Gender & Society*, 16(3): 345–365, 2002.

Carrington, K, *Offending Girls: Sex, Youth and Justice*. Allen & Unwin, Sydney, 2003.

Casey, EA and Lindhorst, TP, "Toward a multi-level, ecological approach to the primary prevention of sexual assault prevention in peer and community contexts." *Trauma, Violence, & Abuse*, 10(2): 91–114, 2009.

CDC National Center for Chronic Disease Prevention and Health Promotion n.d. *School Health Policies and Programs Study (SHPPS)*. Available at <www.cdc.gov/HealthyYouth/shpps/index.htm>.

Claes, T and Reynolds, P, "Why sexual ethics and politics? And why now?" *Journal of the International Network of Sexual Ethics and Politics*, 1(1): 5–18, 2013.

Coker, AL, Cook-Craig, PG, Williams, CM, Fisher, BS Clear, ER, Garcia, LS, and Hegge, LM, "Evaluation of green dot: An active bystander intervention to reduce sexual violence on college campuses." *Violence Against Women*, 17(6): 777–796, 2011.

Connell, RW and Messerschmidt, JW, "Hegemonic masculinity: Rethinking the concept." *Gender & Society*, 19: 829–859, 2005.

Cowling, M, "Rape, communicative sexuality and sex education" in Cowling, M and Reynolds, P (eds), *Making Sense of Sexual Consent*. Ashgate, Aldershot, UK, pp. 17–28, 2004.

Cox, D, "Working with indigenous survivors of sexual assault." *Australian Centre for the Study of Sexual Assault Newsletter: ACCSA Wrap* (5): 1–7, 2008.

Crimes Act 1900 (NSW)

Culpitt, I, *Social Policy and Risk*. Sage, London, 1999.

Cupples, JB, Zukoski, AP, and Dierwechter, T, "Reaching young men: Lessons learned in the recruitment, training, and utilization of male peer sexual health educators." *Health Promotion Practice*, 11(3) suppl 3: 19S–25S, 2010.

DeGue, S, Holt, MK, Massetti, GM, Matjasko, JL Tharp, AT, and Valle, LA, "Looking ahead toward community-level strategies to prevent sexual violence." *Journal of Women's Health*, 21: 1–3, 2012.

de Visser RO, Smith AM, Rissel CE, Richters J, and Grulich AE, "Sex in Australia: Experiences of sexual coercion among a representative sample of adults." *Australian New Zealand Journal Public Health*, 27(2): 198–203, 2003.

Di Censo, A, Borthwick, VW, Busca, CA, and Creatura, C, "Completing the picture: Adolescents talk about what's missing in sexual health services." *Canadian Journal of Public Health*, 92(1): 35–38, 2001.

Dyson, S, Mitchell, A, Dalton, D, and Hillier, L, *Factors for Success in Conducting Effective Sexual Health and Relationships Education with Young People in Schools: A Literature Review*. La Trobe University, Melbourne, 2003.

Dyson, S and Flood, M, *Building Cultures of Respect and Non-Violence: A Review of Literature Concerning Adult Learning and Violence Prevention Programs with Men*. AFL Respect & Responsibility Program & VicHealth, Melbourne, 2008.

Dyson, S and Smith, E, "'There are lots of different kinds of normal': Families and sex education- styles, approaches and concerns." *Sex Education: Sexuality, Society and Learning*, 12(2): 219–229, 2012.

Egan, D and Hawkes, G, *Theorizing the Sexual Child in Modernity*. Palgrave Macmillan, New York, 2010.

Elliott, DS and Mihalic, S, "Issues in disseminating and replicating effective prevention programs." *Prevention Science*, 5(1): 47–53, 2004.

Ellis, J, *Preventing violence against women and girls: A study of educational programmes for children and young people, final report for WOMANKIND Worldwide*, 2004. Available at <www.womankind.org.uk>.

Ellis, J, "Literature review: Better outcomes for children and young people affected by domestic abuse: Directions for good practice" in C Humphreys, C Houghton and J Ellis (eds), *Primary Prevention of Domestic Abuse Through Education*, Scottish Government, Edinburgh, 2008.

Ellison, MM, "Beyond sexual fundamentalism: The call for an ethical eroticism, sexual addiction & compulsivity." *The Journal of Treatment & Prevention*, 8(1): 3–11, 2001.

Ferguson, RM, Vanwesenbeeck, I, and Knijn, T, "A matter of facts and more: An exploratory analysis of the content of sexuality education in the Netherlands." *Sex Education: Sexuality, Society and Learning*, 8(1): 93–106, 2008.

Fields, J, *Risky Lessons: Sex Education and Social Inequality*, Rutgers University Press, New Brunswick, 2008.

Fine, M, "Sexuality, schooling and adolescent females: The missing discourse of desire." *Harvard Educational Review*, 58(1): 29–53, 1998.

Fine, M, "Sexuality education and desire: Still missing after all these years." *Harvard Educational Review*, 76(3): 297–338, 2006.

Fisher, B, Cullen, F, and Turner. M, *The Sexual Victimization of College Women: Findings from Two National-Level Studies*. National Institute of Justice and Bureau of Justice Statistics, Washington, DC, 2000.

Fisher, D, Lang, KS, and Wheaton, J, *Training Professionals in the Primary Prevention of Sexual and Intimate Partner Violence: A Planning Guide*. Centers for Disease Control and Prevention, Atlanta, United States, 2010.

Flaming, D, "The ethics of Foucault and Ricoeur: An underrepresented discussion in nursing." *Nursing Inquiry, 13*(3): 220–227, 2006.

Fleming D (Executive Producer), *The Mourning After,* television broadcast, *Australian Story*. Australian Broadcasting Corporation, Sydney, May 8, 2006.

Flood, M, "Changing men: Best practice in sexual violence education." *Women Against Violence, 18*: 26–36, 2006.

Flood, M, "Involving men in efforts to end violence against women." *Men and Masculinities, 14*: 358–377, 2011a.

Flood, M, "Building men's commitment to ending sexual violence against women." *Feminism & Psychology, 21*: 1–6, 2011b.

Foubert, JD, "Answering the questions of rape prevention research: A response to Tharp et al." *Journal of Interpersonal Violence, 26*(16): 3393–3402, 2011.

Foucault, M, *The History of Sexuality: An Introduction,* vol. 1. Vintage Books Edition, New York, 1990.

Franzway, S, Connell, C, and Court, D, *Staking a Claim: Feminism and the State*. Allen & Unwin, Sydney, 1989.

Froese, K, *Ethics Unbound: Chinese and Western Perspectives on Morality*. The Chinese University Press, The Chinese University of Hong Kong, Hong Kong, 2013.

Furlong, A, and Cartmel, F, *Young People and Social Change*. Open University Press, Maidenhead, UK, 2007.

Gavey, N, "Sexual victimization among Auckland University students: How much and who does it?" *New Zealand Journal of Psychology, 20*(2): 63–70, 1991a.

Gavey, N, "Sexual victimization prevalence among New Zealand university students." *Journal of Consulting and Clinical Psychology, 59*(3): 464–466, 1991b.

Gavey, N, "Unsexy sex: Unwanted sex, sexual coercion and rape" in Gavey, N *Just Sex? The Cultural Scaffolding of Rape*. Routledge, London, pp. 136–168, 2005.

Gibson, S, "The language of the right: Sex education debates in South Australia." *Sex Education: Sexuality, Society and Learning, 7*(3): 239–250, 2007.

Gidycz, CA, Orchowski, LM, and Berkowitz AD, Preventing sexual aggression among college men: An evaluation of a social norms and bystander intervention program. *Violence Against Women, 17*(6): 720–742, 2011.

Gilbert, J, "Between sexuality and narrative: On the language of sex education, youth and sexualities" in Rasmussen, ML, Rofes, E, and Talbutt, S (eds), *Pleasure Subversion and Insubordination In and Out of Schools*. Palgrave Macmillan, New York, pp. 109–126, 2004.

Glanz, K, Rimer, BK, and Viswanath, K (eds), *Health Behavior and Health Education: Theory, Research, and Practice* (4th ed.). John Wiley & Sons, New York, 2008.

Gordon, C (ed.), *Foucault, M Power/Knowledge: Selected Interviews and Other Writings 1972–1977.* Harvester, Brighton, UK, 1980.

Gourlay, P, "Sexuality education: Fact, fiction of fallopian tubes" in Laskey, L and Beavis, C (eds), *Schooling Sexualities: Teaching for a Positive Sexuality.* Deakin University, Geelong, Victoria, pp. 37–52 1995.

Grello, C, Welsh, D, and Harper, M, "No strings attached: The nature of casual sex in college students." *The Journal of Sex Research, 43*(3): 255–267, 2006.

Gross, AM, Winslett, A, Roberts, M, and Gohm, C, "An examination of sexual violence against college women." *Violence Against Women, 12*(3): 288–300, 2006.

Hall, DS, *Consent for Sexual Behaviour in a College Student Population.* PhD thesis, Institute for Advanced Study of Human Sexuality, San Francisco, California, 1995.

Hall, R, "It can happen to you: Rape prevention in the age of risk management." *Hypatia, 19*(3): 1–18, 2004.

Halstead, M and Waite, S, "'Worlds Apart': The sexual values of boys and girls." *Education and Health, 20*: 17–23, 2002.

Harden, A, Oakley, A, and Oliver, S, "Peer-delivered health promotion for young people: A systematic review of different study designs." *Health Education Journal, 60*(4): 339–353, 2001.

Harvey, A, Garcia-Moreno, C, and Butchart, A, *Primary Prevention of Intimate-Partner Violence and Sexual Violence: Background Paper for WHO Expert Meeting May 2–3, 2007*: World Health Organization, 2007.

Haydon, D and Scraton, P, "Sex education as regulation" in Goldson, B, Lavalette, M. and McKenzie, J. (eds), *Children, Welfare and the State,* Sage, London, pp.152–168, 2002.

Heise, L, Ellsberg, M, and Gottemoeller, M, "Ending violence against women." *Population Reports, 27*(4): 1–43, 1999.

Heppner, MJ, Humphrey, CF, Hillenbrand-Gunn, TL, and DeBord, KA, "The differential effects of rape prevention programming on attitudes, behavior, and knowledge." *Journal of Counseling Psychology, 42*(4): 508–518, 1995.

Hercus, N and Carmody, M, *Reflections on Implementing the Sex & Ethics Violence Prevention Program.* University of Western Sydney, Australia, December, 2011.

Hickman, SE and Muehlenhard, CL, "By the semi-mystical appearance of a condom: How young women and men communicate sexual consent in heterosexual situations." *The Journal of Sex Research, 36*(3): 258–272, 1999.

Hillier, L, Turner, A, and Mitchell, A, *Writing Themselves In Again: 6 Years On; The 2nd National Report On The Sexuality, Health & Well-Being*

Of Same Sex Attracted Young People In Australia. Australian Research Centre in Sex, Health and Society, La Trobe University, Melbourne, Australia, 2005.

Hillier, L and Mitchell, A, "'It was as useful as a chocolate kettle': Sex education in the lives of same-sex attracted young people in Australia." *Sex Education: Sexuality, Society and Learning, 8*(2): 211–224, 2008.

Hilton, N, Harris, GT, Rice, ME, Krans, TS, and Lavigne, SE, "Antiviolence education in high schools: Implementation and evaluation." *Journal of Interpersonal Violence, 13*(6): 726–742, 1998.

Hilton, GLS, "Listening to the boys: English boys' views on the desirable characteristics of teachers of sex education." *Sex Education: Sexuality, Society and Learning, 3*(1): 33–45, 2003.

Hilton, GLS, "Listening to the boys again: An exploration of what boys want to learn in sex education classes and how they want to be taught." *Sex Education: Sexuality, Society and Learning, 7*(2): 161–174, 2007.

Hirst, J, "Researching young people's sexuality and learning about sex: Experience, need, and sex and relationship education." *Culture, Health & Sexuality, 6*(2): 115–129, 2004.

Hogg, R and Brown, D, *Rethinking Law and Order*. Pluto, Sydney, 1998.

Hogg, R and Carrington, K, *Policing the Rural Crisis*. The Federation Press, Sydney, 2006.

Holland, J, Ramazanoglu, C, and Thomson, R, "In the same boat? The gendered (in)experience of first heterosex" in Richardson, D (ed.), *Theorising Heterosexuality*. Open University Press, London, pp.143–160, 1996.

Humphreys, TP, "Understanding sexual consent: An empirical investigation of the normative script for young heterosexual adults" in Cowling, M and Reynolds, P (eds), *Making Sense of Sexual Consent*. Ashgate, Aldershot, UK, pp. 209–225, 2004.

Humphreys, T, "Perceptions of sexual consent: The impact of relationship history and gender." *Journal of Sex Research, 44*(4): 307–315, 2007.

Hurley, M (ed.), *Cultures of Care and Safe Sex amongst HIV Positive Australians. Papers from the HIV Futures I and II Surveys and Interviews*. Monograph Series Number 43. The Australian Research Centre in Sex, Health and Society, La Trobe University, Melbourne, Australia, 2002.

Irvine, J, *Talk about Sex: The Battles over Sex Education in the United States*. University of California Press, Berkeley, CA, 2002.

James-Traore, TA Finger, W Ruland, CD, and Savariaud, S, *Teacher Training: Essential for School-Based Reproductive Health and HIV/AIDS Education Focus on Sub-Saharan Africa*. Family Health International, YouthNet Program, Arlington, VA, 2004.

Johnson, J and Holman, M (eds), *Making the Team: Inside the World of Sports Initiations and Hazing*. Canadian Scholars Press, Toronto, 2002.

Johnson, B, *An Evaluation of the Trial Implementation of the Sexual Health and Relationships Education (SHARE) Program 2003–2006*. University of South Australia, Adelaide, 2006.

Jones, TM, "Saving rhetorical children: Sexuality education discourses from conservative to post-modern." *Sex Education: Sexuality, Society and Learning*, 11(4): 369–338, 2011.

Jordan, J, "Worlds apart? Women, rape and the police reporting process." *British Journal of Criminology*, 41(4): 679–706, 2001.

Kaaya, SF Mukoma, W, Flisher, AJ, and Klepp, K, "School-based sexual health interventions in sub-Saharan Africa: A review." *Social Dynamics*, 28(1): 64–88, 2002.

Katz, J, "Reconstructing masculinity in the locker room: The mentors in violence prevention project." *Harvard Educational Review Special Issue: Violence and Youth*, 65(2): 163–174, 1995.

Katz, J, Heisterkamp, HA, and Fleming, WM, "The social justice roots of the Mentors in Violence Prevention model and its application in a high school setting." *Violence Against Women*, 17: 684–702, 2011.

Kelly, L, *Surviving Sexual Violence (Feminist Perspectives)*. Polity Press, Cambridge, UK, 1988.

Kelly, P, "The dangerousness of youth-at-risk: The possibilities of surveillance and intervention in uncertain times." *Journal of Adolescence*, 23(4): 463–476, 2000.

Kelly, L, *Rape in the 21st Century: Old Behaviours, New Contexts and Emerging Patterns*. Full Research Report (no. RES-000–22–1679). Swindon: ESRC, 2007.

Kiely, E, "Where is the discourse of desire? deconstructing the Irish relationships and sexuality education (RSE) resource materials." *Irish Educational Studies*, 24(2–3): 253–266, 2005.

King, D, "Inside the cabin where death sparked burning shame." *The Australian*, p. 3, March 22, 2006.

Kitzinger, C and Frith, H, "Just say no? The use of conversation analysis in developing a feminist perspective on sexual refusal." *Discourse & Society*, 10(3): 293–316, 1999.

Knowles, M, *The Adult Learner: A Neglected Species*. Gulf, Houston, 1973.

Kontula, O, "The evolution of sex education and students' sexual knowledge in Finland in the 2000s." *Sex Education: Sexuality, Society and Learning*, 10(4): 373–386, 2010.

Koss, MP, Gidcyz, CA, and Wisniewski, N, "The scope of rape: Incidence and prevalence of sexual aggression and victimization in a national sample of higher education students." *Journal of Consulting and Clinical Psychology*, 55(2): 162–170, 1987.

Koss, M, "Hidden rape: Sexual aggression and victimization in a national sample in higher education" in Burgess, A (ed.), *Rape and Sexual Assault: A Research Handbook*, vol. 2. Garland, New York, 1988.

Krug, EG Dahlberg, L Mercy, J Zwi, A, and Lozano, R (eds), *World Report on Violence and Health*. World Health Organization, Geneva, 2002.

Lamb, S, "Feminist ideals for a healthy female adolescent sexuality: A critique." *Sex Roles*, 62(5): 294–306, 2010.

Lamb, S, *Sex Ed for Caring Schools: Creating an Ethics Based Curriculum*. Teachers College Press, Columbia University, New York, 2013.

Lambek, M (ed.), *Ordinary Ethics: Anthropology, Language, and Action*. Fordham University Press, Bronx, NY, 2010.

Langhinrichsen-Rohling, J, Foubert, JD, Hill, B, Brasfield, H, and Shelley-Tremblay, S, "The Men's Program: Does it impact college men's bystander efficacy and willingness to intervene?" *Violence Against Women*, *17*(6):743–759, 2011.

Lauder, S (Writer), *Brimble inquest hears police interview* (radio broadcast), *PM*. Australian Broadcasting Corporation, Sydney, June 16, 2006.

Lees, S, *Ruling Passions: Sexual Violence, Reputation and the Law*. Open University Press, Philadelphia, 1997.

Levy, A, *Female Chauvinist Pigs: Women and the Rise of Raunch Culture*. Free Press, New York, 2005.

Lievore, D, *Non-reporting and hidden recording of sexual assault: An international literature review*. Commonwealth of Australia, Canberra, 2003.

Lindgren, K, Schacht, R, Pantalone, D, Blayney, J, and George, W, "Sexual communication, sexual goals, and students' transition to college: Implications for sexual assault, decision-making and risky behaviors." *Journal of College Student Development*, *50*(5): 491–503, 2009.

Lipkins, S, *Preventing Hazing: How Parents, Teachers and Coaches Can Stop the Violence, Harassment and Humiliation*. Jossey-Bass, San Francisco, 2006.

Lonsway, KA and Archambault, J, "The 'justice gap' for sexual assault cases: Future directions for research and reform." *Journal of Violence Against Women*, *18*(2): 145–168, 2012.

Lorde, A, *Sister Outsider: Essays and Speeches*. Crossing Press, Trumansburg, NY, 1984.

Luker, K, *When Sex Goes to School: Warring Views on Sex and Sex Education Since the Sixties*. WW Norton & Company, New York, 2006.

MacIntyre, A, *A Short History of Ethics: A History of Moral Philosophy from the Homeric to the Twentieth Century*. Routledge, London and New York, 1998.

McCarthy, M, *The Group*. Harcourt Inc., New York, 1963.

McClelland, SI and Fine, M, "Over-sexed and under surveillance: Adolescent sexualities, cultural anxieties and thick desire" in Allen, L, Rasmussen, ML, Quinlivan, K (eds), *The Politics of Pleasure in Sexuality Education: Pleasure Bound*. Routledge, New York, pp. 12–34, 2014.

McMahon, N and Jacobsen, G, "Everyone let her down." *Sydney Morning Herald*, p. 29, March 26, 2006.

Measor, L, *Young People's Views on Sex Education*. Routledge, London, 2000.

Mezirow, J, "An Overview on Transformative Learning" in Illeris, K (ed.), *Contemporary Theories of Learning: Learning Theorists—In Their Own Words*. Routledge, Oxon and New York, 2009.

Mitchell, A, *Sexual health education in Australia: Brief background paper for the parliamentary group on population and development*. Commonwealth of Australia, Canberra, ACT, 2007.

Mitchell A, Patrick K, Heywood W, Blackman P, and Pitts M, *5th National Survey of Australian Secondary Students and Sexual Health 2013*, (ARCSHS Monograph Series No. 97), Australian Research Centre in Sex, Health and Society, La Trobe University, Melbourne, Australia, 2014.

Mukoma, W, Flisher, AJ, Ahmed, N, Jansen, S, Mathews, C, Klepp, KI, and Schaalma, H, "Process evaluation of a school-based HIV/AIDS intervention in South Africa." *Scandinavian Journal of Public Health, 37*(2) suppl 2:37–47, 2009.

Moosa-Mitha, M, "A difference-centered alternative to theorization of children's citizenship rights." *Citizenship Studies, 9*(4): 369–388, 2005.

Morrison, S, Hardison, J, Mathew, A, and O'Neil, J, *An Evidence-based Review of Sexual Assault Preventive Intervention Programs.* National Institute Justice, US Department of Justice, Washington, DC, 2004.

Nation, M, Crusto, C, Wandersman, A, Kumpfer, KL, Seybolt, D, and Morrissey-Kane, E, "What works in prevention: Principles of effective prevention programs." *American Psychologist, 58*(6/7): 449–456, 2003.

Neame, A and Heenan, M, "What lies behind the hidden figure of sexual assault? Issues of prevalence and disclosure." *Australian Centre for the Study of Sexual Assault Newsletter, 1*: 1–15, 2003.

NSW Bureau of Crime Statistics and Research, Attorney-General's Department, Sydney, 2005.

NSW Bureau of Crime Statistics and Research (BOCSAR) n.d., Sexual Assault: NSW Recorded Crime Statistics: January 2004 to December 2004: Top 50 local government areas ranked by rate of recorded criminal incidents (LGAs with population under 3000). Available at <www.bocsar.nsw.gov.au/lawlink/bocsar/ll_bocsar.nsf/pages/bocsar_lgaranks_sexualassault04>.

NSW Bureau of Crime Statistics and Research (BOCSAR) Sexual Assault: NSW Recorded Crime Statistics: January 2005 to December 2005: Top 50 local government areas ranked by rate of recorded criminal incidents (LGAs with population under 3000). Available at <www.bocsar.nsw.gov.au/lawlink/bocsar/ll_bocsar.nsf/pages/bocsar_lgaranks_sexualassault05>.

O'Byrne, R, Rapley, M, and Hansen, S, "'You couldn't say "no," could you?': Young men's understandings of sexual refusal." *Feminism & Psychology, 16*: 133–154, May 2006.

O'Malley, P and Sutton, A, *Crime Prevention: Issues in Policy and Research.* Federation Press, Sydney, 1997.

Oregon State University Cascades, http://www.osucascades.edu/campus-crime-report-clery-act, accessed October 2, 2014.

Parrot, A, "*Do rape education programs influence rape patterns among New York state college students?*" Paper presented at the Society for the Scientific Study of Sex, Minneapolis, MN, USA, 1990.

Patton, P, "Ethics and post-modernity" in Grosz, EA, Threadgold, T, Kelly, D, Cholodenko, A, and Colless, E (eds), *Futur*fall: Excursions into Post-Modernity.* Power Institute of Fine Arts, University of Sydney, Sydney, pp. 128–145, 1986.

Patton, M, *Qualitative Research and Evaluation Methods*. Sage, California, 2002.

Payne, M, "Social work theories and reflective practice" in Adams, R, Dominelli, L, and Payne, M (eds), *Social Work: Themes, Issues and Critical Debates*, 2nd edn. Palgrave Macmillan, Basingstoke, pp. 123–138, 2002.

Pease, B, "Men against sexual assault" in Weeks, W and Wilson, J (eds), *Issues Facing Australian Families*, 2nd edn. Longman, Melbourne, 1995.

Piccigallo, JR, Lilley, TG, and Miller, SL, "It's cool to care about sexual violence: Men's experiences with sexual assault prevention." *Men and Masculinities*, 15(5): 507–525, 2012.

Pini, B and Pease, B (eds), *Men, Masculinities and Methodologies*. Palgrave Macmillan, UK, 2013.

Powell, A, "Youth 'at risk'? Young people, sexual health and consent." *Youth Studies Australia*, 26(4): 21–27, 2007a.

Powell, A, "Sexual pressure and young people's negotiation of consent." *Aware*. Australian Centre for the Study of Sexual Assault Newsletter, (14): 8–16, 2007b.

Powell, A, *Sex, Power and Consent: Youth Culture and the Unwritten Rules*. Cambridge University Press, Melbourne, 2010.

Powell, A, "Bystander approaches: Responding to and preventing violence against women: Preventing violence men's violence against women." Australian Centre for the Study of Sexual Assault, *ACSSA Issues*, No 17: 1–20, 2014.

Rabbi Winer LN, RJE, "Sacred choices: Adolescent relationships and sexual ethics: The reform movement's response to the need for faith-based sexuality education." *American Journal of Sexuality Education*, 6(1): 20–31, 2011.

Rabinow, P (ed.), *Michel Foucault: Ethics, the Essential Works 1*. Allen Lane, The Penguin Press, London, 1997.

Race, K, "Revaluation of risk among gay men." *AIDS Education and Prevention*, 15(4): 369–381, 2003.

Race, K, "The use of pleasure in harm reduction: Perspectives from the history of sexuality." *International Journal of Drug Policy*, 19(5): 417–423, 2007.

Race, K, *Pleasure Consuming Medicine. The Queer Politics of Drugs*. Duke University Press, Durham and London, 2009.

Ramazanaglou, C (ed.), *Up Against Foucault: Explorations of Some Tensions between Foucault and Feminism*. Routledge, London, USA, 1993.

Rasmussen, M, "Pleasure/desire sexularism and sexuality education" in Allen, L, Rasmussen, ML, Quinlivan, K (eds), *The Politics of Pleasure in Sexuality Education: Pleasure Bound*. Routledge, New York, pp. 153–167, 2014.

Remez, L, "Oral sex among adolescents: Is it sex or abstinence?" *Family Planning Perspectives*, 32(6): 298–304, 2000.

Robertson, B, *The Aboriginal and Torres Strait Islander Women's Task Force on Violence Report*, rev. edn. Department of Aboriginal and Torres Strait Islander Policy and Development (DATSIPD), Brisbane, Queensland, 2000.

Robinson, KH, *Innocence, Knowledge and the Construction of Childhood: The Contradictory Nature of Sexuality and Censorship in Children's Contemporary Lives.* Routledge, Oxford, 2013.

Rolston, B, Schubotz, D, and Simpson, A, "Sex education in Northern Ireland schools: A critical evaluation." *Sex Education: Sexuality, Society and Learning,* 5(3): 217–234, 2005.

Russell, DEH, *Rape in Marriage,* rev. edn. Indiana University Press, Bloomington, 1990.

Santelli, J, Ott, MA, Lyon, M, Rogers, J, Summers, D, and Schleifer, R, "Abstinence and abstinence-only education: A review of US policies and programs." *Journal of Adolescent Health,* 38(1): 72–81, 2006.

Sawicki, J, *Disciplining Foucault: Feminism, Power and the Body.* Routledge, London, 1991.

Schewe, PA, "Guidelines for developing rape prevention and risk reduction interventions" in Schewe, PA (ed.), *Prevention Violence in Relationships: Interventions Across the Lifespan.* American Psychological Association, Washington, DC, 2002.

Schroeder, WR, "Continental ethics" in Lafollette, H (ed.), *The Blackwell Guide to Ethical Theory.* Blackwell, Malden, MA, 2000.

Scott, J, "Children ask the damndest questions: Sex(uality) education as a social problem" in Hawkes, G and Scott, J (eds), *Perspectives in Human Sexuality.* Oxford University Press, Melbourne, Australia, pp.168–186, 2005.

SHARE Newsletter July 2006 <www.shinesa.org.au>.

SMH 2009. Available from http://www.smh.com.au/technology/elite-college-students-proud-of-prorape-facebook-page-20091108-i3js.html.

Smith, A, Rissel, CE, Richters, J, Grulich, AE, and Visser, R, "Sexual identity, sexual attraction and sexual experience among a representative sample of adults." *Sex in Australia Special Edition, Australian and New Zealand Journal of Public Health,* 27(2): 138–145, 2003.

Sriranganathan, G, Jaworsky, D, Larkin, J, Flicker, S, Campbell, L, Flynn, S, and Erlich, L, "Peer sexual health education interventions for effective programme evaluation." *Health Education Journal,* 71(1): 62–71, 2010.

Svendsen, SHB, "Elusive sex acts: Pleasure and politics in Norwegian sex education." *Sex Education: Sexuality, Society and Learning,* 12(4): 397–410, 2012.

Thompson, S, *Going All the Way: Teenage Girls' Tales of Sex, Romance and Pregnancy.* Hill and Wang, New York, 1995.

Tolman, DL, "Doing desire: Adolescent girls' struggles for/with sexuality." *Gender & Society,* 8(3): 324–342, 1994.

Tolman, DL, *Dilemmas of Desire: Teenage Girls Talk About Sexuality.* Harvard University Press, Cambridge, MA, 2002.

Tutty, L, Bradshaw, C, Thurston, WE, Barlow, A, Marshall, P, and Tunstall, L, *School-Based Violence Prevention Programs, a Resource Manual: Preventing Violence against Children and Youth,* rev. edn. 2005. Available at <www.ucalgary.ca/resolve/violenceprevention/>.

UNESCO, 2009. International guidelines on sexuality education: An evidence informed approach to effective sex, relationships and HIV/STI education. Available at http://www.fpq.com.au/21st/pdf/International GuidelinesSexualityEducation.pdf

United Nations Economic and Social Council. *Report of the United Nations Development Fund for Women on the Elimination of Violence against Women.* No. 8, 2005.

UN General Assembly, In-depth study on all forms of violence against women: Report of the Secretary General, 2006. A/61/122/Add. 1. 6 July United Nations *In-depth study on all forms of violence against women: Report of the Secretary-General A/61/122/Add.1.* United Nations General Assembly, Geneva, 2006.

Victorian Health Promotion Foundation (VicHealth), *Preventing Violence before It Occurs: A Framework and Background Paper to Guide the Primary Prevention of Violence against Women in Victoria.* Victorian Health Promotion Foundation, Victoria, Australia, 2007.

Victorian Health Promotion Foundation (VicHealth), *National Survey on Community Attitudes to Violence against Women 2009; Changing Cultures, Changing Attitudes—Preventing Violence against Women.* Victoria, Australia, 2010.

Victorian Health Promotion Foundation (VicHealth), *More than Ready: Bystander Action to Prevent Violence against Women in the Victorian Community.* Victorian Health Promotion Foundation (VicHealth), Carlton, Australia, 2012.

Vladutiu CJ,. Martin, SL, and Macy RJ, "College -or university-based sexual assault prevention programs: A review of program outcomes, characteristics and recommendations." *Trauma, Violence, Abuse, 12*: 67–86, 2011.

Walker, SJ, "When 'no' becomes 'yes': Why girls and women consent to unwanted sex." *Applied & Preventive Psychology, 6*(3): 157–166, 1997.

Walsh, A, Parker, E, Cushing A, "'How am i gonna answer this one?': A discourse analysis of fathers' accounts of providing sexuality education for young sons." *The Canadian Journal of Human Sexuality, 8*(2): 103–114, 1999.

Weaver, H, Smith, G, and Kippax, S, "School-based sex education policies and indicators of sexual health among young people: A comparison of the Netherlands, France, Australia and the United States." *Sex Education: Sexuality, Society and Learning, 5*(2): 171–188, 2005.

Welch, D, "Dianne Brimble: DPP recommends manslaughter charges." *Sydney Morning Herald* <www.smh.com.au>, September 11, 2008.

Weston, A, *A Practical Companion to Ethics.* Oxford University Press, New York,1997.

Whitaker, DJ, Morrison, S, Lindquist, C, Hawkins, SR, O'Neil, JA, Nesius, AM, "A critical review of interventions for the primary prevention of perpetration of partner violence." *Aggression and Violent Behavior, 11*(2): 151–166, 2006.

White House, http://www.whitehouse.gov/the-press-office/2014/04/29/fact-sheet-not-alone-protecting-students-sexual-assault, accessed September 17, 2014.

Wilkinson, K, "It's not just black and white: Why gen-Y needs to break societal standards of sexuality" http://elitedaily.com/life/just-black-white-understanding-sexual-fluidity/654164/, accessed September 18, 2014.

Wissink, L, "Reshaping the future: Student peer support for sexual harassment and assault." *Association for University and College Counselling Journal (AUCC)*, British Association for Counselling and Psychotherapy, 2004.

World Bank, *World Development Report 1993: Investing in Health.* Oxford University Press, New York, 1993.

World Health Organization, *WHO Multi-country Study on Women's Health and Domestic Violence against Women: Summary Report of Initial Results on Prevalence, Health Outcomes and Women's Responses.* World Health Organization, Geneva, 2005.

Wright, L and Carmody, M, *Guidelines for the Delivery of the Sex + Ethics Respectful Relationships Program with Indigenous Young People.* University of Western Sydney, Australia, 2012.

Zalewski, M, *Feminism after Postmodernism: Theorizing Through Practice.* Routledge, London, 2000.

9 News, 2014, http://www.9news.com.au/national/2014/10/04/10/22/uni-response-to-sex-photo-inadequate-says-student-head.

Index

Printed in the United States
By Bookmasters